cornish place names & language

craig weatherhill

Reprinted: 1998, 2002

Published by Sigma Leisure – an imprint of
Sigma Press, 1 South Oak Lane, Wilmslow, Cheshire SK9 6AR, England.

British Library Cataloguing in Publication Data
A CIP record for this book is available from the British Library.

ISBN: 1-85058-462-1

Typesetting and Design by: Sigma Press, Wilmslow, Cheshire.

Cover photograph: Mousehole from the air

Cover design: MFP Design and Print

Printed by: MFP Design and Print

Preface:

Of what use is Cornish, a language which at no time in its long history was spoken by more than 35,000 people? If it died, then why not leave it to rest in peace? Doesn't its revival reflect a politically nationalistic attitude? Such questions really represent the negative view; the positive side is seldom put.

In a nation which is rightly proud of its heritage, and in a Duchy which has conserved so much of its past, it would make little sense to ignore or neglect such a vital element as one of these island's oldest languages. In a tourist-orientated place as Cornwall, the language is a positive asset; an additional source of fascination which strengthens that feeling of being in a different place, and there are thousands of signposts constantly reminding us that the language never really went away.

Few Cornish people are under any illusion that it will ever again be a first language but it has the potential to be a useful second one. It is still closely related to the Celtic language of Brittany, Cornwall's neighbour and cousin across the Channel, where close to a million people speak Breton. In purely economic terms, not to mention those of diplomacy and friendship, Cornish is a vital element, too valuable to be cast aside.

Equally important is its symbolism of identity, that basic need of every region and individual and most especially so to a minority culture, but the Cornish language is not only part of Cornwall's heritage. It is an integral part of the heritage of Britain and of Europe, as equally worthy of the protection afforded to those monuments and buildings of archaeology and history, and it exists for everyone to enjoy.

This book contains only authentic forms of Cornish from its various historical periods, with the its most recent evolutionary form, Modern (or Late) Cornish appearing in word-lists, poems, grammar, proverbs, phrases and the story of John of Chyanhor. It is unfortunate that unauthentic, theoretical forms of the tongue also exist, so beware imitations, however well packaged they may be.

Craig Weatherhill, Bosloggas Warha, An Dreav, Penzans, Kernow: meez Ebral 1995.

Contents

Introduction

A Sense of Difference

Amalveor – Baldhu – Chysauster – Egloshayle – Feock – Goonhilly – Heligan – Kehelland –
Liskeard – Marazanvose – Polyphant – Stenalees – Tintagel – Warleggan – Zennor

Such are examples of the utter strangeness of the place names which assail the
visitor to Cornwall from the moment the River Tamar is crossed and the
familiar world of English place names is left behind. To further befuddle the
mind, road signs at each of the Tamar crossings boldly announce:

CORNWALL
KERNOW

For most people, the explanation for this is not readily apparent and the aim
of this book is to answer the questions asked by not only visitors to Cornwall
but also by many who live in the Duchy. Why are these place names so
different? What do they mean? How are they pronounced? (local TV and radio
presenters have endless trouble with this and often, when told how, still insist
on their own pronunciation – "Dunnaw an wun't be tawld" as the Cornish
might say.) Why does Cornwall differ so much from England and, come to
that, who are the Cornish?

In 1935, listeners to BBC radio were astonished to hear a Cornish choir
singing in a strange language vaguely reminiscent of Welsh. The BBC
switchboard was jammed by callers demanding more information but the staff
could tell them little other than what they had heard was one of Britain's
least-known but most ancient of tongues; one that the very few who had ever
heard of it had thought was long dead. The nation had been listening to the
Cornish language.

In The Beginning

In the early part of the 1st millenium BC, a powerful and brilliant society
emerged in West Central Europe around the headwaters of the River Danube.
Calling themselves *Keltoi*, these people formed a wealthy clan-based society
ruled by powerful princes, and grew to develop a diverse and dynamic culture.

From their original Transalpine homeland, the Celts spread east, west and south across Europe, extensively settling Gaul (modern France) in the 5th century BC. Some, bent on conquest, headed south towards Italy at the end of the same century, with 300,000 of them on the move and settling in the Po valley, rich in Celtic place names to this day. By 400 BC, the Celts of the Po valley were moving south again. In 386 BC, they captured, sacked and occupied Rome under the leadership of Brennos.

Those who had headed east were in Hungary at the end of the 5th century BC and, soon afterwards, were in south-west Slovakia and Transylvania, where they recalled by the name Wallachia (*Wal-, Gal-* normally denotes "Celts"). In 280 BC, a strong Celtic army was in Macedonia where they defeated the army of Ptolemy Ceraunius. Another band settled an area of Asia Minor, modern Turkey, where, although strongly Hellenised, their isolated community kept their Celtic language and culture into Christian times. These were the Galatians to whom St Paul addressed his Epistle.

The westward expansion of what has been loosely termed the "Celtic Empire" was generally a peaceful programme of colonisation and settlement. The westernmost extent of Celtic Europe was the north-west corner of the Iberian peninsula, settled in the 1st century BC and still known as Galicia.

The extent of Celtic Europe c. 200 BC (stippled). Modern Celtic nations, with their native names, are shown in solid black (C. Weatherhill)

The British Isles were Celtic in the 5th century BC, with the existing native population being assimilated and absorbed into the new culture. Late in the following century, Celtic place names in Britain were recorded by the Greek explorer Pytheas. *Belerion*, meaning something like "The Shining One" was present day Land's End; *Iktis*, perhaps an Early Celtic *ek-tiros*, "off the land", was undoubtedly St Michael's Mount. Two other names recorded by Pytheas are preserved to this day: *Kantion* is our present Kent, and *Orcas* the present day Orkneys. Britain itself was, in Early Celtic, *Predanno-s*, the Romans being to blame for replacing the original P with B in their *Britannia*. The original P remains in modern Welsh *Prydein*, and the Cornish place name *Predannack*.

The Celtic language in the British Isles consisted of two distinct groups, Goidelic (Gaelic or Q-Celtic) and Brythonic (British or P-Celtic). Gaelic is spoken in Ireland, the Highlands and Islands of Scotland and the Isle of Mann where the last native speaker, Ned Maddrell, died in 1974, although a healthy revival of Manx is well under way.

The rest of Britain, from the Lowlands of Scotland southward, spoke Brythonic throughout the Iron Age (500 BC – AD 43) and the Roman period (AD 43 – AD 410). After the final Roman withdrawal in the early 5th century AD, groups of Germanic peoples began to cross the North Sea and colonise south-eastern Britain: Jutes from the Danish peninsula; Frisians from the Low Countries; Angles and Saxons from Germany. These groups, generally lumped together under the name Anglo-Saxons, were the forbears of the English and their language, also to be called Anglo-Saxon, was the precursor of the English language.

Historians now tend to believe that the westward spread of the English was more a progression of piecemeal colonisations rather than a planned pro-gramme of invasions although both the Anglo-Saxon Chronicles and the British Easter Annals, among other sources, record a number of bitter and bloody battles between the English newcomers and the Romano-Celtic British over a five century period. The Celtic population were not so much pushed westward, as popularly believed, as absorbed into the new Anglo-Saxon culture. Intermarriage was commonplace and Saxons with Celtic names such as Cerdic crop up surprisingly frequently. The Celtic west, though, resisted fiercely while the English fought equally hard to isolate these Celtic areas from each other. A Saxon victory at Dyrham near Bath in 577 succeeded, after a century of trying, in driving a wedge between the Celts of the south-western peninsula and those of Wales. From that moment, the Brythonic language spoken in both (although there were almost certainly regional dialects) began to diverge and develop independently. Another isolated area in north-western Britain, Cumbria (a name which includes the same Celtic word as the Welsh *cymru*, "compatriots") also developed its own branch of the tongue which died out in the 14th century, although Celtic place names such as Penrith survive to this day.

The Cornish language developed from the south-western dialect of Brythonic, as did Breton. The Armorican peninsula of Gaul, lying due south of Cornwall, was extensively settled from the 5th century AD by people from south-western Britain to become Brittany, "little Britain". The Breton language, still spoken by nearly a million people, remains the closest relative of Cornish.

After the Roman period, and probably both during and before, Cornwall was the westernmost part of the Celtic kingdom of Dumnonia, a name from which modern Devon is derived. The separate name was first recorded by the Romans in the place name *Durocornovio*. Identified as Tintagel, this name meant "fortress of the Cornish". *Cornubia*, recorded in the 8th century, probably represents a Latin *Cornouia*, itself derived from a Celtic name.

Here, then, is the explanation of the KERNOW of the road signs by the Tamar. It is the Cornish name for Cornwall, with a meaning approximating to "(land of the) promontory people". The modern name, Cornwall, first recorded as *Cornwalas* in 891, is a hybrid name in which the Anglo-Saxon word *wealhas*, their name for the Celtic Britons, was added to the then current form of Kernow, *Corneu*. It is also the word from which Wales is derived.

Contrary to the claims by some history books that Cornwall was conquered by the English King Ecgberht, the English advance in fact neither conquered nor subjugated it. Cornwall first faced the advance when King Centwine of Wessex won a battle in north Devon in 682. This resulted in extensive Anglo-Saxon settlement in north-eastern Cornwall, north of the River Ottery where English names predominate. In 705, the Cornish King Gerent II reacted derisively to a dictate from the Synod of Whitby that the Celtic Church of Cornwall — itself much older than the barely century-old English Christianity — conform to the doctrines of Rome. An army led by the Wessex King Ine and his kinsman Nonna attempted to enforce the directive in a fight against Gerent. The outcome is not known but the fact that lands at *Linig*, perhaps on the River Lynher, were given to Glastonbury Abbey by Ine may indicate that Gerent's resistance was unsuccessful.

At the Battle of *Hehil* (possibly on the Camel estuary, or even Hele near Bude) in 722, the Cornish pushed back a Saxon offensive. Other battles took place in the 8th century, although locations and results are not known. In 766, King Cynewulf of Wessex gave land in Somerset to the church at Wells for: " . . . love of God, atonement of my sins and also . . . for certain harassment of our enemies, the race of the Cornish". Evidence suggests that Cornwall stood firm during this period until King Ecgberht, in 815, ravaged the Cornish "from east to west", probably an offensive pushing down north-eastern Cornwall as far as the Camel. The Battle of *Gafalforda*, probably Galford on the Devon side of the Tamar, took place ten years later but, once again, the victor is not known.

It would appear that, at this time, the Cornish were allowing Danish Vikings to use Cornish harbours as bases from whence they could raid Wessex ports.

Ecgberht was not amused and his army crossed the Tamar to face a combined Cornish-Viking army at *Hengestesdun* (Hingston Down, Callington) in 838. The result was victory for Ecgberht, but he could not follow it up with outright conquest. Instead, renewed Viking activity on Britain's east coast called his forces away from Cornwall and within a year Ecgberht was dead. This was the last known battle on Cornish soil between the Cornish, or the West Welsh as they were often called at the time, and the English. Nearly a century of apparent peace reigned, with Cornish kings still on their thrones; in 875 or thereabouts, it was recorded that "Dungarth, king of Cornwall, was drowned.

Early in the 10th century, King Edward of Wessex created the bishopric of Crediton, to which lands in East Cornwall were given. Bishop Eadwulf was charged "that there every year he should visit the Cornish race, to stamp out their errors, for previously as much as they could they resisted the truth and did not obey papal decrees". Edward's successor, Aethelstan, the "father of England", expelled the "filthy race of the Cornish" from Exeter in the year 926 and fixed the left (east) bank of the Tamar as the boundary between the Cornish kingdom and that of Wessex into which Cornwall had never been incorporated. The following year, it was recorded that "Aethelstan had power over all the kings that were in this island; first Huwal, king of the West Welsh (then others) guaranteed peace both with pledge and with oaths". Huwal of the West Welsh (Cornish) should not be confused with Hywel Dda, king of Dyfed and, subsequently, of the enlarged South Welsh kingdom of Deheubarth during this same period.

By now, there were a number of Anglo-Saxon landowners in the eastern-most parts of Cornwall. In the north-eastern corner, north of the River Ottery, English place names were in the majority, and scattered concentrations of them were to be found along the Tamar. Some of these landowners even had Cornish slaves. The freeing of many of these slaves are recorded in the 10th century Bodmin Gospels and their Celtic names stand out clearly. Also freed in these manumissions were Anglo-Saxon slaves in the service of Cornish masters, but these are much in the minority. It is clear from these Celtic names that, by this time, the Cornish tongue had developed into a distinct language in its own right and would continue to do so while the Cornish monarchy diminished to an Earldom and, eventually, a Duchy as it is today.

Little was known of this early form of Cornish until about 1700 when Edward Lhuyd, keeper of the Ashmolean Museum, realised that an ancient 12th century document formerly believed to record an older form of Welsh was, in fact, Cornish. The mistake was easy to understand; for a long time Gwenhwyseg, the Gwent dialect of Welsh, was remarkably similar to Cornish. The document itself was a Vocabulary of Old Cornish, containing 960 words, with their glosses in Latin.

The Three Ages of Cornish

Old Cornish is the language from about 800 to 1250, whose remnants survive in the manumissions written on the flyleaves and margins of the Bodmin Gospels, the Old Cornish Vocabulary, place names in ancient charters and surviving place names in parts of East Cornwall in particular where, as the language died out at an early stage, their old form remained fossilised. The most obvious characteristic of these are the hard endings to elements which later softened; for example, Old Cornish *nant*, "valley", preserved in names such as Trenant, was to become *nans* and *nance* in later periods. This is a peculiarity of Cornish not present in Welsh and Breton where the hard endings have remained.

Middle Cornish or Medieval Cornish refers to the development of the language in the period from 1250 to 1550. The beginning of this period saw the softening process complete. Final *nt* became *ns*; final and medial *d* became a *dj* sound (a change which is believed to have taken place before 1200), or *z*; between vowels, *d* tended to become a soft *th*; and the guttural sound of *ch*, *gh* became a softly breathed *h*. Middle Cornish yielded a great deal of literature and the oldest surviving sentence in Cornish, from a 15th century Cartulary of the Collegiate Church of St Thomas at Glasney, Penryn. *Yn Polsethow ywhylyr anethow* was a reputed prophecy of c.1200 foretelling the founding of the church in 1265. It means, "In Polsethow shall be seen dwellings," but is ambiguous in that *anethow* can also mean "marvels".

It was also certainly at Glasney that the great works of Middle Cornish were written. Chief among these was the cycle of three long religious plays known as the *Ordinalia*. Played consecutively over three days in open air arenas known, in the Cornish of the time, as *plenys an gwary*, "playing places" they related events from the creation of the world until the resurrection of Christ. There was also a long poem based on the Passion of Christ and, from the closing years of this period, the play *Beunans Meryasek*, "Life of St Meriasek", the patron of Camborne, and written in 1504 by one Radulphus Ton. A few further scraps, such as a group of sermons translated from English, complete the surviving literature of Middle Cornish.

Late Cornish, or Modern Cornish, was the period of the language from about 1550 until its demise in the 19th century. It should be said that *Beunans Meriasek* and the series of twelve Homilies written in Cornish by John Tregear c.1555 are often regarded as a transitional or Tudor Cornish, resembling Middle Cornish but containing many characteristics of the Late period of the language.

Surviving texts in Late Cornish are many and varied, from folk-tales – notably *Jooan Chy a Horr*, "John of the Ram's House" and also called "The Three Points of Wisdom", to translations from the Bible, personal letters, poems, folk songs, narratives and family mottoes, in all about half as much again as the surviving remnants of the Middle Period. Surprisingly, these Late Cornish texts contain significantly less loan words from English and other languages than do the great plays of the Medieval phase. In 1707, the Welsh Celtic scholar Edward Lhuyd became the only person to carry out a detailed study of Cornish while it was a living vernacular. His spelling system is somewhat curious, differing strikingly with the spellings employed by the native writers of the time, and only recently has it been recognised that his system is phonetic, recording for the first and only time the actual pronunciation of the living tongue. The last piece of native prose to be written was the letter to Daines Barrington in 1776 by a Mousehole fisherman, William Bodinar, while the last native verse, known as "The Crankan Rhyme" was written down in the late 19th century.

As will be mentioned, problems have arisen within the movement to revive the language. In the author's view, however, the logical path is the continuation of the language, as unaltered as possible, from its last naturally evolved form; that is, Modern (Late) Cornish but only since 1980 has the necessary research into that period of the language taken place. This work, including a painstakingly careful standardisation of its spelling, is now complete and the Cornish in this book, except where otherwise stated, is Modern Cornish.

How Many People Spoke Cornish?

The westward retreat of Cornish was a gradual and somewhat irregular affair. Anglo-Saxon predominance north of the Ottery probably saw the language in that area die out at a very early date, probably well before 1200. Place names show that it lingered a little longer around Launceston, to the south-west of the Ottery and in the area south and west of the River Inny. English names are common on Bodmin Moor, due to settlements founded at a later date, but the Moor also contains many Cornish names, including its Cornish name *Goen Bren*, "upland grazing of the hill", recorded in the 12th century.

With Lanseme Travers, vicar of Quethiock, teaching his congregation the Lord's Prayer, Ten Commandments and Apostles' Creed in English in 1529, and Dr John Moreman doing likewise at Menheniot in 1540, it seems likely that Cornish was moribund in south-east Cornwall by the Tudor period, if not earlier. Place names also seem to indicate that the language had declined even earlier further west, around Lostwithiel.

At the time when Cornish was spoken from the Tamar westward, at around 1100, the population of Cornwall was about 21,000, 20,000 of whom spoke the language. In 1400, at the beginning of the era which saw the production of the great miracle plays, the population is estimated at 55,000. Of these, perhaps 34,000 were Cornish speakers. By this time, the language had re-

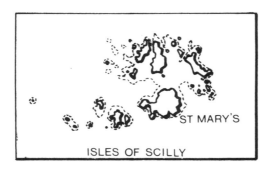

ISLES OF SCILLY

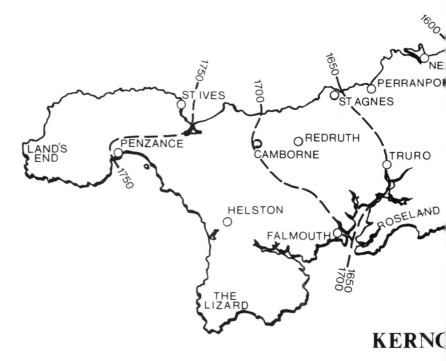

KERNO

THE WESTWARD RET

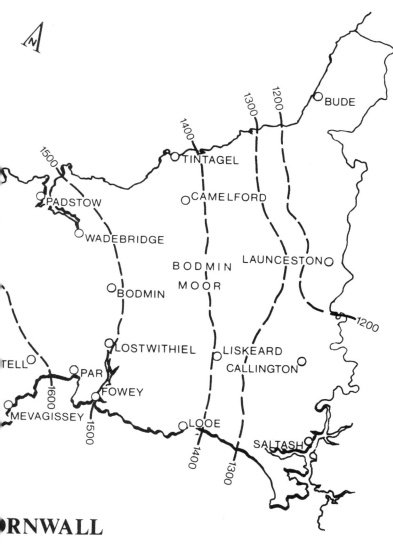

>RNWALL

E CORNISH LANGUAGE

treated to the area west of a line between Tintagel and Looe. A century later, it had fallen back as far as Bodmin. About 69,000 people then lived in Cornwall, of whom about half spoke Cornish.

The beginning of the 17th century saw the language's use confined to the west of Truro, with only a quarter of the Duchy's 84,000 people speaking it.

Cornish was reportedly spoken at St Ewe, near Mevagissey as late as 1595. Richard Carew, writing in 1602, stated that while Cornish was spoken everywhere west of Truro, most people were bilingual; however, in the Land's End peninsula, no English was spoken. Monoglot Cornish speakers survived at Feock in 1640 and forty years later, William Scawen affirmed that Cornish was still the only language that people of the Land's End and Lizard peninsulas knew. The last known Cornish sermon was preached at Landewednack, close to the Lizard, in 1678.

Nicholas Boson, who wrote extensively in Cornish at about that same time, and Edward Lhuyd in 1707, both stated that Cornish was still used in West Penwith (the Land's End peninsula), the coastal parishes of the Lizard, and towards Falmouth but, by 1750, it was confined to West Penwith.

It is difficult to say with any real accuracy when the Cornish language died out as a native vernacular. What is certain is that Dolly Pentreath of Mousehole (died 1777) was not the last speaker of Cornish despite the claims of all too many guide books. However, she was one of the very last to have been brought up as a monoglot Cornish speaker. Small pockets of people who could speak the tongue survived Dolly, and could be found well into the 19th century.

Memorial to Dolly Pentreath at Paul

The revival of the language

The instigator of the revival was Henry Jenner, born at St Columb in 1848. In the latter part of the 19th century, he pieced the language together, finally publishing his "Handbook of the Cornish Language" in 1904. His original intention was to continue the language in the form to which it had evolved in its last historic period but, in fact, he fed in a considerable amount of Medieval Cornish and left most of the modern form unexplored. Like almost everyone else who came after him, Jenner ignored Edward Lhuyd's study of the pronunciation and instead introduced a system which was virtually a mixture of Welsh and West Cornwall dialect. It was, nevertheless, a brave attempt to refloat the language but too much of it was missing.

Jenner died in 1934, aged 86, by which time the mantle of revival leadership had been taken over by Robert Morton Nance. Nance's approach was to begin again, widening the scope of the revived tongue by incorporating into it every scrap of Cornish he could find, from every historic period from the 12th to the 18th century. There had been no dictionary of Cornish, and therefore the texts of Middle and Late Cornish contained many variations in spelling. To overcome this problem, Nance devised his own system but with a more detailed and factual guide to pronunciation than Jenner. This new system was named "Unified Cornish", and has been the standard form of the language from the 1920s until recent years. Ironically, he launched it by issuing the Late Cornish folk story of "Jooan Chy a Horr", completely altering its linguistic character in the process. Hybrid and inaccurate it may have been but, over the years, Unified Cornish attracted a strong following and, in 1967, the Cornish Language Board was formed.

The success of the Language Board, though, became its undoing. As more, and often better informed, people became involved, so questions regarding the validity, inaccuracies and shortcomings of Unified Cornish began to be aired. The crisis came to a head in 1984 when Professor Glanville Price's book "The Languages of Britain" severely criticised Unified Cornish. It was, as most were aware, a concocted version of the tongue. As a result, Celtic scholars, linguists and academics were not prepared to take it seriously. In the end, the Language Board felt compelled to seek an alternative. Curiously, the Board refused to look at the suggestion that Henry Jenner's original intention, to pick up from where the language had left off in its Late period, but instead were persuaded to adopt a new system devised by Dr Ken George.

George's system, originally called Phonemic Cornish, was based on his 1984 doctorial dissertation presented at the Universite de Bretagne Occidentale in Brittany. This had studied the language of the Medieval period and, with the aid of a computer, had attempted to determine the pronunciation of the language at that time. The result introduced a spelling system so radically different to anything which had been seen before in Cornish that it provoked fierce opposition, not only within the language movement, but among academics who felt that Phonemic Cornish, or Common Cornish as it was renamed, had not only altered the spelling to an unacceptable degree, but had also failed to address any of the problems which had beset Nance's Unified System.

In the early 1980s, a group of Cornish enthusiasts led by Richard Gendall, perhaps the most experienced expert in the Cornish language decided to do what Jenner, Nance and all who had followed had failed to do; to study every scrap of Late, or Modern, Cornish and to pick it up from where it had left off. Authenticity was the desired goal, and this caused protracted and painstaking work in producing a standardised spelling in which only textual precedent could be used. Lhuyd's pronunciation study was also scrutinised in minute detail. The texts of Late Cornish provided details of traditional speech absent from the Middle Cornish on which both Unified and Common Cornish were based, and which exists only as religious verse. These enthusiasts formed the Cornish Language Council in 1986, a body which not only promotes Modern Cornish as a revived language, but encourages studies of the language from all its historic periods. It should perhaps be added here that the academics, linguists and Celtic scholars accept revived Late, or Modern, Cornish as an authentic tongue. This form of the tongue is also simpler in construction than those of earlier periods. For example, Middle Cornish inflected almost every verb, requiring literally thousands of verb parts to be learned. In contrast, all verb parts are handled by five auxiliary verbs, and the infinitive form of the main verb. The number of verb parts to be learned in the Late system is only about 150.

This book concerns itself only with authentic spellings from all periods of the language in the case of place names and their elements, and with standardised Modern (Late) Cornish in vocabularies, phrases and elementary lessons. The author is grateful to the Cornish Language Council and to its cultural sister group Teere ha Tavas (Land and Language) for assistance and support in the production of this book. However, it must be stressed that the responsibility for any errors are mine alone.

How many can speak Cornish today?

In truth, not very many, and the answer to this question really depends on the degree of fluency. Hundreds, perhaps more than a thousand people have passed examinations in Cornish of one form or another but, if fluency means the ability to hold spontaneous, unrehearsed speech on any normal subject, unarmed with dictionary and without breaking sentences down into words, or words into syllables or, for that matter, sounding like an English person attempting to speak a foreign language, then the number must be less than a hundred. The chances of hearing Cornish speech in the streets are pretty slim, but the odds are improving.

Do native speakers of Cornish exist?

Quite simply, no. A native speaker can only be one who has learned the language from another native speaker and so none can have existed since the language's demise. Arguably, the last native speaker was John Davey (died 1891), who learned the tongue from his father. A number of modern families have brought up their children to be bilingual in Cornish and English but, because the parents had to learn the language from scratch, they cannot be described as native speakers.

Abbreviations used in the text

B – Breton; Eng. – English; F – French; LC – Late Cornish; MC – Middle Cornish; OC – Old Cornish; OE – Old English; W – Welsh. C14, C15 etc. – 14th century, 15th century etc.

Cornish place name prefixes
– the 21 most common explained

"By Tre, Lan, Ros, Car, Pol and Pen; ye shall know most Cornishmen". So says the rhyme quoted by many guide books and Cornish surnames which begin with these elements are derived from place names. The following list explains what these common prefixes mean:

BOS: Also found as BOT-, BO-, BOJ-, BUS-, and BOD-. This means "dwelling, home" and, in many cases, is followed by a person's name, often an old and Celtic one. Old Cornish BOD-, BOT- often survives in East Cornwall with the later, softened forms occurring further west. The word survives in place-names despite becoming obsolete in the language before 1500, its meaning being absorbed by CHY.

CAR: Also GEAR, CAER and CR-. Possibly related to Latin *castrum*, this word means an enclosed settlement and can be loosely translated as "fort" or "enclosure". It was often applied to late prehistoric farmsteads within circular or oval enclosures or "rounds", and also to much larger and stronger Iron Age forts.

CARN: Still in general use in local speech, particularly in West Cornwall, CARN (the A is pronounced as in "hat", and the R is strongly sounded) applies to prominent rock formations. On hilltop sites, the translation is "tor" while at other locations, particularly coastal ones, "rockpile" or "crag". In one or two instances, it applies to artificial mounds of Neolithic or Bronze Age date where it means "cairn".

CHY: Also found as CHE-, CH-, and TY-. The modern tendency is to pronounce this to rhyme with "cry", but the final Y is in fact a peculiar sound not found in English and best described as quickly running together the sounds "er-ee". Where unstressed in place-names, this final sound tends to disappear. Originally meaning "cottage", CHY can be translated as "house".

GOON: Also occurring as GUN-, GON-, GOEN- and WOON. This is properly pronounced with a short OO, as in "good". Usually translated as "downs", it refers to open moorland, usually upland, and often used as unenclosed common pasture.

HAL: Also HALE- and HALL-. Often interpreted as "moor", this word rarely applies to upland moorland. Instead, it refers to the more archaic sense of "moor" – "marsh, wetland", usually the kind in which willow carr is found. LC *helack*, "willows", is almost certainly a related word. The great majority of HAL- place names occur near low-lying marshes of this type.

HAYLE: Occasionally HEL- or HELE. This means "estuary" in locations where expanses of mud or sand are exposed at low water. "Saltings" might be an equally good translation. ABER, "estuary", is found in Old Cornish but rarely in the Duchy's place names despite being common in Wales or Brittany where the same word exists. Instead, Cornish locations tend to use LOE, which also means "lake, pool".

HEN: This means "old" in the sense of "ancient, former". The commonest of all Cornish place names, HENDRA, literally means "old farm" but is better interpreted as "farm which still stands on its original site".

LAN: Like BOS-, this word became obsolete in the language before 1500 but is preserved in place names. Meaning "church enclosure", it normally described an Early Christian foundation of the Celtic Church within a round or oval earthwork, usually a re-used prehistoric site. Parish churches still occupy many of these sites, but a few which fell out of use at an early date are recalled by such names as HELLAND (*hen lan* – "former church enclosure"). LAN also occurs as a suffix to mean "fold, pound, enclosure" in words such as BOWLAN, "cattle-pound" and CORLAN, "sheep-fold" (it can also mean "cemetery"). Care is needed in translation as some place names with LAN actually contain NANS.

LES: Also found as LIS- and LEZ-. This normally means "court" in the sense of a local administrative centre, but can also mean "ruin", usually of an old fortified site. In place names, then, LES- can be interpreted as "court" or "ruined fort".

MELLAN: Also occurs as MELAN-, VELLAN- and BOLIN-. Derived from Latin, this means "mill" and is often found in mutated form with an initial V, implying a lost definite article. In Late Cornish, this initial sometimes became B, as in the place name BOLINGEY, "millhouse". Confusion with MELYN, "yellow, tawny", can often arise.

MEN: Also found as MAEN and MAYON. Pronounced "MAI-en", this word means "a stone". It is often found on maps and sign-posts with a circumflex over the E, a device borrowed from Lhuyd's phonetic records of the spoken language (1707) to de-note this peculiar vowel sound.

NANS: Also NAN-, NANT-, NANJ- and NANCE-. Some names which now begin with LA- or LAN- actually contain NANS, which means "valley". The form NANT, common in East Cornwall, preserves the hard ending of the Old Cornish word.

PEN: Also PEDN. This word has to be translated according to its context, as it can mean "head", "end", "top", "principal". There are even some cases where it derives from an Old Cor-nish *ben*, meaning "foot, bottom end". After about 1500, the original PEN became PEDN, although the intrusive D was often dropped if the word was used as a prefix to a compound word, e.g. PEDN KEI, but PENZANCE. In most coastal names, the usual translation is "headland".

POL: Sometimes found as POLL. Pronounced "pole", the meaning of this word is "pool", "pit", and occasionally "cove". In some names it replaces an earlier PORTH.

PORTH: Also occurs as POR-, PAR- and PR-. Coastal names with
           PORTH denote "a cove", normally one in which a boat can be
           safely landed, or where a valley meets the sea. This leads on to
           its secondary meaning, "entrance, gateway", mostly applying
           to inland sites. Modern maps which add "Cove" to names with
           PORTH ought to delete it.

RES: Also RET-, RED- and RE-. "Ford". The hard ending of Old
           Cornish *rit* survives in some place names, particularly in East
           Cornwall and also where it precedes an original letter H. For
           example, the Old Cornish name *ret hir* is now RETIRE, while
           the modern RETALLACK preserves the hard sound of Old
           Cornish *rit heloc*, "willow ford".

ROSE: Often ROS-. Perhaps the trickiest word to translate, the best
           clue is usually the landscape context of the place name. Its
           original meaning appears to have been "promontory", as in the
           Welsh *rhos*, developing to include "hillspur" and "coastal
           slope". Further meanings, "uncultivated valleyside" and, even-
           tually, "area of roughland surrounded by farmland" became
           covered by ROSE. In Late Cornish, the variant ROSH (pro-
           nounced "roe-sh") came to mean "uncultivated valley bot-
           tom". The oft-given interpretation of ROSE as "heathland" is
           not very strongly supportable and, where not obviously mean-
           ing a promontory, coastal slope or hillspur, ROSE is perhaps
           best translated as "roughland".

TRE: Also TREV- and TR-. Pronounced "tray", this originally meant
           a farming settlement but later expanded its scope to include
           larger communities. In place names, it can be taken to mean
           "farm" or "village", and sometimes forms a suffix, -DRA or -
           DREA. In many cases, TRE- is followed by a person's name,
           presumably the settlement's founder or, at least, a prominent
           early occupant.

VENTON: Sometimes FENTON. Derived from the Latin *fons*, this means
           "a well" in the sense of a natural spring (an artificially dug
           well is PEETH). Many of Cornwall's "holy wells" have this
           word in their names, often followed by the name of a local
           saint (VENTON UNY, "St Euny's well"), or a word describ-
           ing its qualities (VENTON SAURAS, [LC *saworez*], "fla-
           voured well").

ZAWN: A West Cornwall dialect word still in common use and derived
          from Late Cornish *sawan*. It describes a precipitous chasm-
          like formation in a sea cliff, usually where the action of the sea
          has eroded a narrow vertical lode of mineral ore from the
          harder country rock on either side. It can therefore be trans-
          lated as "cleft" or "cliff-chasm".

Common place name elements

The list which follows is of words commonly found within Cornish place
names, in their Late, Middle and Old forms (where known). Also included are
equivalent words in Welsh and Breton, which clearly show the relationship
between the three languages.

Late	Middle	Old	Welsh/Breton	English
-ack	-ek	-oc/-ic	W. -og; B. -ek/eg	adjectival ending
agolan	agolen		W. agalen; B. higolenn	whetstone
ambel (amal-)	ammal		W. ymyl	hillside, edge
an	an	en	W. y/yr; B. an	the
	ar		W. ar; B.ar	facing, beside
are	arth	ard	W. ardd; B. arz	high place
aulz	als	alt	W. allt; B. aod	cliff, slope, shore
awan	avon	auon	W. afon; B. auoun	river
bal				a mine, tinworks
bean	byghan/byan	bochan	W. bychan; B. bihan	small, little
bear	ber	ber	W. byr; B. berr	short
beath	beth		W. bedd; B. bez	grave, tomb
belin/melin	melyn	melin	W. melin; B. milin	mill
beuh	bugh/bewgh	buch	W. buch; B. bu	cow
bezow	besow	bedou	W. bedw; B. bezo	birch trees
	bos	bod	W. bod; B. bot	dwelling, home
bounder	bownder	bounder		lane
bowgy	bughjy	buchti	W. beudy; B. boutig	cowshed
broaz	bras	bras	W. bras; B. bras	great, large, big
brea	bre		W. bre; B. bre	hill
breh	bregh	brech	W. braich; B. brec'h	arm
brith	bregh		W. brych; B. brec'h	speckled, dappled
	bro		W. bro; B. bro	district, region
cabm (cam-)	cam	cam	W. cam; B. kamm	crooked, bent, curved
cadgwith	caswyth		W. cadwydd	thicket
carn	carn/kern		W. carn; B. karn	tor, crag
carbons	carbons		B. karrbont	paved road, causeway
carrack	carrek	carrec	W. carreg; B. karreg	a rock
carow	carow	caruu	W. carw; B. karv	stag (red deer)
castell	castel		W. castell; B. kastell	castle

Late	Middle	Old	Welsh/Breton	English
cauns	cauns		W. cawsai; B. chaoser	causeway, slipway
chy (-gy)	chy (-jy)	ti	W. tŷ; B. ti	house, cottage
cligar	clegar		W. clegr; B. kleger	crag
cooz	coys	cuit	W. coed; B. koad	a wood
corn	corn	corn	W. corn; B. korn	horn, corner
cownans	kewnans		W. ceunant	ravine
creaz	creys		W. craidd; B. kreiz	middle, centre
creeb	cryb		W. crib; B. krib	crest, reef
creeban	cryben		W. cribin; B. kribenn	little crest, reef
creeg	cruk	cruc	W. crug; B. krug	tumulus, barrow
crow	crow		W. crau; B. kraou	hut, shed
crowgy	crowjy			hut, hovel
crowz	crows	crois	W. crwys/croes; B. kroaz	a cross
crubm	crom		W. crwm; B. kromm	curved, bent
crumbla	cromlegh		W. cromlech; B. krommlec'h	quoit, dolmen
cudin	cudyn	cudin	W. cudyn; B. kudenn	curl, tress
cuthan	cuthen			hidden place, submerged reef
davas	davas	dauat	W. dafat; B. danvad	a sheep
deen	dyn	din/dun	W. din; B. din	cliff castle, hill fort
devrow	devra	dofer	B. douriev	waters
dinas	dynas	din/dun	W. dinas	cliff castle, hill fort
diserth	dyserth		W. diserth	precipitous, a bluff
doer (dor-)	dor	doer	W. daear; B. douer	ground, earth
dowr	dour	douer	W. dŷr; B. dour	water, river
drein	dreyn	drein	W. drain; B. drein	thorn bushes
dreiz	dreys	dreis	W. drys; B. drez	brambles
drym	trum		W. drum/trum	ridge
due	du	duw	W. du; B. du	black, dark
deaw/dew	deu/dyw	dui	W. dau/dwy; B. daou/diu	two
eball	ebal	ebol	W. ebol; B. ebeul	colt, foal
effarn	yfarn		W. uffern; B. ifern	hell, underworld
eglos	eglos	egglos	W. eglwys; B. iliz	church
elerh	elergh	elerhc	W. eleirch; B. elerc'h	swans
en	yn			in, in the
ennis	enys		W. ynys; B. enez	island, remote place
espack	epscop	escop	W. esgob; B. eskob	bishop
esse	eys	yd	W. ŷd; B. ed	corn, chaff
faw	faw		W. ffaw-; B. faou	beech trees
fose	fos		W. ffos; B. foz	wall, dyke
froze	fros	frot	W. ffrwd; B. froud	current, stream
garan	garan	garan	W. garan; B. garan	crane (bird)
garow	garow		W. garw; B. garv	rough, rugged
gew	keow		W. cau; B. kev	enclosure, paddock
glaze	glas		W. glas; B. glas	grey-green, blue
godreav	godref		W. godref	little farm, smallholding
gool (gol-)	gol		W, gŵyl; B. gouel	fair, feast, festival
golva	golva	guillia	W. gwylfa	watchplace, lookout
goon	goen	guen	W. gwaun; B. geun	downs, moorland

Late	Middle	Old	Welsh/Breton	English
gooth	goyth	guit	W. gŵydd; B. gwaz	goose
gover	gover	guuer	W. gofer; B. gouer	stream
gullas	goles	goeles	W. gwaelod; B. gouelet	lower, bottom
gulow	golow	golou	W. golau; B. goulou	light
gurgo	gorge		B. gour-gleuz	broken-down hedge
gwarha	gwartha		W. gwarthaf	higher, upper
gwavas	gwavos	guaevos	W. gaeafod	winter dwelling/farm
gweal	gweyl/guel	guil		open field
gweall				sight, view
gwearn	gwern	guern	W. gwern; B. gwern	alders, alder-marsh
gweeth	gweyth	guid	W. gwŷdd; B. gwez	trees
gwelz	guels		W. gwellt; B. geot	grass
gwennol	gwennol	guennol	W. gwennol; B. gwennel	swallow (bird)
gwenz	guyns	guins	W. gwynt; B. gwent	wind
gwethan	guethen	guiden	W. gwydden; B. gwezenn	tree
gwidn	gwyn/guen	guyn	W. gwyn; B. gwenn	white, light-coloured
gwlaze	gwlas	gulat	W. gwlad; B. glad	land, territory, nation
ha/hag	ha/hag		W. a/ac; B. ha/hag	and
hale	hal/haal		W. hâl; B. hal	marshy moor
havern	havar		W. hafar; B. havreg	summer fallow
hayl	heyl	heill		estuary, salting
hean (hen-)	hen		W. hen; B. hen	old, ancient, former
heel (hel-)	hel	hel		hall
hendra	hendre		W. hendref	old farm, farm on original site
heer	hyr	hir	W. hir; B. hir	long, tall
hellan	henlan		W. henllan	former church site
helles	henlys		W. henllys	ancient court, old ruins
helly	helhy	helh-	W. hely; B. helc'hi	hunting
hewas	havos		W. hafod; B. hanvod	summer dwelling, shieling, rough pasture
hily	hyly		W. heli; B. hili	salt water, brine
-iall/-all	-yel/-el		W. -iol/-ol; B. -iol/-ol	adjectival ending
idn	yn		W. yng; B. enk	narrow
idniall	enyal		W. ynial	wild, desolate
-in	-yn			diminutive ending
kear	car/cair	caer	W. caer; B. kêr	fort, enclosure
kein/kil	keyn/kyl	chein	W. cain/cefn; B. kein	back, ridge
kelyn	kelyn	kelin	W. celyn; B. kelenn	holly
killy	kelly	kelli	W. celli; B. killi	grove, copse
	kevil		W. ceffyl	horses
	lan	lan	W. llan; B. lann	church site
lanerh	lanergh	lanherch	W. llannerch	clearing
leaw	lugh	loch	W. llo; B. leue	calf
ledan	ledan	lidan	W. llydan; B. ledan	wide, broad
	lefans	lefant	W. llyffant; B. leffant	toad
leh	legh	lech	W. llech; B. lec'h	slab, flat stone, ledge
les	lys	lis	W. llys; B. lez	court, ruined fort
leven	leven		W. llyfn; B. limn	smooth, level

Late	Middle	Old	Welsh/Breton	English
lew	lyw	liu	W. lliw; B. liv	colour
lidgow	lusow		W. lludw; B. ludu	ashes, cinders
lidn (lin-)	lyn	lin	W. llyn; B. lenn	pool, pond
	lok	loc	W. lloc; B. lok	chapel, cell
loe	logh	loch	W. llwch; B. loc'h	lake, estuary, inlet
looan	lowen	lauen	W. llawen; B. laouen	happy
looar	lowarth	loworch	B. liorzh	garden
looarn	lowarn	louern	W. llywarn; B. louarn	fox
looz	loys	luit	W. llwyd; B. louet	grey
lost	lost		W. llost; B. lost	tail
maanah	managh	manach	W. mynach; B. manac'h	monk
marhas	marghas	marchas	W. marchnad; B. marc'had	market
marh/marth	margh	march	W. march; B. marc'h	horse
mean	men		W. maen; B. maen	a stone
melin/belin	melyn	melin	W. melin; B. milin	mill
melyn	melen	milin	W. melyn; B. melen	yellow, tawny
mena/meneth	meneth	menit	W. mynydd; B. menez	hill, hillside
mere	meyr	maur	W. mawr; B. meur	great, large
merther	merther		W. merthyr; B. merzher	saint's grave
miniz	munys		B. munut	little
moel	mol	moyl	W. moel; B. moal	bare, bald, domed
moer (mor-)	mor	mor	W. mor; B. mor	sea
nans	nans	nant	W. nant; B. ant	valley
noer (nor-)	nor	noer		ground, land, the earth
noweth	nowyth	newyth	W. newydd; B. nevez	new
oan	on/oyen		W. oen; B. oan	lamb
-ow	-ow	-ou	B. -ev	plural ending
park	park		W. parc; B. park	field
	perveth/parva		W. perfedd; B. permed	middle, inner
peal	peul		B. peul	steeple, pillar
pedn (pen)	pen	pen	W. pen, B. penn	head, end, top
				headland, principal
peebell	pybel	pybell	W. pibell	pipe, culvert
pell	pell		W. pell; B. pell	far, distant
penare	penarth		W. penardd; B. pennard	prominent headland
penteer	pentyr		W. pentir; B. penn-tir	headland
pillas	pylas		B. piled	naked oats (avena nuda)
plain	pleyn			arena
plewe	plu	plui	W. plwyf; B. ploue	parish, local
poll	pol	pol	W. pwll; B. poull	pool, cove, pit, creek
pons	pons	pont	W. pont; B. pont	bridge
por/porth	porth	porth	W. porth; B. porzh	cove, gateway
praze	pras		B. prad	meadow
prevan	preven		W. pryfan; B. prenven	snake, reptile, worm
pyg	pyk		W. pig; B. pig	point, beak
redan	reden	redan	W. rhedyn; B. raden	bracken
reen/ridn	ryn		W. rhyn; B. rinn	spur of land
res	res	rit	W. rhyd; B. red	ford

Late	Middle	Old	Welsh/Breton	English
rooz	ruyth	rud	W. rhudd; B. ruz	red
rose	ros		W. rhos; B. ros	promontory, hillspur roughland, valleyside coastal slope
royn	ruen		W. rhon; B. reunig	seal
sawan	savan		W. safn; B. saon	cliff-chasm, cleft
scathe	schath		W. ysgraff; B. skaf	open boat
scaw	scaw		W. ysgaw; B. skav	elder trees
scawan	scawen		B. skavan	elder tree
sevi	sivy		W. syfi; B. sivi	strawberries
spearn	spern			thorns
stampez				tin-stamping mill ("stamps")
stean	sten		W.ystaen; B. staen	tin
stenack	stenak		W. ystaenog; B. staeneg	tin-ground, tin-streaming works
straze	stras	strat	W. ystrad	flat-bottomed valley
	stum		W. ystum; B. stumm	bend
	tagell		W. tagell; B. tagell	collar, noose
talle (tal-)	tal/taal	tal	W. tal; B. tal	brow, gable
teer	tyr	tir	W. tir; B. tir	land
tew	tew			fat, thick
tewl	teul		W. tywyll; B tenwal	dark
towan	tewyn		W. tywyn; B. tevenn	sandhill(s)
	te-	to-	W. to-; B. de-	honorific prefix, "thy", to saint's name
todn	ton		W. ton; B. tonnen	turf, pasture
tol	toll		W. twll; B. toull	hole, boundary mark
tre(a)/tre(a)v	tre/tref	treu	W. tre/tref; B. trev	farm, settlement
treath	treyth	trait	W. traeth; B. treizh	beach, sand, strand
trethan	trethan			sand-bar
try/teir	try/tre		W. try; B. tri	three, triple
venton	fynten	funten	W. ffynnon; B. feunteun	well, spring
vorr	forth	ford	W. ffordd	way, road
war	war		W. ar; B. war	on, upon
wheal	wheyl			a mine, works
yeat	yet		W. giât	gate
yein	yeyn/eyn	iein	W. iaen; B. yen	cold, bleak
yorth	yorgh	yorch	W. iwrch; B. yourc'h	roebuck
		yuv	W. udd; B. iud	lord
zans	sans	sent	W. sant; B. sant	holy, sacred, saint
zeah	seygh		W. sych; B. sec'h	dry
zeath	seth	sait	W. saeth; B. saezh	arrow

Moaz Lowz

Tho ve scathe
nevra war an moer a neidga,
gen an todnow leskez,
gen an gwendgow heltheze. . .
na oar den'eth gwelhas
pelea reeg ve kerras.

Tho ve quillan
war askall goolan,
pub ear pell a vaggia
pelea vo daa gonga,
ubma ha enna,
skesy nevra
me nan veth.

Cran o ve,
nevra andro therama a moaz,
nag eze dallath,
nag eze duath,
della me ra boaz
tereba merwall.
Dew gwerras thebm a fall.

Drifting

I am a boat
ever on the sea drifting,
by the waves rocked,
by the winds driven. . .
no man can see
where I have gone.

I am a feather
on a gull's wing,
ever travelling far
where it pleases her,
here and there,
escape never
shall I be able.

I am a circle,
ever around I go,
there is no beginning,
there is no ending,
thus shall I be
until I die.
God help to me my failure.

Richard Gendall

*   *   *

Pronunciation

The pronunciation of Cornish words and place names can be a baffling exercise to the uninitiated as they are seldom spoken quite as expected. Often, the placing of stress can come as a surprise. This does not tend to follow the pattern of English and frequently catches out the media presenters in particular (despite the existence of a BBC pronunciation dictionary).

In general, stress is placed on the penultimate syllable of words with more than two syllables; for example, "bosWARthen" not "BOSwarthen". With two syllable words, the stress is often on the second one so, for Penzance, Redruth and Liskeard, we have "p'n-ZANSS", "r'DROOTH", "l's-KARD" and not the "PEN-zanss", "RED-rooth" and LISS-kard" we hear only too often.

Throughout this book, pronunciation guides are given for some of the more difficult or unexpected words. These guides are necessarily approximate as some sounds of Cornish do not occur in Standard English and, as mastery of the International Phonetic Alphabet is an art in itself, a simplified system is used here and explained below.

a – as in "cat"
aa – as *ai* of "air"
au – midway between "aw" and "ah"
aia – roughly, "ai(r)-a"
ar – *a* as in "cat", *r* lightly rolled
aou – "ai-oo" spoken quickly
dh – soft th, as in "this"
e – as in "pen"
ei – roughly, "er-ee"
ee – as in "seen"
eu – "ee-oo"
ew – as in "dew"
g – hard, as in "gate"
h – as last letter, lightly breathed

i – as in "pin"
j – as in "jet"
lh – the peculiar sound of Cornish *ll*, "l'hl"
o – as in "dog"
oe – as in "toe"
oi – as *oy* of "boy"
oo – as in "pool"
ooi – as "coo-ee"
rr – lightly roll
ss – as in "hiss"
th – hard *th*, as in "thin"
u – as in "bun"
û – as *u* of "bull"
zh – as *s* in "leisure"

All other letters and combinations as in Standard English. Stress is shown by capital letters

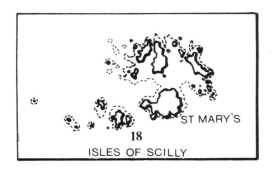

18
ISLES OF SCILLY

ST MARY'S

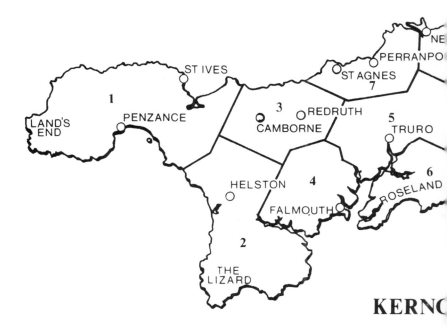

ST IVES

1

LAND'S
END

PENZANCE

3

REDRUTH

CAMBORNE

ST AGNES
7

PERRANPO

NE

5

TRURO

6

ROSELAND

HELSTON

4

FALMOUTH

2

THE
LIZARD

KERN

BUDE
14

TINTAGEL
13

CAMELFORD

PADSTOW

11 WADEBRIDGE

15
LAUNCESTON

BODMIN
12 MOOR

BODMIN

9

STELL

LOSTWITHIEL

LISKEARD

PAR **10**

CALLINGTON

FOWEY

16

17

MEVAGISSEY

LOOE

SALTASH

CORNWALL

1

Place Names of Penzance, St Ives & Land's End

AIRE POINT: after rock formation called Carn Aire, LC *carn are*, "outcrop on a height".

ALSIA: probably MC *alsyow*, "slopes", but pronounced "AI-lia".

AMALEBRA: "amal-EB-ra". LC *amal-*, "hillslope" and unknown second element. Padel suggests an unrecorded Cornish equivalent of Welsh *obry*, "down, below".

AMALVEOR: LC *amal vere*, "great hillslope".

ANGARRACK: LC *an garrack*, "the rock".

ARDENSAWETH/ARDENSAWAH: LC *arrans aweth*, "silver stream".

AVARACK: possibly an ironic name for this wave-swept rock, LC *havrack*, "fallow ground".

BALLESWIDDEN: LC *bal Leswidn*, "Leswidden Mine", after nearby farm, LC *les widn*, "white ruins", after nearby earthwork (now destroyed), or "white mud" from extensive china-clay deposits.

BALLOWALL: "b'LAOU-el". Early forms such as C13 *Bolouhal* suggest that this name is MC *bos Louhal*, "Louhal's dwelling".

BARTINNEY: "bar-TIN-ee". A little obscure. C13 form *Breteny* might support the traditional meaning, "hill of fires", LC *brea tanow*.

BEAGLETODN: "big'l-TUD'n". LC *beagel todn*, "pasture hillock".

BELLOWALL: this name results from a mapmaker's error and was *Bolowan* in the C17. MC *bos lowen*, "happy dwelling", and still locally pronounced "b'LOO-an".

BOJEWYAN: MC *bos Uyon*, "Uyon's dwelling".

BOLEIGH: "b'LAI". MC *bos legh*, "dwelling by a slab".

BOLOGGAS: MC *bos logas*, "dwelling of mice".

BOSAVERN: MC *bos Awern*, "Awern's dwelling".

BOSCASWELL: MC *bos Caswal*, "Caswal's dwelling". Locally pronounced "b'SKAAL".

BOSCAWEN-ÛN: "b'scaun-OON". MC *bos*, "dwelling"; LC *scawan an oon*, "elder tree on the downs".

BOSCEAN: MC *bos*, "dwelling"; LC *sehan*, "waterless place".

BOSIGRAN: "b'SIG-run". C14 spellings *Bosygarane/Boschygarn* reveal the curious inclusion of both MC *bos*, "dwelling", and MC *chy*, "house/cottage" (see also BOSULLOW). How this translates is not clear, perhaps "dwelling by Geren's house".

BOSKEDNAN: MC *bos*, "dwelling"; LC *kednan*, "reeds".

BOSLOW: MC *bos*, "dwelling"; LC *loe*, "pool".

BOSOLJACK: MC *bos*, "dwelling"; LC *howlgack*, "sunny".

BOSPORTHENNIS: MC *bos*, "dwelling", LC *porth ennis*, "gateway to an isolated spot (or "to Ninnes")". A lonely moorland track leads south towards Ninnes, LC *an ennis*, "the isolated place". Pronounced "b'z-PREN-iss".

BOSTRAZE: MC *bos*, "dwelling"; LC *straze*, "flat-bottomed valley".

BOSULLOW: C14 *Boschiwolou*. MC *bos chy wolow*, "dwelling by a house of light".

BOSWARTHAN: MC *bos Warthan*, "Gwarthan's dwelling".

BOSWARVA: *Bosworveth* C15. MC *bos*, "dwelling"; LC *war veth*, "on a grave".

BOSWENS: MC *bos*, "dwelling"; LC *wenz*, "wind".

BOSWORLAS: MC *bos Worlas*, "Gorlas's dwelling".

BOTALLACK: "b'TAL-ek". MC *bos Talek*, "Talek's dwelling". The personal name Talek, still found as the surname Tallack, means "big/heavy browed".

BOWGYHEERE: "baou-jee-HEER". LC *bowgy heer*, "long cowshed".

BRANE: *Bosvran* C14. MC *bos vran*, "crow's dwelling" or "Bran's dwelling". The nearby Iron Age hill fort of Caer Brane is LC *kear Brane*, "hill fort at Brane".

BREA: "brai". LC *brea*, "hill".

BRISONS: these great rocks off Cape Cornwall have a French name, *brisant*, "reef".

BRUNNION: LC *brudnian*, "hills".

BURNEWHALL: "ber-NEW-el". *Bodynewel* C14. MC *bos yn newl*, "dwelling in the mist".

ST BURYAN: from patroness of church, St Beriana. The Cornish name for the churchtown was *Eglosberria* C11, OC *egglos Beriana*, "church of St Beriana".

BUSVARGUS: MC *bos*, "dwelling"; LC *vargez*, "buzzard".

CANON'S TOWN: C19 settlement, founded by Canon John Rogers of Penrose, Helston (1778-1856).

CAPE CORNWALL: so named by chartmakers from about 1690. Its Cornish name was *Kulgyth East* C16, *The Kilguthe* C17; LC *kil gooth East*, "gooseback of St Just", from the headland's distinctive shape. Claims that this is the only so-called "cape" south of Scotland are not quite correct: the headland of Pencabe in the Roseland peninsula, near Portscatho, contains MC *capa*, "cape".

CARBIS BAY: A modern name. The bay is actually *Porthreptor* c.1580 (still Barrepta Cove on some maps); LC *porth*, "cove" and an unknown second element. *Carbons*, C14, was a nearby farm, LC *carbons*, "paved road, causeway".

CARN BARGUS: Confusingly respelt "Carn Barges" by the Ordnance Survey, the name contains a hard G. LC *carn bargez*, "buzzard outcrop".

CARN BARRA: LC *carn bara*, "bread (shaped) outcrop".

CARN BEAN: "carn BEE-an". LC *carn bean*, "little tor".

CARN DU: LC *carn due*, "black outcrop".

CARNEQUIDDEN: the C14 form *Kernegwyn* shows that this name does not contain *carn*. LC *kernick widn*, "white corner".

CARN EUNY: "carn YOO-nee". LC *carn Euny*, "St Euny's tor". The rock outcrop above the prehistoric village which has adopted its name also stands near the twin holy wells and site of a former chapel dedicated to St Euny.

CARN GALVA: the erroneous spelling by the Ordnance Survey, since adopted by others, "Carn Galver", alters the pronunciation of this name which is LC *carn golva*, "lookout tor".

CARN GLOOSE: a fairly recent respelling of *Careg Glouse* C17, *Carrick Gloose* C19; LC *carrack looz*, "grey rock".

CARN GREEB: LC *carn greeb*, "crest outcrop".

CARN GUTHENSBRAS: LC *carn guthan broaz*, "outcrop by a great sunken reef".

CARN KENIDJACK: The C16 form *Kern-nusack*, and the C17 and 18 *Karnusak, Carnidjack, Carn Nusack*, clearly show that this name is not the same as that of Kenidjack Farm a couple of miles to the west, which was *Kenygiek* C14, *Keniggiack* C16, *Caniack* C18; MC *kunyjek*, "fuel-ground". The Carn has never been part of Kenidjack land but on the holding of Carnyorth. The "Carn" of the present name is superfluous and was only added in the C19. The derivation would seem to bear out its traditional translation, LC *carn eedgack*, "hooting tor", from the sound of the wind blowing through its weird shapes.

CARN LES BOEL: LC *carn les boell*, "ruined fort at an axe-shaped outcrop". The site of an Iron Age cliff castle.

CARN LESKYS: LC *carn leskez*, "burnt outcrop".

CARN NAUN: Ordnance Survey misprint of C19 *Carnmen Point*; LC *carn mean*, "stone outcrop". Its alternative and older name, Pensowssen, C16, is LC *pen- Sausen*, "Englishman's headland".

CARN SCATHE: LC *carn scathe*, "boat outcrop".

CARN VESLAN: LC *carn vesklan*, "mussel outcrop".

CARNYORTH: LC *carn yorth*, "roebuck tor".

CARRACK GLADDEN: LC *carrack gladn*, "waterside rock".

THE CARRACKS: LC *carrack*, "rock", with Eng. plural. These are the rocks advertised by St Ives boatmen as "Seal Island". The two groups of rocks are more precisely known as the Western Carracks and Carrack an Ethan, LC *carrack an ethen*, "the birds' rock".

CASTALLACK: "c'STAL-ek". LC *castellick*, "little castle" from prehistoric enclosure nearby.

CASTLE AN DINAS: Eng. *castle*: LC *an dinas*, "the hill fort".

CASTLE HORNECK: A former mansion of the Borlase family, now a Youth Hostel, the name is LC *castell hoarnack*, "iron-strong castle", possibly a former name of the nearby hill fort now called Lesingey Round (see LESINGEY).

CHAIR LADDER: Usually interpreted as Eng. *chair* and LC *ledra*, "cliff", an alternative emerges from a c.1700 folk-tale "The Duchess of Cornwall's Progress". In this, Harry the Hermit of Chapel Carn Brea is accused of sorcery; one charge being that he habitually sat without fear in a natural chair on the brink of this stupendous cliff. The chair is referred to as *Tutton Harry an Lader*, "Seat of Harry the Thief", and it is suggested from this that the name is LC *cheer lader*, "thief's chair".

CHAPEL CARN BREA: Confusingly named "Carn Brea" on most maps (another Carn Brea stands above Redruth), the chapel recalled by this name no longer exists. It stood on a huge Neolithic cairn on the summit of the hill whose name would appear to be LC *chapall carn brea*, "chapel of the cairn hill".

CHÛN: "choon". LC *chy oon*, "house on downland".

CHYANDOUR: LC *chy an dowr*, "house by the water/stream".

CHYENHAL: LC *chy an hale*, "house by the marsh". The pronunciation "chei-an-HAIL" would be more correct than the current "chei-an-HAWL".

CHYKEMBRO: LC *chy Kembro*, "Welshman's house".

CHYPONS: LC *chy pons*, "bridge house".

CHYPRAZE: LC *chy praze*, "meadow house".

CHYSAUSTER: LC *chy Silvester*, "Sylvester's house" (*Chysalvestre* C14). The current pronunciation, "chei-ZAW-ster" is incorrect; traditionally, it is "ch'ZOI-ster".

CHYTODDEN: LC *chy todn*, "house on pasture".

CLODGY POINT: LC *clodgy*, from *clave-gy*, "lazar-house".

COLDHARBOUR: Eng. term meaning "shelter".

COLLURIAN: No Cornish derivation can be found for this name. A healing well reputed to cure diseases of the eye exists here and, curiously, the Greek *kolorion* means "eye-salve".

CONNOR DOWNS: A C19 settlement named after the former manor of Conarton (*Conarditone* C11), Eng. *Conar tun*, "Conor's farm".

COWLOE: The name of this flat reef surrounded by swirling foam off the breakwater at Sennen Cove may derive from LC *cowla*, "curdling", or from LC *carla/carlath*, "ray-fish". Smaller seaward rocks, Bo Cowloe and Little Bo, contain LC *boh*, "buck".

CRIBBA HEAD: LC *creebow*, "crests, reefs".

CRIPPLES' EASE: A C19 hamlet, so named from its position at the top of a long, tortuous hill.

CROWLAS: "KRAOU-lus". The C14 form *Croures* suggests MC *crow res*, "hut on a ford".

CROWNER ROCKS: Off Porthmeor Beach, St Ives, these are wrongly named by the Ordnance Survey. The correct name is Gawna, LC *gowna*, "farrow cow".

CROWS AN WRA: LC *crowz an wrah*, "the hag's/witch's cross". Pron. "kraouz an RAI".

CUDDEN POINT: Possibly from LC *cudin*, "tress", from its outline, or from the fringe of kelp around its base.

DERVAL: C20 shortening of the earlier *Deveral*; LC *dever-ell*, "watery".

DOWRAN: LC *dowr-an*, "place of water".

DRIFT: LC *(an) dreav*, "the settlement/farm".

EBAL ROCKS: LC *eball*, "colt, foal".

EMBLA: LC *emblow*, "hillslopes".

ENESTREVEN: LC *ennis treven*, "isolated houses".

ST ERTH: after dedication of its church to the Irish priest Erc. The former name of the churchtown was Lanuthnoe, MC *lan Uthno*, "church-site on the manor of Uthno".

ESCALLS: LC *hesk aulz*, "sedge cliff".

FOAGE: "foej". A strangely mutated fossilisation of MC *bos*, "dwelling".

GALA ROCKS: *Carlow Rocks* C19. LC *carla/carlath*, "ray fish".

GAZELL: the maps appear to attach this name to rocks but, in fact, it belongs to a nearby indentation in the coast; LC *an gazall*, "the armpit/hollow".

GAZICK: in contrast to the above, this name applies to a rock and not a cove as the maps suggest. LC *an gasack*, "the mare".

GEAR: LC *an gear*, "the fort".

GEEVOR MINE: The present name derives from an early tinwork on the site which was *Stenak an gever;* LC *stenack an gever,* "the goat's tinstream". The name has a hard G and the pronunciation "GEE-vaw" commonly used by the media should be discouraged in favour of the more correct "GEE-ver".

GEORGIA: LC *gurgow*, "broken field walls".

GERMOE: pronounced with a hard G, this name is from the dedication of the church to the early Celtic priest Germoch.

GODOLPHIN: "g'DOL-fin". Some have expressed doubts about the derivation of this word from a suggested MC *godolghyn*, "hillock", but no alternative has been found.

John Norden's c.1580 map of the Lands's End peninsula

GODREVY: LC *godrevi*, "smallholdings".

GOLDSITHNEY: LC *gol- Sithny*, "St Sithny's feast". The traditional feast of Sithney, near Helston, was transferred to this location in Medieval times.

GRUMBLA: LC *an grumbla*, "the dolmen". The remains of a megalithic structure still survive nearby.

GULVAL: apparently named after an obscure Celtic saint, Welvela. The name formerly given to the churchtown was *Lanestli* C13; MC *lan Estli*, "Estli's church-site".

GURNARD'S HEAD: Eng., from the resemblance of the headland's profile to that of a red gurnard. This name does not appear to be older than the mid C18. In C16, the headland was known as *Innyall*; LC *idniall*, "desolate place", a name recalled by St Ives fishermen in 1935 as "The Isnarl".

GWAVAS: "GWAW-vus". LC *gwavas*, "winter farm".

GWENVER: LC *gwin- vorr*, "white way".

GWINEAR: from Early Christian Irish priest Fionngar, the patron of the church.

GWITHIAN: from early Celtic priest Gothian, to whom the church is dedicated.

HAILGLOWER: LC *helack looar*, "willow garden".

HALSETOWN: named after its founder, James Halse (1769-1838), owner of the St Ives Consols Mine and MP for St Ives.

HANNIBAL'S CARN: possibly named after the legendary giant Holiburn of nearby Carn Galva, but more likely after Hannibal Thomas, a C18 farmer at Bosporthennis, below the hill. The name does not appear to be older than his time.

HAYLE: A C18/19 settlement named after the lake-like estuary; LC *hayl*, "estuary, saltings", as is the principal river flowing into it.

HEAMOOR: Eng., from OE *gehaeg mor*, "enclosure by a marsh".

HELLANGOVE: LC *hel- an gove*, "the smith's hall".

HELLESVEAN: LC *helles vean*, "little Helles" (LC *hen- les*, "old ruins").

HELLESVEOR: LC *helles vere*, "great Helles".

HENDRA: LC *hendra*, "old farm, farm on original site". With at least 34 examples, this is the most common place name in Cornwall.

ST HILARY: from St Hilarius, patron of the church.

HOR POINT: LC *horr*, "ram".

ST IVES: from foundation of church by the Irish priestess St Ia (pron. "EE-a"). The mistaken forms *Ive/Ithe* appeared briefly in C14, but the original form persisted until the C17. The harbour was *Porthia* C13, *Poreea* C18; LC *por(th) Eia*, "St Ia's harbour".

JOPPA: LC *shoppa*, "workshop".

ST JUST: named after the patron of the church, thought by some to have been Yestin, son of King Gerent I of Dumnonia. The medieval name for the churchtown was *Lanuste* C14 (pron. lan-AIST"); MC *lan Uste*, "St Just's church-site".

KEIGWIN: LC *kea gwidn*, "white hedge" and traditionally pronounced "gwid'n". The alternative pronunciation is "KEG-win".

KELYNACK: LC *kelynack*, "holly grove". The modern pronunciation, "k'LIE-nek", is actually in error, and ought to have been "k'LIN-ek".

KEMYEL: LC *kea Mehale*, "Michael's hedge".

KENEGIE: LC *kenegi*, "marshes". A modern tendency to pronounce this "k'NEE-gee" by mistaken analogy with Carnegie Hall should be discouraged in favour of the correct "k'NEG-ee".

KENYTHON: "k'n-EI-thun". LC *kea an eithin*, "the furze hedge".

KERRIS: LC *kearez*, "fortified". The remains of an Iron Age enclosure stand nearby.

KERROW: LC *kerrow*, "forts", or LC *carow*, "stag".

KERROWE: formerly *Nancarrow* C18; LC *nans carow*, "stag's valley".

LAMORNA: *Nansmorana* C13; MC *nans moranow*, "valley of blackberries", showing an archaic plural form.

LAND'S END: Eng., dating from C14. A Cornish equivalent was recorded in C16/17, *Pen an Gluas, Pedden an Wolas*; LC *pedn an wlase*, "end of the land".

LANYON: now rather different from its early form, *Liniein* C13; MC *lyn yeyn*, "cold pool". The modern pronunciation "lan-YON" is incorrect. Traditionally it is "l'n-EIN", which reflects its true derivation.

LEAH: also spelt LEHA; LC *lehow*, "slabs".

LEEDSTOWN: C19 settlement founded by the Dukes of Leeds. Attempts by some to Cornucise the name to "Treleeds" are somewhat absurd as its Eng. name was coined after the demise of Cornish.

LELANT: properly UNY LELANT, from the dedication of its church to St Euny. The older name of the churchtown, *Lananta* C13; MC *lan Anta*, "Anta's church-site", is thus preserved. A chapel to St Anta (Chapel Anjier) stood on a low cliff north of the present church.

LESINGEY: LC *les en gea*, "ruined fort within a hedge". The Iron Age hill fort, Lesingey Round, is enclosed within a circular stone hedge (see also CASTLE HORNECK).

ST LEVAN: the church saint, Selevan, has suffered the shortening of his name to St Levan. He may have been Selyf, brother of St Just, and the "Selus" named on the early inscribed memorial stone in St Just church. Porth Chapel, LC *porth chapall*, "chapel cove", nearby and below the ancient remains of St Levan's chapel and holy well was, in C16, *Porth Selleven*, "St Selevan's cove".

LOGAN ROCK: Dialect, *logging*, "rocking" and properly pronounced "LOG-un", rather than the "LOE-gun" often heard today. This natural formation was formerly known as *Men Amber*, LC *mean omber*, "balance stone", as is another rocking stone near Nancegollan.

LONGSHIPS: Eng. "long ships" from a fancied resemblance of this reef to a fleet of vessels and dating from the C16. Individual rocks within the reef include Cein, LC *kein*, "back"; Tal-y-maen, LC *talle an mean*, "the stone gable", also called Farkell Carn, LC *carn forhel*, "forked outcrop"; Hy-jail Rock, LC *an jowl*, "the devil"; Carn Brâs, LC *carn broaz*, "great outcrop" (the rock on which stands the lighthouse); Plassek, LC *plasack*, "plate-like"; Herly, LC *heer leh*, "long ledge"; and Meinek, LC *meinack*, "stony".

LUDGVAN: The St Ludevon often referred to appears not to have existed. The place name, traditionally pronounced "LID-jan", may be LC *lidgow-an*, "place of cinders".

MADRON: "MAD-ern". The name is derived from the church saint, Madern. The churchtown was once known as *Landithy*, MC *lan Dethy*, "Tetha's church-site". Is this the same person commemorated at St Teath near Camelford?

MAEN DOWER: LC *mean dowr*, "water stone".

MARAZION: formerly twin settlements, each with its medieval market: MC *marghas vyan*, "little market", and MC *marghas Iou*, "Thursday market". The first remains as the present name of the town, while the second is remembered by Market Jew Street, Penzance, LC *marhas Jeu*, "Thursday market", which led towards the original market three miles away. The name of the town is pronounced "ma-ra-ZEI-an", rather than the "ma-ra-ZEE-an" which would have been truer to the language.

MAYON: LC *mean*, "stone". Named after a former *carrack zans*, ("sacred rock") which still exists. Also known as the Table-maen, local traditions and Arthurian tales are linked with it.

MÊN-AN-TOL: LC *mean an tol*, "stone of the hole". A famous Neolithic holed stone, recently shown to have been a component of a stone circle.

MÊN SCRYFA: LC *mean screffa*, "stone of writing"; also called MÊN

SCRYFYS, LC *mean screffez*, "written stone". A C5/6 inscribed memorial stone.

MERRY MAIDENS: a C19 name for the famous stone circle formerly known as the *Dawns Myin*; LC *dauns mein*, "dance of stones".

MERTHEN POINT: LC *mor- theen*, "sea-fort".

ST MICHAEL'S MOUNT: the C12 priory on the summit of this island was dedicated to St Michael and was, for a time, administered by its Breton equivalent, Mont St Michel. The island has a traditional Cornish name, *Cara Clowse in Cowse* C17; LC *carrack looz en cooz*, "grey rock in the wood", which, if genuine, would be a remarkable folk-memory: the Mount was once surrounded by a forest which was inundated by the sea c.2500 BC.

MINACK THEATRE: named after the coastal rock above which this open-air cliffside theatre was built; LC *meinack*, "stony".

MORVAH: *Morveth* C14. Apparently named after an obscure St Morwetha to whom the chapel whose scanty ruins lie on the cliff north of the present church (uniquely dedicated to St Brigid of Sweden) was dedicated in medieval times. Padel rejects St Morwetha, preferring LC *mor- veth*, "sea grave".

MOUSEHOLE: despite endless arguments and attempts to find a Cornish derivation, this place name is Eng., though *Musehole* C13 is surprisingly early, and presumably after the great sea cave nearby. The harbour was *Portheness* C13, *Porth Ennis* C17; LC *porth ennis*, "island harbour", after St Clement's Isle which shields its entrance. Mousehole and Porth Ennis were, at one time, adjacent communities. Pronounced "MAOU-zl".

MULFRA: LC *moel vrea*, "bare/domed hill".

NANCLEDRA: *Nanscludri* C14. MC *nans Clodri*, "Clodri's valley". Pronounced "nan-KLED-ra", but traditionally "KLED-ri".

NANJIZAL: LC *nans esall*, "low valley". Pronounced "nan-JIZ'l".

NATHAGA ROCKS: Formerly *Lethega Rocks*; LC *lethegow*, "milky ones" from the foam around their bases.

NAVAX POINT: MC *kynyavos*, "autumn farm".

NEWBRIDGE: C19 Eng. name coined after building of road bridge over Carthew Water (Newlyn River). Its former name was *Hallentacken*, LC *hale an tegan*, "the pretty marsh".

NEWLYN: Early misspelling of C13 *Lulyn*; MC *lu lyn*, "fleet pool".

NEWMILL: *Mulfra Newe Mill* C17. An earlier name of this settlement may have been *Chynoey*, LC *chy Noy*, "Noah's house" or "house of the Noy family".

NINNES: LC *an ennis*, "the isolated place" (see also BOSPORTHENNIS).

NOON BILLAS: LC *an oon billa*s, "the downs of naked oats (*avena nuda*, locally "pillas")".

NUMPHRA: LC *an oon vrea*, "the downs by a hill".

PARK AN GROWES: LC *park an growz*, "field of the cross". Pronounced "park an GRAOUZ".

PAUL: after St Paul Aurelian (St Pol de Leon).

PEDNAVOUNDER: LC *pedn a vounder*, "end of the lane".

PEDN KEI: LC *pedn kye*, "dog's head".

PEDN MEN AN MERE: LC *pedn mean an mere*, "the great stone headland". Its earlier name was *Tallmer/Talmena Point* C16, LC *tal- mere*, "great brow"; LC *tal- mena*, "hillside brow".

PEDN OLVA: LC *pedn olva*, "lookout headland".

PENBEAGLE: LC *pen- beagel*, "top of a hillock".

PENBERTH: LC *pen- berth*, "bush end".

PENDEEN: LC *pen- deen*, "cliff castle headland". No such fortification is known here but, as the headland was extensively mined in the C18/19, all trace of one could have been destroyed.

PENDOWER COVE: LC *pen- dowr*, "water's end". PENDOUR COVE at Zennor has the same meaning.

PENDREA: LC *pen- drea*, "principal farm". Pronounced "p'n-DRAI".

PEN ENYS POINT: LC *pedn ennis*, "island/remote headland". The word "Point" on the maps is unnecessary.

PENGERSICK: "p'n-GER-zek". LC *pen- gorsack*, "end of a marshy area".

PENLEE POINT: LC *pen- leh*, "slab headland". Pron. "p'n-LEE". Again, "Point" is not necessary.

PENNANCE: "p'NANSS". LC *pen- nans*, "valley end".

PENROSE: "p'n-ROEZ" and not "PEN-roez". LC *pen- rose*, "end of rough-land".

PENTREATH: LC *pen- treath*, "beach end". Properly, "p'n-TRETH".

PENWITH: an ancient name for Cornwall's western Hundred, traceable back to at least the year 997. Nance's translation of LC *penwith* as "furthest end, extremity" was rejected by Padel, who suggests "end-district".

PENZANCE: LC *pen- zans*, "holy headland", from an ancient chapel which stood on the low headland near the present church.

PENZER POINT: LC *pen- ser(th)*, "steep headland".

PERRANUTHNOE: LC *Perran en Uthno*, "St Perran in the manor of Uthno".

PHILLACK: after St Felec or Felicitas. Until the C17, the churchtown was *Egloshayle*, LC *eglos hayl*, "church by an estuary".

POLKINGHORNE: LC *poll Kenhoarn*, "Kenhoarn's pool", from an early Celtic personal name meaning "iron hound/chieftain".

POLOSTOC ZAWN: LC *sawan por lostack*, "cliff-chasm by fox's cove". *Lostack*, "bushy-tailed", is a local nickname for the fox, otherwise LC *looarn*.

POLPRY COVE: LC *pollprye*, "claypit".

POLTEGGAN: LC *poll tegan*, "pretty pool".

PONJOU: LC *pondgow*, "bridges".

PONSANDANE: LC *pons edn dean*, "one-man bridge", from its former narrowness.

PONSHALLOW: LC *pons hallow*, "bridge by marshes". Pron. "ponz-HAL-oe", not the increasingly popular "pon-SHAL-oe".

PORN BOE: LC *por an boh*, "the buck's cove".

PORTHCOLLUM: a name of uncertain meaning. Early forms suggest MC *pol keyl lom*, "shelterless pool".

PORTHCURNO: *Porth Cornowe* C16. LC *porth cornow*, "cove of horns", from the peculiar cliff formations here.

PORTHERAS: LC *porth erez*, "cove by ploughed land".

PORTHGLAZE: LC *porth glaze*, "grey-green cove".

PORTHGUARNON: LC *porth gwernan*, "alder-tree cove".

PORTHGWARRA: apparently LC *porth gwarra*, "higher cove", after its steep slipway from sea level to the settlement on the clifftop. However, it was *Porthgorwithou* C14 (probably a misspelling), *Porth Cluythen/Kilwethan* C16, LC *porth collwethan*, "hazel-tree cove". The present name appears to have been coined c.1700.

PORTHGWIDDEN: LC *porth gwidn*, "white cove".

PORTH KIDNEY: *Polkemyes* C16, *Polkidnow* C19, LC *poll kibmiaz*, "cove of farewell".

PORTHLEDDEN: LC *porth ledan*, "wide cove". In the C18, it was alternatively known as *Port Caniack*, "cove/landing place for Kenidjack hamlet".

PORTHLOE: often pronounced "por-LOE". LC *porth loe*, "inlet cove".

PORTHMEOR: LC *porth mere*, "great cove".

PORTHMINSTER: MC *porth mynster*, "cove by an endowed church".

PORTH NANVEN: locally pronounced "p'NAN-wel". C14 *Porthangwin*, C18 *Porthanwen*, LC *porth an gwidn*, "the white cove".

PRAA SANDS: also spelt PRAH SANDS, both are pronounced "prai" and not "prah". LC *porth wrah*, "hag's cove" or "wrasse cove".

PRIEST COVE: the recent Ordnance Survey spelling, "Priest's Cove" is mistaken. *Porthuste* C14, *Porth Juste* C16, *Porth-easte*, C18. The pronunciation "por-AIST" has led to the present spelling, LC *porth East*, "St Just's cove".

PROGO: LC *por ogo*, "cave cove", after its natural arch.

RAGINNIS: LC *rag ennis*, "facing an island". This clifftop farm overlooks St Clement's Isle, off Mousehole.

RECEVEN: LC *res sevian*, "strawberry ford".

RED RIVER: Eng., from the discoloration of its waters from tin mining upstream. Until C18, the river was *Dour Conor*, LC *dowr Conor*, "Connerton River" (*dowr*, "water" was also used to mean "river" in river names).

REJARNE: *Rosenhoern* C14. Apparently MC *ros an horn*, "the iron hillspur".

RELUBBUS: *Rellehoubes* C14. MC *res Lehoubes*, "Lehoubes's ford".

ROSE AN GROUSE: LC *rose an growz*, "roughland of the cross".

ROSEMERGY: properly pronounced "rose-MER-jee". LC *rose mergy*, "roughland with a stable".

ROSEMODRESS: LC *rose Modres*, "Modret's roughland".

ROSEMORRAN: LC *rose moran*, "blackberry hillspur".

ROSEVIDNEY: LC *rose vidny*, "roughland with moorgrass". Purple moorgrass is still locally called "fynny grass".

ROSEWALL: *Ryswall* C14, Possibly MC *res wal*, "ford by a wall".

ROSKENNALS: LC *res Kenwal*, "Kenwal's ford". This features an old Celtic personal name, derived from the Brythonic *cuno-ualos*, "powerful hound/chieftain", and the same name as the C5/6 Cunoval named on the Mên Scryfa inscribed stone.

ROSKESTAL: LC *rose castell*, "roughland by a castle". An intriguing name as no remains of a fortified site are known within a mile of the site.

ROSPANNEL: LC *rose banoll*, "roughland with broom".

ROSUDGEON: LC *rose odgan*, "oxen's roughland".

RUNNEL STONE: Eng., from OE *rynel stan*, "channel stone".

SANCREED: from the church saint, Sancred, although the church is mistakenly dedicated to a St Credan. In C12, the churchtown was known as *Eglossant*, OC *egglos sant*, "saint's church".

SENNEN: from the dedication of the church to St Senan, possibly the Early Christian Irish abbot Senan of Inis Cathaig (Scattery Island).

SENNEN COVE: so called only since C19, it was formerly *Porth Gone Hollye*, C16, LC *porth Goonhily*, "port serving Ganilly (Isles of Scilly)". Of interest here is the legend which tells that, after the destruction of the lost land of Lyonesse – probably a folk memory of the inundation of Scilly – a survivor, the Lord of Goonhily, landed at Sennen Cove and founded a chapel in thanks for his deliverance. This was Chapel Idne, LC *chapall idn*, "narrow chapel" (now destroyed and replaced by a car park).

SKEWJACK: LC *scawgack*, "place of elder trees".

SPARNON: LC *spernan*, "thorn tree".

SPERRIS CROFT: LC *croft speres*, "spirit's rough pasture".

SPLATTENRIDDEN: LC *splat an redan*, "the bracken plot".

STAMPS AND JOWL ZAWN: LC *sawan stampez an jowl*, "chasm by the devil's stamping mill".

STENNACK: LC *stenack*, "tin-stream".

TATER-DU: LC *torthell due*, "little black loaf".

TOLCARNE: LC *tal- carn*, "tor brow".

TOLDAVAS: *Treloghdevas* C14, *Trelodavas* C19. LC *tre- loe devez*, "sheep-pool farm".

TOL PEDN PENWITH: LC *tol pedn Penwith*, "holed headland of Penwith". This name was in common use (often in the shortened form "Tol-pedn") until the 1970s, when it was strangely supplanted by the baffling replacement "Gwennap Head". This first appeared in 1888 and presumably has some connection with the local family of that name. The "hole" referred to is a huge funnel connecting with a large sea cave.

TOL PLOUS: LC *tol ploos*, "dirty hole".

TOWEDNACK: MC *to-*, "thy", added to *Wednack*, the LC form of OC *Winnoc*, the pet-name given to St Winwalo, the real patron of the church rather than the excruciatingly made-up dedication to a "St Tewennochus". Pron. "t'WED-nek".

TOWNSHEND: C19 settlement named after the Townshend family (the Dukes of Leeds).

TRANNACK: The farm near Madron was *Trewethenoc* C14, MC *tre Wethenoc*, "Gwethenoc's farm"; while the Trannack by Sancreed was *Trevranek* C14, MC *tre Vranoc*, "Branoc's farm".

TREASSOWE: pron. "TRAZ-a", the early forms of this name, *Trefrasou* C13 and *Trevrassowe* C14 suggest MC *tre vrassa*, "greater farm" or, possibly, "Brasou's farm".

TREAVE: *Treyef* C13, *Treyuff* C14. OC *treu yuf*, "lord's farm".

TREDAVOE: pron. "tr'DAV-a" or, traditionally, "DAA-va". The modern "tre-DAH-voe" or, worse, "tred-a-VOE" must be deplored. This was *Treworthavou* C14, MC *tre Worthavo*, "Gorthavo's farm".

TREDINNICK: *Treredenek* C13. LC *tre- redanack*, "fernbrake farm".

TREEN: *Trethyn* C14. LC *tre- theen*, "farm by a cliff castle". An Iron Age fort called TRERYN DINAS stands near both settlements of this name.

TREGADGWITH: LC *tre- gadgwith*, "thicket farm".

TREGAMINION: LC *tre- geminian*, "commoners' farm".

TREGAVARAH: possibly LC *tre- goverow*, "farm by streams".

TREGEMBO: *Trethigember* C14. MC *tre chy gember*, "farm by a house where streams join".

TREGENNA: LC *tre- Genna*, "Kenna's farm".

TREGEREST: LC *tre- Gerest*, "Cerest's farm". Pron. "tr'-GEH-rest".

TREGERTHEN: LC *tre- gerthan*, "rowan-tree farm".

TREGESEAL: *Tregathihael* C13. Possibly MC *tre Gathihael*, "Catihael's farm".

TREGIFFIAN: MC *tre Gifyan*, "Gifyan's farm".

TREGILLIOWE: LC *tre- gilliow*, "farm by groves".

TREGLISTIAN: *Treclyston* C16. MC *tre cellestron*, "farm of pebbles".

TREGONEBRIS: MC *tre Genebres*, "Kenhebres's farm". "treg-un-EB-riss".

TREGURTHA: MC *tre Gortha*, "Gortha's farm".

TRELEW: LC *tre- Lew*, "Lew's farm" or LC *tre- leaw*, "calf's farm".

TREMBATH: LC *tre- an bath*, "the boar's farm".

TREMBETHOW: LC *tre- an bethow*, "farm by the graves".

TREMEADER: also spelt and pronounced TREMEDDA. LC *tre- meader*, "field-mouse farm".

TREMELLING: LC *tre- melin*, "mill farm".

TREMENHEERE: "trem-en-HEER". LC *tre- menheer*, "standing-stone farm".

TREMETHICK: LC *tre- methag*, "doctor's farm".

TRENCROM: LC *tre- an crubm*, "farm on the curve", probably referring to the flank of Trencrom Hill (also known as Trecrobben Hill), which was *Torcrobm* C18, LC *toer crubm*, "hunched bulge".

TRENDRINE: LC *tre- an drein*, "farm by the thorn bushes".

TRENEERE: *Trenyer* C13. LC *tre- an year*, "the hens' farm".

TRENGWAINTON: LC *tre- an gwainten*, "the springtime farm".

TRENUGGO: *Trewarnogou* C14. LC *tre- war an ogo*, "farm on the cave". A cave below the farm, now covered over, was used as a dairy store in the C19.

TREREIFE: pron. "treev". *Treweruf/Treruf* C13. OC *treu en yuf*, "the lord's farm".

TRERYN DINAS: modern name replacing *Castle of Trethyn* C15, *Castle Trereen* C19. As Treen/Treryn/Trethyn derives from LC *tre- theen*, "farm by a cliff castle", the modern introduction of LC *dinas*, "fort", was unnecessary.

TRESVENNACK: *Tressevenek* C14. LC *tre- sevienack*, "strawberry-land farm".

TRETHEWEY: LC *tre- Theawi*, "Deawi's (David's) farm".

TREVAIL: also spelt TREVEAL, both are pronounced "tr'VAIL". MC *tre Veli*, "Beli's farm".

TREVALGAN: LC *tre- Valgan*, "Maelgon's farm".

TREVARRACK: LC *tre- varack*, "horseman's farm".

TREVAYLOR: LC *tre- Vailor*, "Melor's farm".

TREVEAN: LC *tre- vean*, "little farm". Pronounced "tr'VEE-an".

TREVEGA: Properly pronounced "tr'VEJ-a", although "tr'VEE-ja" is now popular. LC *tre(a)v esa*, "lowest farm". The adjacent farm of TREVESSA in fact shares the same name.

TREVESCAN: LC *tre(a)v heskan*, "sedge farm".

TREVETHOE: LC *tre- vethow*, "farm by graves".

TREVILLEY: MC *tre Veli*, "Beli's farm".

TREVORRIAN: LC *tre- Vorrian*, "St Buryan's farm".

TREVORROW: LC *tre- vorrow*, "farm by roads".

TREWELLARD: LC *tre- Welard*, "Welard's farm".

TREWERN: pron. "TROO-an". MC *tre Uren*, "Uren's farm".

TREWEY: pron. "TROO-ee". LC *tre- (Th)eawi*, "Deawi's (David's) farm".

TREWHELLA: LC *tre- euhella*, "higher farm".

TREWINNARD: MC *tre war an arth*, "farm on a height".

TREWOOFE: pron. "troev". *Trewoeff/Trewoef* C14. Probably OC *treu woyf*, "winter farm".

TREZELAH: LC *tre- zeahla*, "farm in a waterless place". Pron. "tr'ZEE-la".

TRINK: *Trefrenk* C14. LC *tre- Frenk*, "Frenchman's/freeman's farm".

TRUNGLE: a contraction of LC *tre- vungla*, "quarry farm".

TRUTHWALL: the hamlet near St Just has the pronunciation "TRUH-thel", ana a possible derivation from LC *tre- wothal*, "thicket farm". The Truthwall near Marazion is "TROO-el" and from MC *tre Iudihael*, "Judihael's farm".

VARFELL: *Varwhell* C17. Possibly named after the Hampshire manor of Wherwell which owned land in Penwith at one time, though apparently not near Varfell itself. A second possibility is that the name could be LC *vorr euhall*, "high road".

VELLANOWETH: Pron. "vel-an-AOU-eth". LC *an velin noweth*, "the new mill".

VELLANSAGA: "vel-an-SAI-ja". LC *an velin saya*, "the fulling mill".

VELLANDRUCHIA: "vel-an-DROO-sha". LC *an velin drokkia*, "the tucking mill".

VENTONLEAGUE: LC *venton leh*, "slab well".

WATCH CROFT: Eng. "watch"; LC *croft*, "rough pasture". The remains of a Napoleonic Wars lookout hut survive on the summit of Penwith's highest hill. So called after 1840, its former names being *Trevean Hill* and *Morvah Hill*, from settlements near its foot.

WHEAL OWLES: LC *wheal aulz*, "cliff mine".

WHEAL REETH: LC *wheal reeth*, "red mine". *Reeth* is a variant of *rooz*, "red".

WHITESAND BAY: Eng., "bay of white sand". The name dates from the C16.

WOON GUMPUS: LC *an woon gumpas*, "the level downs". Locally known as "The Gump".

THE WRA or THREE STONE OAR: C16 *Enys Hore*, LC *ennis horr*, "ram island". As the reef consists of three principal rocks, *ennis* was later replaced by Eng. "three stone".

ZAWN BRINNY: LC *sawan brini*, "crows' chasm".

ZAWN BROS: LC *sawan broaz*, "great chasm".

ZAWN BUZZ AND GEN: *Zawn Bosangean* C18, possibly LC *sawan bos an gean*, "chasm by the giant's dwelling".

ZAWN DUEL: LC *sawan tewl*, "dark chasm".

ZAWN KELLYS: LC *sawan kellez*, "lost chasm".

ZAWN ORGAN: LC *sawan organ*, "pennyroyal chasm".

ZAWN REETH: LC *sawan reeth* (variant of *rooz*), "red chasm". Formerly *Savyn Marake* C16, LC *sawan marack*, "horseman's chasm". The great crumbling stack within the zawn, with its noticeably red rocks, is still known as "The Diamond Horse".

ZENNOR: from St Senara, to whom the church is dedicated, possibly the Breton priestess Azenor. Pronounced "ZEN-er".

Mutations

It will have been noticed from this first list of place names that some words have suffered changes to their initials which, under certain circumstances, have been altered or even dropped. For example, in the case of *bean*, "small", CARN BEAN is found, but also TREVEAN.

This is the result of mutation, a feature of Celtic languages, but not even English is wholly free of them: one example is where F becomes V; *wife, knife*, but *wives, knives*. Cornish mutation only affects initial letters or combinations, and their effect is to keep the spoken language flowing. There are a set of rules governing mutation in Cornish but those common to place names are:

i. Adjectives after feminine singular nouns

ii. Feminine singular nouns after *a/an*, "the"

iii. Masculine plural nouns after *a/an*, "the"

iv. Feminine singular nouns after *edn*, "one"

v. All singular nouns after *deaw/dew*, "two"

B	becomes	V	G	becomes	W, or is dropped
C/K	becomes	G	GW	becomes	W
CH	becomes	soft G	M	becomes	V
D	becomes	soft TH	P	becomes	B
F	becomes	V	T	becomes	D or soft TH

Other initials are not affected. Late Cornish applies these rules a little less stringently than in earlier periods and some words, such as *venton*, "well, spring" (MC *fynten*), and *vorr*, "road, way" (MC *forth*) became almost permanently mutated.

Months, Days and Seasons

Months of The Year: *Meeziow an vlethan*

MONTH: *meez* (meez) pl. *meeziow* (MEEZ-yau), masc.
YEAR: *blethan* (BLEDH-an) pl. *blethidniow* (bleth-ID-nyau), fem.

JANUARY: *meez Jenuar* (ZHEN-wer), m.
FEBRUARY: *meez Whevral* (HWEV-rel), m.
MARCH: *meez Merh* (MAIR'h), m.
APRIL: *meez Ebral* (EB-ral), m.
MAY: *meez Mea* (mai), m.
JUNE: *meez Efan* (EF-an), m.

JULY: *meez Gorefan* (gor-EF-an), m.
AUGUST: *meez East* (AA-st), m.
SEPTEMBER: *meez Gwedngala* (gwed'n-GAL-a), m.
OCTOBER: *meez Hedra* (HED-ra), m.
NOVEMBER: *meez Due* (d'yoo), m.
DECEMBER: *meez Kevarthue* (kev-AR-dh'yoo), m.

Days of The Week: *Journiow an seithan*

DAY: *death* (daith), pl. *deathiow* (DAITH-yau), m. Used for the daytime or daylight hours. A shortened form, *de* (dai), precedes the names of the days.
　　: *journa* (JOO-er-na) pl. *journiow* (JOO-er-n'yau), m.
WEEK: *seithan* (ZEI-then) pl. *seithednow* (zei-THED-nau), f.

SUNDAY: *de Zeel* (zeel), m.
MONDAY: *de Leen* (leen), m.
TUESDAY: *de Merh* (MAIR'h), m.
SATURDAY: *de Zadarn* (ZAD-ern), m.

WEDNESDAY: *de Marhar* (MAR-her), m.
THURSDAY: *de Jeu* (zh-EU), m.
FRIDAY: *de Gwenar* (GWEN-er), m.

Seasons: *Seasons*

SPRING: *gwainten* (GWAIN-ten), m.
SUMMER: *have* (haav), m.

AUTUMN: *kidniaz* (KID-n'yez), m.
WINTER: *gwave* (gwauv), m.

2

Place Names of Helston & The Lizard

ANGROUSE: LC *an growz*, "the cross".

ANHAY: LC *an*, "the"; OE *(ge)haeg*, "enclosure".

ST ANTHONY IN MENEAGE: from At Antenin. The former name of the churchtown was *Lanyntenyn* C14, MC *lan Antenyn*, "St Antenin's church-site". (see also MENEAGE).

John Blight's engraving of St Anthony in Meneage, c. 1863

ANVOASE: LC *an vose*, "the wall/dyke".

ARROWAN: LC *war awan*, "on a river", does not fit the site The name might be LC *erow-an*, "acre place" (a Cornish acre was the equivalent of about 120 English acres).

ASHTON: C19 settlement. Eng., "ash-tree farm".

BALMYNHEERE: LC *bal menheer*, "standing-stone mine".

BEREPPER: F. *beau repair*, "pleasant retreat". Pronounced "b'REP-er".

BINNERTON: OE *Binna tun*, "Binna's farm".

BLACK HEAD: a direct Eng. translation of its former name, *Peden Due* C17, LC *pedn due*, "black headland".

BOCHYM: "buk-IM". A rather obscure name, possibly LC *boh-in*, "little buck", but a name containing MC *bos*, "dwelling" and an unknown second element is also possible.

BODILLY: MC *bos Deli*, "Deli's dwelling". "b'DIL-ee".

BONYTHON: MC *bos*, "dwelling"; LC *an eithin*, "the furze". Pron. "b'NEI-then".

BOSCADJACK: "b'SCAD-jek". MC *bos*, "dwelling"; LC *cadgack*, "place of daisies".

BREAGE: from the patron of the church, St Breaca. Pronounced "breeg" or, more correctly, "braig". The churchtown was also once known as *Eglospenbro* C13, MC *eglos Penbro*, "church of Penbro", the name of a nearby farm which is MC *pen bro*, "end of a region".

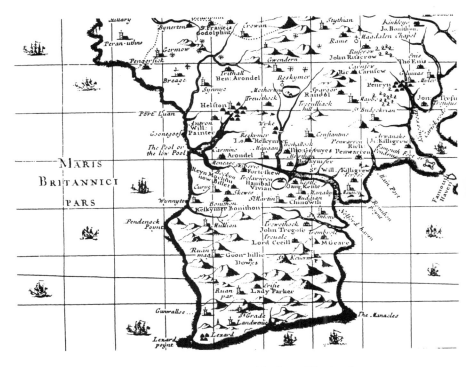

John Norden's c.1580 map of the Lizard Peninsula

CADGWITH: LC *cadgwith*, "thicket".

CAERVALLACK: LC *kear Vallack*, "Maeloc's fort".

CARLEEN: *Carleghyon* C13. MC *car leghen*, "fort of shale/slate".

CARMINOWE: LC *carn meanow*, "outcrop of stones".

CARN MEAL: LC *carn Mehale*, "Michael's tor".

CARRAG-A-PILEZ: LC *carrack a pilla*s, "rock of the naked oats (*avena nuda*)".

CARRAG LUZ: LC *carrack looz*: "grey rock".

CHENHALE: LC *chy an hale*, "house by the marsh".

CHYANVOUNDER: LC *chy an vounder*, "house by the lane".

CHYNHALLS: LC *chy an aulz*, "house by the cliff".

CHYREEN: LC *chy reen*, "house on a spur of land".

CHYVARLOE: LC *chy war loe*, "house by a lake".

RIVER COBER: possibly LC *cober*, "copper".

CORGERRICK: MC *cogeryk*, "little winding stream".

COVERACK: Originally *Porthcovrec* C13, with MC *porth*, "cove, landing place". LC *goverack*, "place of streams". Locally pronounced "KUV'rek".

COW-Y-JACK: a name wrongly split up in recent times for a "more Cornish" look. LC *kewedgack*, "hollowed".

CROFT PASCO: LC *croft Pasco*, "Pasco's rough grazing land".

CROUSA: *Crouswrah* C10. LC *crowz wrah*, "hag's cross".

CULDROSE: LC *kil rose*, "ridge with roughland".

DEGIBNA: from St Decuman, a chapel to whom once stood close by.

DENNIS POINT: LC *dinas*, "cliff castle".

DOLLAR OGO: LC *(an) dalar ogo*, "the sea-stack cave". LC *talar*, literally "auger", is applied to a number of sea-stacks, from their tall, narrow shapes.

DOLOR POINT: LC *(an) dalar*, "the sea-stack".

DRYM: LC *(an) drym*, "the ridge".

ST ELVAN: from St Elvan or Elwyn.

ERISEY: possibly LC *erow-gy*, "acre-house".

THE GAIDER: LC *(an) gader*, "the chair".

GARLIDNA: LC *grelidnow*, "cattle-ponds".

GARRAS: LC *garow rose*, "rough hillspur".

GEW GRAZE: LC *(an) gew greaz*, "the middle enclosure/paddock".

GILLAN CREEK: LC *(an) gilan*, "the creek". The "creek" of the present name is therefore unnecessary.

GILLY GABBEN: LC *(an) gilly gabm*, "the crooked grove".

GOONHILLY DOWNS: "Downs" is a superfluous addition to this name which is LC *goon helhy*, "hunting downs". Pronounced "gûn-HIL-ee".

GRADE: from St Grada, possibly the same as St Crida of Creed, Grampound.

GRAMBLA: LC *(an) grumbla*, "the dolmen".

GRUGWITH: *Cruk heyth* C15. MC *cruk heyth*, "stag's barrow/tumulus".

Gunwallde: J.T. Blight's 19th century engraving

GUNWALLOE: from the church saint, Winwalo.

GWARDER: LC *gwear doer*, "green ground".

GWARTH-AN-DREA: LC *gwarra an drea*, "above the farm".

GWEALHELLIS: LC *gweal Helles*, "Helston field" (see HELSTON).

GWEEK: MC *gwyk*, "wooded village".

GWENDREATH: LC *gwin- dreath*, "white beach". Pronounced "gwen-DRETH".

GWENTER: LC *gwin- teer*, "white land".

HALESTROW: LC *hale laister*, "marsh of flag-irises". "hal-ES-trau".

HALLIGYE: LC *helagi*, "willow-groves".

HALNOWETH: LC *hale noweth*, "new marsh".

HALSFERRAN CLIFF: also known as HALZAPHRON CLIFF: LC *aulz effarn*, "hell cliff".

HAYLE KIMBRO: LC *hale Kembro*, "Welshman's marsh".

HELFORD: LC *hayl*, "estuary; Eng. "ford". The name would seem to centre on Helford village, where there is a fordable creek.

HELSTON: LC *helles*, "old court"; OE *tun*, "farm". Although the Eng. suffix dates back to at least C11, the town was still known as *Helles* into the C17.

HENSCATH: MC *hens scath*, "slipway".

HERLAND: LC *heer lidn*, "long pool".

HOT POINT: LC *hat*, "hat, hood".

HUTHNANCE: MC *huthnans*, "happy valley".

HYRLAS ROCK: LC *heer laze*, "tall grey-green one".

KENNACK SANDS: LC *kenack*, "marshy".

ST KEVERNE: *St Achebrannus/Lannachebran* C11; *St Akaveran/Kaveran* C13. After St Achebran.

LANARTH: LC *lanerh*, "clearing".

LANDEWEDNACK: MC *lan*, "church-site", MC *to-*, "thy", LC *Wednack*, the late form of MC *Winnoc*, pet-form of the name St Winwalo. (see also TOWEDNACK in Section 1, and GUNWALLOE). "lan-de-WED-nek".

LANDRIVICK: the early forms of this name show that it is MC *hendrevyk*, "little Hendra".

LESNEAGE: *les-manaoc* C11. MC *lys managhek*, "court of a place of monks". Pronounced, "lez-NEEG".

LESTOWDER: LC *les Teudar*, "Teudar's court". Legend and the miracle play *Beunans Meriasek* tell of a Cornish King Teudar, who persecuted Irish Early Christian priests.

LEZEREA: LC *les wrah*, "hag's court".

LIZARD: the oft-quoted Cornish derivation, MC *lys arth*, "high court", is frankly doubtful and makes no geographical sense. It is more likely an English or French (*lesart*) chartmaker's name, from the likeness of the peninsula's long, low profile to a lizard's tail.

LOE POOL: another unnecessary and recent repetition. This used to appear on maps as THE LOE, LC *loe*, "lake".

MANACCAN: "m'NAK-en". MC *managh-an*, "place of monks" or, possibly, after a St Managhan who is also found at Lanreath. In C13/14, the name *Ministre/Menstre* was applied to Manaccan, MC *mynster*, "endowed church".

MANACLES: LC *mein eglos*, "church stones". The spire of St Keverne church stands prominently on the mainland above this lethal reef.

MANHAY: LC *menehy*, "monastery".

ST MARTIN-IN-MENEAGE: after St Martin of Tours. In C14, this was also known as the parish of *Dydemin*, an obscure name but perhaps linked with the family name Dudeman. See also MENEAGE.

J.T. Blight's 19th century engraving of St Martin-in-Meneage

MAWGAN-IN-MENEAGE: after dedication of the church to St Maugan. See also MENEAGE.

MELLANGOOSE: LC *melin gooz*, "woodland mill".

MENADARVA: MC *merther Derwa*, "saint's grave of St Derwa".

MÊN AMBER: LC *mean omber*, "balance stone". This former rocking stone was a famous natural phenomenon until its deliberate displacement during the Civil War.

MENEAGE: "m'NEEG" or, more correctly, "m'NAIG". A district covering the northern parishes of the Lizard peninsula, bordering the southern banks of the Helford River. The name is MC *managhek*, "place of monks", *Manahec* C13.

MÊN-TE-HEUL: LC *mean tewl*, "dark stone".

MERTHERUNY: MC *merther Uny*, "saint's grave of St Euny".

THE MORAH: LC *morah*, "dolphin".

MULLION: after St Melan. The churchtown was *Eglosmeylyon* C14.

MULLION COVE: a modern name, directly adapted from the Cornish one, *Porth Mellin*, C19. Although there was formerly a mill (LC *melin*) here, it is more likely that this is LC *porth Melan*, "St Melan's cove".

MULLION ISLAND: a C19 name, replacing the *Gull Rock* of C17/18. This in turn replaced the island's Cornish name which was *Inispriven* C16, LC *ennis preven*, "snake/reptile island".

NANSLOE: LC *nans Loe*, "valley of the Loe", i.e. Loe Pool.

NARE POINT: contraction of LC *penare*, "prominent headland".

OGO-DOUR: LC *ogo dowr*, "water cave".

OGO-PONS: LC *ogo pons*, "bridge-like cave".

PADJAGARRICK COVE: LC *pager garrack*, "four rocks".

PEDNGWINION: LC *pedn gwidn*, "white headland", with an archaic adjectival plural.

PEDN MYIN: LC *pedn mein*, "end of the stones", in this case, the Manacles.

PENGWEDNA: LC *pen-*, "head"; and stream-name Gwedna, from LC *gwidn*, "white".

PENHALE JAKES: LC *pen- hale*, "marsh end", and obscure second word, possibly a personal name, LC *Jakkez*, "Jack, Jake, Jacques".

PENHALLICK: LC *pen- helack*, "willows' end".

PENOLVER: LC *pen- olva*, "lookout headland".

PENROSE: "p'n-ROEZ". LC *pen- rose*, "end of a hillspur".

PIGEON OGO: Eng., "pigeon"; LC *ogo*, "cave".

PISTIL OGO: LC *pistill ogo*, "waterfall cave". With Pistil Meadow on the clifftop above, (sometimes corrupted to Pistol Meadow),this is the only recorded Cornish equivalent of W. *pistyll*, "waterfall".

POLBREAM COVE: MC *pol breyn*, "foulwater pool".

POL CORNICK: LC *poll kernick*, "little corner cove".

POLDHU COVE: An artificial and wrong respelling of a name which was *Polsewe* C16 and *Poljew* C19. LC *poll jue*, "black pool".

POLDOWRIAN: LC *pen- dowr-an*, "end of a watery place".

POLPEOR COVE: LC *poll pure*, "clear pool".

POLTESCO: LC *poll*, "pool"; and an obscure word which might be a Cornish equivalent of B. *tuska*, "moss".

POLURRIAN COVE: possibly LC *belerian*, "cress-beds". The name appears to be unconnected with the Iron Age native name for the Land's End peninsula, *Belerion*, which is derived from a root meaning "bright, shining".

PONSONGATH: LC *pons an gathe*, "the cat's bridge".

PONSONJOPPA: LC *pons an shoppa*, "bridge by the workshop".

PORKELLIS: LC *por(th) kellez*, "lost/hidden gateway".

PORTHALLOW: LC *porth Alaw*, "cove of the Alaw stream". The stream name is pre C10 and might mean "water-lily". Pronounced "PRAL-a".

PORTHCEW: LC *porth gew*, "enclosure/paddock cove".

PORTHKERRIS: possibly LC *porth kerith*, "heron cove".

PORTHLEVEN: LC *porth leven*, "smooth cove", really does not fit the site, unless *Leven*, "smooth" was the name of the stream which flows into it. A further possibility is that the name might once have been MC *porth Elvan*, "St Elvan's cove" (St Elvan church is only a mile inland), though such a form is not recorded.

PORTHOUSTOCK: *Portheustech* C13. LC *porth Ustick*, "Ustick's cove". The surname Ustick was a West Cornish family name meaning "of St Just". This name is pronounced "PRAOU-stek".

PRAZE: LC *praze*, "meadow".

PREDANNACK: this name might have been the original name of the Lizard peninsula and must be one of the oldest surviving place names in the country. Meaning "(headland) of Britain", it is the Brythonic *predanniko-s*, still preserving the original initial P which altered to B when the name was Latinised by the Romans. Similarly, the W. *Prydein*, "Britain", also retains the original initial. Variably pronounced "PRAD-nek" and "pr'DAN-ek".

PROSPIDNICK: LC *prisk pidnack*, "bush in a place of pines".

QUILLETS: Dialect, *quillets*, "paddocks".

REDALLEN: OC *rit*, "ford"; and river name *Alan*.

RELEATH: LC *res leh*, "slab ford".

RESKYMER: MC *res kember*, "ford where streams join".

THE RILL: LC *ryll*, "cleft".

RINSEY HEAD: LC *reen-gy*, "promontory house".

ROSCROWGEY: LC *rose crowgy*, "hut dwelling on roughland". "roz-KRAOU-jee".

ROSELADDON: LC *res ledan*, "wide ford".

ROSENITHON: "roze-NEI-then". LC *rose an eithin*, "the furze roughland".

ROSKRUGE: MC *ros cruk*, "roughland with a barrow/tumulus". Pronounced "ros-KROOJ".

ROSUIC: "roz-YOO-ik". MC *ros ewyk*, "hind's roughland".

RUAN MAJOR: after St Rumon. This place was *Rumon in Woen*, C14, becoming *Ruan in Woon* in C18, LC *Rumon en woon*, "St Rumon in downland".

RUAN MINOR: This name has existed since the C15, before which it was *Rumon Parva*, MC *Rumon perveth*, "inner/middle St Rumon".

RUTHDOWER: LC *rooz dowr*, "red water".

SCOVARN: LC *scovarn*, "ear".

SEWORGAN: *Reswoethgen* C14. MC *res Woethgen*, "Goethgen's ford". Locally pronounced "se-VER-gen".

SITHNEY: from St Sithny, possibly the Breton priest Sizni. In 1230, the name *Merthersitheny*, "St Sithny's saint's grave", suggested that he might have been buried here.

SKYBURRIOWE: LC *skeburiow*, "barns".

SPERNIC COVE: LC *spernack*, "place of thorns, thorny".

TENDERRA: "ten-DEH-ra". Possibly LC *chy an dowrow*, "house by the waters".

TOLDHU: as with POLDHU, this is a recent and mistaken respelling of LC *tol due*, "black hole".

TOLVEN: LC *tolvan*, "holed stone". A famous example of these enigmatic Neolithic monuments stands here behind a private house.

TRABOE: "TRAI-bo". *Trefwurabo* C10. OC *treu Worabo*, "Gorabo's farm".

TREGADJACK: LC *tre- gadgack*, "farm in a place of daisies".

TREGARNE: LC *tre- garn*, "tor farm".

TREGIDDEN: *Treguthyn* C14. Possibly LC *tre- guthan*, "farm in a concealed place".

TREGONNING HILL: *Tregonan* C13/14. MC *tre Gonan*, "Conan's farm".

The Iron Age hill fort on its northern summit, now Castle Pencaire, was *Pencair* C16, LC *pen- kear*, "principal fort".

TRELAN: MC *tre lan*, "cemetery farm". MC *lan*, normally "church-site, church enclosure", can mean cemetery. An Iron Age cemetery was found nearby.

TRELEAGUE: LC *tre- leh*, "slab farm".

TRELEASE: LC *tre- les*, "farm by a ruined fort".

TRELOAR: LC *tre- looar*, "garden farm".

TRELOWARREN: *Trellewaret/Treluueren* C11. Possibly MC *tre lowarn*, "fox's farm", or "Lewaret's farm". Pronounced "trel-a-WARN".

TREMAYNE: LC *tre- mean*, "farm by a stone".

TREMENHEERE: LC *tre- menheer*, "standing-stone farm". Pronounced "trem-en-HEER".

TRENANCE: LC *tre- nans*, "valley farm".

TRENARTH: MC *tre an arth*, "farm on the height".

TRENEAR: LC *tre- an year*, "the hens' farm".

TRENETHICK: possibly LC *tre- menethack*, "farm at a place of hillsides".

TRESOWES: LC *tre- Saws*, "Saxon's/Englishman's farm".

TREVENEN: LC *tre- venen*, "woman's farm".

TREWAVAS: "tr'WAU-vuss". LC *tre- wavas*, "farm of winter grazing".

TREWENNACK: LC *tre- whennack*, "farm in a place of weeds".

VELLAN DRANG: LC *(an) velyn drang*, "the yellow passage".

VELLAN HEAD: possibly LC *(an) velin*, "the mill". A windmill once stood not far away. Alternatively, LC *(an) velyn*, "the yellow one", might be the meaning.

VENTON ARIANCE: LC *venton arrans*, "silver spring/well".

VENTON VEDNA: LC *venton vedna*, "flowing spring/well".

THE VRO: possibly MC *(an) vrogh*, "the badger", although *brogh* should not be mutated in this case.

WATER-MA-TROUT: Eng. dialect, "wet my throat", a name for a dry field.

WENDRON: after St Gwendern. The churchtown was known as *Eglossiga*, C13, apparently "Siga's church".

*   *   *

Wheelas Taze!

Seeking a Father!

Edn metten ha me a moaz war an vorr,
Me a vettias gen moze, ha clave o e thoer.
Deez! meth hye,
Gero nye deaw gweel try!
Ter me an breze,
Nag o che vaze,
Devethez gen floh gen orrol
Ha vedn gweel ve taze!

One morning as I went along the way,
I met with a maid and sick was her belly.
Come! said she,
Let us two make three!
I think to myself,
Thou art up to no good,
Got with child by another,
And want to make me Father!

Traditional, 18th century

*   *   *

Counting and Telling the Time

Cornish Numbers: *Neverow Kernuack*

0: *man* (man); *traveeth* (tra-VEETH) – or *tra* (tra).
1: *edn* (edn); *un* (un) – only used for counting; *onen* (UN-en) – used only as a pronoun, as in the Cornish motto: *Onen hag oll*, "One and all".
2: *deaw* (daou) m.; *dew* (d'YOO) f.
3. *try* (trei) m.; *teir* (tair) f.
4: *pager* (PAJ-er) m.; *peder* (PED-er), f.

5: *pemp* (pemp)	20: *igans* (IG-ens)	40: *dogans* (DOE-gens)
6: *whee(ath)* (hwee[-eth])	21: *edn warn igans*	41: *edn ha dogans*
7: *seith* (zeith)	22: *deaw warn igans*	42: *deaw ha dogans*
8: *eath* (Al-eth)	23: *try warn igans*	43: *try ha dogans*
9: *nawe* (naou)	24: *pager warn igans*	44: *pager ha dogans*
10: *deag* (daig)	25: *pemp warn igans*	45: *pemp ha dogans*
11: *ednack* (ED-nek)	26: *whee warn igans*	50: *deag ha dogans*
12: *dowthack* (DAOU-thek)	27: *seith warn igans*	60: *try igans*
13: *tarthack* (TAR-thek)	28: *eath warn igans*	70: *deag ha try igans*
14: *pazwarthack* (p'z-WAR-thek)	29: *nawe warn igans*	80: *pager igans*
15: *pemthack* (PEM-thek)	30: *deag warn igans*	90: *deag ha pager igans*
16: *whethack* (HWAI-thek)	31: *ednack warn igans*	100: *cans* (canz)
17: *seithack* (ZEI-thek)	32: *dowthack warn igans*	200: *deaw cans*
18: *eathack* (Al-thek)	33: *tarthack warn igans*	500: *pemp cans*
19: *nawngack* (NAOUN-jek)	34: *pazwarthack warn igans*	1000: *meel* (meel)

Rules To Remember:

edn – causes fem. singular nouns to mutate (B to V; C/K to G; CH to G; D to TH; F to V; G to W or dropped; GW to W; M to V; P to B; T to D or TH).

deaw/dew – causes masc. or fem. nouns to mutate as above.

After a number, the noun always remains singular: *edn dean,* "one man"; *deag dean,* "ten men", literally, "ten man".

From 21 onwards, the noun follows the first word of the number: *deag dean warn igans,* "30 men", literally, "ten man on twenty".

50 can be expressed as *hantercans,* "half a hundred", but only in isolation. It can't be used to form numbers such as 51, 52, etc. Fifty pence is: *hantercans dinar* (han-ter-CANZ DEE-ner).

1st: *kensa* [1a] (KEN-za)	16th: *whethegvas* [16vas] (hweth-EG-vaz)
2nd: *nessa*[2a] (NESS-a)	17th: *seithegvas* [17vas] (zei-THEG-vaz)
3rd: *tridga* [3a] (TRIJ-a)	18th: *eathegvas* [18vas] (ai-THEG-vaz)
4th: *pagwera* [4a] (pazh-WEH-ra)	19th: *nawngegvas* [19vas] (naoun -JEG-vaz)
5th: *pempas* [5a] (PEMP-az)	20th: *igansvas* [20vas] (IG-enz-vaz)
6th: *whethas* [6as] (HWETH-az)	21st: *kensa warn igans* [21a]
7th: *seithas* [7as] (ZEI-thaz)	22nd: *nessa warn igans* [22a]
8th: *ethas* [8as] (AI-thaz)	23rd: *tridga warn igans* [23a]
9th: *nawas* [9as] (NAOU-az)	24th: *pagwera warn igans* [24a]
10th: *degvas* [10vas] (DEG-vaz)	25th: *pempas warn igans* [25as]
11th: *edndegvas* [11vas] (edn-DEG-vaz)	26th: *whethas warn igans* [26as]
12th: *dowthegvas* [12vas] (daou-THEG-vaz)	27th: *seithas warn igans* [27as]
13th: *tarthegvas* [13vas] (tar-THEG-vaz)	28th: *ethas warn igans* [28as]
14th: *pazwarthegvas* [14vas] (pazh-wer-THEG-vaz)	29th: *nawas warn igans* [29as]
15th: *pemthegvas* [15vas] (pem-THEG-vaz)	30th: *degvas warn igans* [30vas]

The Time

What time is it? *Pe owr ew?* (pee AOU-r yoo)
Do you have the time? *Eze gena che an owr?* (aiz GEN-a chee an aou-r)
It's . . . *Thew* . . . (th'yoo).   Midday: *Hanterdeath* (han-ter-DAITH)
Midnight: *Hanternoze* (han-ter-NAUZ)
1 o'clock: *Edn owr* (edn aou-r)   2 o'clock: *Deaw owr* (daou aou-r)
3 o'clock: *Try owr* (trei aou-r)   Minute: *Minisan* (MIN-iz-en)
Quarter: *Quarter* (KWOR-ter)   After: *ouga* (OO-ja)   To: *tho* (thoe)
2.05: *Pemp minisan ouga deaw owr*   1.15: *Quarter ouga edn owr*
3.30: *Hanter ouga try owr*   4.50: *Deag minisan tho pemp owr*
About 4 o'clock: *Dro tho pager owr*   5 o'clock exactly: *Pemp owr poran*
Gone 6 o'clock: *Whee owr passiez*   Almost 7 o'clock: *Seith owr ogas*
Come at 9: *Deez tho nawe owr*   Be there at noon: *Bethez enna tho hanterdeath*
Be on time: *Bethez adermen*   Don't be late: *Na vethez holerh*
What time will you be there? *Pe owr vedo whye boaz enna?*

3

Place Names of the Camborne-Redruth Area

ANGEAR: "an-GEER". LC *an gear*, "the fort".

BALROSE: LC *bal rose*, "mine on a hillspur". "bal-ROEZ".

BARIPPER: F. *beau repair*, "pleasant retreat". Pronounced "b'RIP-er".

BARNCOOSE: LC *bar an cooz*, "top of the wood".

BLACKWATER: Eng., "black stream".

BLOWINGHOUSE: Eng., "smelting house".

BOLENOWE: "b'LEN-a". MC *bos lynnow*, "dwelling by pools".

BOLITHO: MC *bos leghow*, "dwelling by slabs". Pronounced "b'LEI-thoe".

BOSPARVA: MC *bos perveth*, "inner/middle dwelling".

BOSPEBO: MC *bos peber*, "baker's dwelling". Now pronounced "b'z-PEE-boe".

BOSWYN: MC *bos wyn*, "white/fair dwelling".

BURRAS: LC *bear res*, "short ford".

BUSVEAL: MC *bos Veli*, "Beli's dwelling". Properly "b's-VAIL".

CALVADNACK: O.J.Padel's suggestion of pointed hill, derived from LC *kal*, "penis" and LC *vadnack*, "place of hills", is not accepted here, there being no obviously pointed hills in the area which would warrant such a name. Instead, LC *gulvidnack*, "place of sparrows", is suggested.

CAMBORNE: the normally offered derivation "curved hill", MC *cam bron* (mutation of *bron* to *vron* would have been expected) is uncertain, especially in the light of a three syllable form from C12, *Camberon*. A word appearing in LC as *cambern*, "dog-leg" could refer to the course of a road or stream and, in 1700, a stone known as "The Camburn" stood in the churchtown. New road signs erected on the approaches to the town express the name in the computer-aided version of Cornish devised in 1986, *Kammbronn*, a noticeably Breton spelling which provoked a huge outcry, as it did not resemble any recorded spelling of the name, and also assumes that the "curved hill" derivation is correct. Medieval *Cambron* or LC *Cambern*, which also reflects its pronunciation "KAM-bern", would be preferable.

CAMBROSE: Formerly *Carnbrose*, this is LC *carn broaz*, "big tor".

CARGENWEN: Pronounced "car-GEN-wen". LC *kear Genwyn*, "Kenwyn's fort", although it is possible that MC *car geyn wyn*, "fort on a white ridge" might be correct.

CARHARRACK: MC *car arthek*, "fort on a high place", with the loss of *th* typical of the Late Cornish period.

CARN ARTHEN: *Carn Arthur* until C15. MC *carn Arthur*, "Arthur's tor".

CARN BREA: Pronounced "carn BRAI". LC *carn brea*, "hill tor".

CARNHELL GREEN: LC *carn heal*, "hall tor", with Eng. *green*, "grassy plot".

CARNKIE: LC *carn kye*, "dog's tor". Pronounced "carn-KEI".

CARNMARTH: LC *carn marth*, "horse tor". Possible is MC *carn Margh*, "Mark's tor".

CARNMENELLIS: LC *carn manalez*, "stacked tor".

CARTHEW: LC *kear thue*, "black fort".

CARVANNEL: LC *kear vanoll*, "broom fort".

CARWYNNEN: LC *carn widn*, "white tor".

CATHEBEDRON: "cath-a-BED-ren". LC *cader Badern*, "Padarn's chair".

CLOWANCE: LC *clowans*, "echo". Pronounced "KLAOU-anss".

COGEGOES: *Cogegowe/Cozejegowe* C17. MC *cos heyjygow*, "ducklings' wood". Locally pronounced "JIG-uz".

COMFORD: probably Eng. "comfort", still the site of an inn.

CONDURROW: LC *kendowrow*, "meeting of waters". Pronounced "k'n-DUH-ra".

COSWINSAWSIN: MC *cos wyn Sawson*, "Englishman's/Saxon's white wood".

CRANE ISLANDS: these sea stacks are the remains of an eroded headland, the stump of which displays the remains of an Iron Age cliff castle. The name could, therefore, be a contraction of LC *kear hean*, "ancient fort" (though *hean* normally precedes the noun).

CREEGBRAWSE: LC *creeg broaz*, "great barrow/tumulus".

CRENVER: contraction of MC *car Genver*, "Kenver's fort". This personal

The Tristan Stone

name originates as the Brythonic *Cuno-moros*, "sea hound/chieftain", which is found on the C5/6 inscribed stone known as the Tristan Stone, Fowey.

CROFTHANDY: LC *croft hengy*, "rough pasture with an old house".

CROWAN: from St Crewenna. The churchtown was *Eggloscrauuen* C12, OC *egglos Crauuen*, "Crewenna's church". Pronounced "KRAOU-en".

ST DAY: from St Dei, also venerated in Brittany.

DOLCOATH: LC *doer coth*, "old ground".

FOUR LANES: Eng. A C19 settlement on a cross-roads.

GEW: LC *gew*, "enclosure/paddock".

GOVERROW: "guh-VEH-ra". LC *goverow*, "streams".

GREGWARTHA: MC *crug gwartha*, "higher barrow/tumulus".

GULLYN ROCK: LC *goolan*, "gull".

GWEALAVELLAN: LC *gweal avallan*, "apple-tree meadow". Pron. "gwail-a-VEL-en".

GWENNAP: from St Wenappa. The churchtown was *Lanwenap* C12, OC *lan Wenap*, "Wenappa's church-site".

HALABEZACK: LC *hale webesack*, "gnat-infested marsh". Pron. "hal-a-BEZ-ek".

ILLOGAN: from St Illogan, and pronounced "il-LUG'n" (locally "LUG'n"). The churchtown was known as *Eglossalau* C13, *Egloshal* C14 and *Eglish Hallow* C19, LC *eglos hallow*, "church inmarshes".

KEHELLAND: "kee-HEL-und". *Kellyhellan* C13. MC *kelly henlan*, "grove at a former church site".

KERRIER: the name of the old Hundred, restored as the name of the local authority district for Camborne-Redruth, Helston and the Lizard in 1974, its derivation is uncertain. It may be MC *car hyr*, "long fort", perhaps with reference to the great elongated prehistoric fortifications on Carn Brea.

KILLIFRETH: LC *killy vrith*, "dappled grove".

KILLIVOSE: LC *killy voze*, "grove by a wall".

LANCARROW: LC *nans carow*, "stag valley".

LANNER: LC *lanerh*, "clearing".

MAGOR: LC *meagor*, "ruin". Pronounced "MAA-ger".

MAWLA: *Maula* C14, *Mola* C17. Possibly LC *moel -la*, "bare place".

MENHERION: LC *menherian*, "standing stones".

MENWINNION: MC *men wynyon*, "white stones", with archaic adjectival plural.

MERROSE: MC *methros*, "middle of a hillspur".

NANCE: LC *nans*, "valley".

NANCEKUKE: *Nancuic* C10, *Lancichuc* C11, *Nanscoyk* C14. LC *nans chycock*, "swallow valley".

NANCEMELLIN: LC *nans melin*, "mill valley".

PEDNANDREA: LC *pedn an drea*, "end of the town".

PENCOYS: MC *pen coys*, "end of a wood".

PENDARVES: MC *pen derves*, "end of an oak wood".

PENGEGON: MC *pen*, "end", and an obscure second word resembling LC *kegen*, "kitchen", but this would make little sense. Padel suggests an equivalent of W. *cegin*, "ridge".

PENGREEP: LC *pen- greeb*, "end of a hillcrest".

PENHALVEAN: LC *pen- hale vean*, "little Penhale" ("marsh-end").

PENHALVEOR: LC *pen- hale vere*, "great Penhale".

PENMARTH: LC *pen- marth*, "horse top".

PENPONDS: LC *pen- pons*, "bridge end".

PENVENTON: LC *pen- venton*, "spring-head".

PLAIN-AN-GWARRY: LC *plain an gwary*, "the playing place", evidently once the site of a medieval amphitheatre for sporting events and the performance of Miracle Plays.

POLCREBO: LC *poll creebow*, "pool by crests" or, possibly, "pool of crested newts".

POLMARTH: LC *poll marth*, "horse pool".

POLSTRONG: LC *poll stronk*, "filth pool".

POOL: LC *poll*, "pool".

PORTH CADGACK: LC *porth cadgack*, "cove by a place of daisies".

PORTREATH: LC *por treath*, "sand cove". Usually pronounced "por-TREETH", instead of the expected "por-TRETH".

PRAZE-AN-BEEBLE: LC *praze an beebel*, "the pipe field".

REAWLA: Norman-French, "royal place".

REDRUTH: MC *red ruyth*, "red ford". *Res*, "ford" tends to retain its archaic hard ending before R. Pronounced "r'DROOTH" or, locally, "DROOTH".

RESKAJEAGE: "res-ka-JEEG". *Roskedek* C13. MC *ros Cadoc*, "Cadoc's roughland".

ROSCROGGAN: "ros-KROG-en". LC *rose crogan*, "skull valleyside".

ROSEWARNE: "roez-WARN". LC *rose wearn*, "roughland with alder trees".

ROSEWORTHY: *Redwori/Reswori* C13. MC *res Worgi*, "Gorgi's ford". Traditionally pronounced "rezh-UH-ree".

ROSKEAR: "ros-KEER". *Resker* C14. LC *res kear*, "ford by a fort".

SAMPHIRE ISLAND: Eng., from growth of samphire.

SCORRIER: Latin, *scoria*, "mining waste". The recent pronunciation "SKUH-ree-er" should be discouraged in favour of the traditional "SKOH-ree-er".

STENCOOSE: MC *stum coys*, "bend by a wood".

TEHIDY: The derivation from a supposed MC *teghyjy*, "retreat", has been recently challenged. An alternative might be MC *chy heyjy*, "ducks' house".

TOLGULLOW: *Talgullow* C13. LC *tal- gulow*, "hillbrow of light".

TOLGUS: LC *tol gooz*, "wood in a hollow".

TOLSKITHY: LC *tal- skezow*, "hillbrow of shadows".

TOLVADDON: LC *tal- vadn*, "high brow".

TREBOWLAND: LC *tre- bowlan*, "cattle-pound farm".

TREDEAGUE: "tr'DEEG". LC *tre- deag*, "beautiful farm".

TREGEA: "tr'GAI". LC *tre- gea*, "farm by a hedge".

TREGULLOW: LC *tre- gulow*, "farm of light".

TRELEIGH: MC *tre legh*, "farm by a slab". Pronounced "tr'LAI".

TRESAVEAN: *Treyusu* C14, *Treyusow vyan* C16: MC *tre wysow vyan*, "little sow's farm".

TRESKILLARD: MC *tre scoul arth*, "kite's hill farm".

TRESWITHIAN: *Treveswythian* C15. LC *tre(a)v ez wethan*, "farm below a tree". Traditionally pronounced "JEDH-en", although "trez-WIDH-yan" is most often heard today.

TRETHARRUP: MC *tre gortharap*, "very pleasant farm".

TREVARTH: LC *tre- varth*, "horse farm".

TREVINCE: LC *tre(a)v ennis*, "isolated farm".

TROON: LC *tre- oon*, "farm on downland".

TUCKINGMILL: Eng., "fulling mill".

VELLYN SAUNDRY: LC *(an) velin Saundry*, "the mill run by Saundry". Saundry, a family name, is also the Cornish form of Alexander.

VENTONRAZE: LC *venton rase*, "well of grace".

VOGUE: LC *(an) voge*, "the kiln/furnace".

WEETH: LC *(an) weeth*, "the trees".

*   *   *

Cornish Names and Origins

Cornish Personal Names:
Henwyn an deez Kernuack.

For the earliest known names borne by Cornish people, the Early Christian inscribed stones dotted throughout Cornwall provide the best testimony. Often altered somewhat by being Latinised, these names, which mostly date from the 5th or 6th century AD, nevertheless show that divergence from the Brythonic parent of Cornish had barely begun. A selection of these names, with their Brythonic origin, give a good idea of the language from which Cornish, Welsh and Breton evolved:

CLOTVALLUS: Bryth. KLUTO-UALOS ("famed powerful one"). Phillack CONETOCUS: Bryth. CUNO-TOCOS ("good hound/chieftain"). Cubert church.

CUNOMORUS: Bryth. CUNO-MOROS ("sea hound/chieftain"). Tristan Stone, Fowey.

CUNOVALUS: Bryth. CUNO-UALOS ("powerful hound/chieftain"). Mên Scryfa.

DRUSTANUS: Bryth. DRUS-TENOS ("oak fire"). Tristan Stone, Fowey.

GUENNCREST: Bryth. UINDO-CAROS ("white/fair friend"). Madron church.

RICATUS: Bryth. RIGO-CATOS ("king of battle"). Penzance.

RIALOBRANUS: Bryth. RIGALO-BRANOS ("kingly raven"). Mên Scryfa.

TEGERNOMALUS: Bryth. TIGERNO-MAGLOS ("princely lord"). Cubert church.

A similar exercise can be carried out by examining the names of kings of post-Roman Dumnonia, or of Cornwall, as they appear in ancient genealogies and records. Among these kings appear the names CYNVAWR, the same as the CUNOMORUS of the list above, and RICATUS, also in the same list.

DONIERT/DUNGARTH: Bryth. DUBNO-GARTOS, ("dark, sleek one").

ERBIN: Bryth. URBO-GENOS ("twin-born").

GERENT: Bryth. CARANTOS ("love").

GURVAWR: Bryth. UOR-MAROS ("very great").

TUDWAWL: Bryth. TOTO-UALOS ("people-powerful").

These same Brythonic roots can be seen in many of the names which appear in the Bodmin Manumissions and it would seem that surnames had not yet come into fashion. The earliest surnames are in fact place names, evidently taken from the place where the family lived, so that Conan of Trenithon eventually became Conan Trenithon. This actually worked both ways, with many place names being named after the people who once lived there. The greater majority of these are the names beginning with BOS-, CAR- and TRE-, or their variants. These, denoting some kind of habitation or settlement, are extremely old, probably originating between the 5th and 11th centuries, with place names beginning with CHY- being introduced at about the 11th century. Family names drawn from place names which describe natural features are more difficult to date.

Strangely, some Cornish surnames come from Anglo-Saxon names, for example EDDY, a diminutive of EDWARD; and also from Norman-French names, RAWE or ROWE deriving from RALPH, and WILLIAMS from GUILLAUME. Religion played a large part too, with Biblical names resulting in names like JOHNS, TOMS, PETERS. Sometimes, the parish from which a family came was adopted into their name: BERRYMAN was the "man from St Buryan", whilst the USTICK family were "of St Just".

People: *Teez*

ARTIST: *limner*, pl. *-s*, m. (LIM-ner)

BAKER: *peber*, pl. *peberian*, m. (PEB-er; peb-UR-yan))

BLACKSMITH: *gove*, pl. *-s*, m. (goev)

BOY: *mawe*, pl. *cosgar*, m. (maab; KOZ-ger))

BROTHER: *broder*, pl. *brederath*, m. (BRUD-er; BRED-er-eth)

BUTCHER: *keger*, pl. *kegerian*, m. (KEG-er; keg-UR-yan)

CHILD: *floh*, pl. *flehas*, m. (flau'h; FLAI-hez)

COMRADE: *soce*, m. (sing. and pl.) (soess)

COUNCILLOR: *cussillier*, pl. *-s*, m. (cu-SSIL-yer)

DAUGHTER: *merth*, pl. *-as*, f. (mairth; MAIR-thez)

FARMER: *teeack*, pl. *teeogian*, m. (TEE-ek; tee-OG-yan)

FATHER: *taze*, pl. *tazow*, m. (taaz; TAZ-au) – only used in formal or religious contexts; *seera*, pl. *seerez*, m. (ZEE-ra; ZEE-rez)

FELLOW: *gwase*, pl. *gwesian*, m. (gwaaz; GWEZH-yan)

FISHERMAN: *poscader*, pl, *-s*, m. (puz-KAD-er)

FOLK: *kemin*, pl. *keminian*, m. (KEM-in; kem-IN-yan)

FRIEND: *coweth*, pl. *cowethas*, m. (KAOU-eth; k'WEDH-ez)

GIRL: *moze* pl. *muzzi*, f. (moez; MUZ-ee)

KING: *matearn*, pl. *maternath*, m. (MAT-airn; m'TER-neth)

LORD: *arleth*, pl. *arlithi*, m. (AR-ledh; ar-LIDH-ee)

MAN: *dean*, pl. *teez*, m. (DAA-en; teez)

MONK: *maanah*, pl. *meneh*, m. (MAA-na'h; MEN-a'h)

MOTHER: *mabm*, pl. *mabmow*, f. (mab'm; MAB-mau) – only used in a formal sense; *daama* pl. *damiow*, f. (DAA-ma; DAM-yau)

NEIGHBOUR: *contrevack*, pl. *contrevegian*, m. (k'n-TREV-ek; kon-tre-VEG-yan)

POLICEMAN: *gwethias*, pl. *gwethidgi*, m. (GWETH-yaz; gweth-ID-jee)

PRIEST: *proanter*, pl. *pronterian*, m. (PRAUN-ter; pron-TER-yan)

QUEEN: *matearnas*, pl. *maternesow*, f. (m'TAIR-nez; mat-ERN-ez-au)

SISTER: *hoer*, pl. *herith*, f. (HOE-er; HEH-rith)

SON: *mabe*, pl. *mibian*, m. (MAAB; MIB-yaN)

TEACHER: *deskadger*, pl. *-s*, m. (d'SKAD-jer)

WIFE: *gwreag*, pl. *gwregath*, f. (g'RAA-eg; g'REG-eth))

WITCH: *gwrah*, pl. *gwrahas*, f. (g'RAA; g'RAA-haz)

WOMAN: *benen*, pl *-as*, f. (BEN-en; BEN-en-ez)

WRITER: *screffer*, pl, *-s*, m. (SKREF-er)

Animals: *Bestas*

BADGER: *dorgy* pl. *dorgean*, m. (DOR-gee; DOR-gai-en)

BEE: *gwanan* pl. *gwenen*, f. (GWAN-en; GWEN-en)

BUCK: *yorth* pl. *-as*, m. (yordh; YOR-dhaz)

BULL: *tarow* pl. *terewi*, m. (TAR-au; te-ROO-ee)

BUTTERFLY: *tikkidew* pl. *-as*, m. (tik-ee-DYOO)

CAT: *cathe*, pl. *cathas*, f. (kaath; KATH-az)

COW: *beuh* pl. *-as*, f. (b'yoo'h; B'YOO-haz)

DEER: *carow* pl. *kervez*, m. (KA-rau; KER-vez)

DOG: *kye* pl. *kean*, m. (kei; KAI-en)

FLY: *gwiban* pl. *gwibas*, f. (GWIB-en; GWIB-ez)

FOX: *looarn* pl. *lewern*, m. (LOO-ern; l'yoo-ERN)

FROG: *cronack melyn* pl. *kernogow melyn*, m. (KRON-ek MEL-in; ker-NOG-au MEL-in)

GOAT: *gavar* pl. *gevar*, f. (GAV-er; GEV-er)

HEDGEHOG: *zart* pl. *-as*, m. (zart)

HORSE: *marth* pl. *merth*, m. (mardh; mairdh)

MOUSE: *logodgan* pl. *logas*, f. (l'GOJ-en; LOG-ez)

OTTER: *dowrgy* pl. *dowrgean*, m. (DAOUR-gee; daour-GAI-en)

PIG: *hoh* pl. *moh*, m. (hoe'h; moe'h)

RABBIT: *cunnen* pl. *-as*, m. (KUN-en; KUN-en-ez)

RAM: *horr*, pl. *horthas*, m. (hor; HOR-dhez)

RAT: *logodgan vroaz* pl. *logas broaz*, f. (l'GOJ-an vrauz; LOG-az brauz)

SHEEP: *davas* pl. *devas*, f. (DAV-ez; DEV-ez)

SLUG: *melwhidgan* pl. *melwhez*, f. (mel-HWID-jen; MEL-hwez)

SNAIL: *bulhorn* pl. *-as*, m. (BÛL-horn)

SNAKE: *preev* pl. *prevas*, m. (preev; PREV-ez)

SQUIRREL: *gwiwer* pl. *-as*, m. (GWI-wer; gwi-WEH-rez)

TOAD: *cronack due* pl. *kernogow due*, m. (KRON-ek d'yoo; ker-NOG-au d'yoo)

Colours: *Lewiow*

BLACK: *due* (d'yoo)	GOLD: *owr* (aour)	ORANGE: *roozvelyn* (rûz-VEL-in)
BLUE: *blou* (bl'yoo)	GREEN: *gwear* (gwair)	RED: *rooz* (rûz)
: *glaze* (glaaz)	GREY: *looz* (lûz)	SILVER: *arrans* (AR-anz)
BROWN: *tewl* (t'yool)	GREY-GREEN: *glaze* (glaaz)	YELLOW: *melyn* (MEL-in)
	WHITE: *gwidn* (GWID'n)	

4

Place Names around Falmouth

ANGARRACK: LC *an garrack*, "the rock".

ANTRON: MC *an troen*, "the nose".

ARGAL: MC *argel*, "retreat".

ARWENACK: "ar-WEN-ek". MC *ar uernek*, "beside an alder grove".

BAREPPA: F. *beau repair*, "pleasant retreat". Pronounced "b'REP-a".

BLACK ROCK: Modern Eng. name, replacing the Cornish one which was *An Garrack Ruen* C15; *Caregroyne* C16; LC *an garrack royn*, "the seal's rock". The sheltered stretch of estuary water called Carrick Roads is named after the rock which lies at its entrance, between the headlands of Pendennis and St Anthony.

BLANKEDNICK: possibly MC *blyn kenak*, "top of a marsh". Pronounced "blan-KED-nek"

BONALLACK: "b'NAL-ek". LC *banollack*, "broom brake".

BOSAHAN: "b'ZAI-en". MC *bos seghen*, "dwelling in a waterless place".

BOSLOWICK: *Preslowyk* C16. LC *pris loe -ick*, "copse by a little pool".

BOSVATHICK: MC *bos Vuthek*, "Budoc's dwelling". Traditionally pronounced "s'VATH-ek".

BRILL: LC *brea helh*, "hunt hill".

BUDOCK: from St Budoc, whose name, meaning "victor", is the masculine form of the famous name Boudicca. From the C15 until the C18, the name softened to *Buthek* and *Vythick* (see BOSVATHICK), but has returned to its old hard D.

BURNCOOSE: LC *bern cooz*, "wood hill".

CALAMANSACK: possibly LC *kil a mingack*, "the pointed ridge". Pronounced "ka-le-MAN-zek" but, traditionally, "k'MAN-zhek".

CARCLEW: LC *creeg lew*, "barrow/tumulus of colour". "kar-KL'yoo".

CARLIDNACK: "Kar-LID-nek". LC *kear lidnack*, "fort by a place of pools", or, possibly LC *kelynack*, "holly grove".

CARNKIE: LC *carn kye*, "dog's tor". Pronounced "karn-KEI".

CARNSEW: LC *carn jue*, "black tor".

CARSAWSEN: MC *car Sawsen*, "Saxons'/Englishmen's fort".

CARVETH: MC *car veth*, "fort by a grave". Pronounced "kar-VETH".

CARWYTHENACK: MC *car Wethenoc*, "Gwethenoc's fort".

CHEGWIDDEN: "sha-GWID'n". LC *chy gwidn*, "white house".

CHENALLS: "sh'n-AULZ". LC *chy an aulz*, "house on the cliff".

CHIRWYN: possibly MC *tyr gwyn*, "white/fair land".

CHYNOWETH: LC *chy noweth*, "new house".

CHYVOGUE: "chei-VOEG". LC *chy voge*, "furnace house".

CONSTANTINE: after St Constantine, probably the C6 Dumnonian king who, in old age, abdicated and entered monastic life. He was condemned by the contemporary monk Gildas as "the unclean whelp of the lioness of Dumnonia". The place name is traditionally pronounced "c's-TEN-ten", and gave rise to the local surname Cossentine.

COSAWES: MC *coys Saws*, "Saxon's/Englishman's wood". "k'SAWZ".

CROWGEY: "KRAOU-jee". LC *crowgy*, "hut, hovel".

CROWSMENEGGUS: "kraouz-m'n-EG-ez". *Rosmeneggas* C16. LC *rose venegas*, "blessed hillspur".

DEVICHOYS: possibly MC *(an) devys coys*, "the mature wood".

DURGAN: An obscure name. However, a version of the Helford River's archaic name *Condefrion* "waters' meet", occurs on the opposite side of the river as Condurrow. Could this be a reversed version of the same word, LC *dowrow gen*, "waters' meet"? A further possibility   might be LC *dowrgean*, "otters".

EATHORNE: LC *eithin*, "furze".

EDGCUMBE: named after the Edgcumbe family.

ENYS: MC *enys*, "isolated/remote place".

RIVER FAL: despite a wealth of early forms; *Faele* C10/11, *Fale* C13, this river name has defied translation and it has even been suggested that it might be a pre-Celtic name. This, however, could be doubtful in view of the probability that the river had a different name in the 1st century AD (see KENWYN in the Truro place names section).

FALMOUTH: this name is surprisingly early for an Eng. name, "mouth of the Fal", being recorded as *Falemue/Falemuth* C13. A settlement of that name existed at least a century before the Charter of 1661 which triggered the growth of the town. A harbourside settlement here was known as Smithick, *Smythwyck* C14, Eng. "smith's village" and in C17, the growing town gained the nickname "Pennycomequick" for its prosperity (although thoroughly unconvincing attempts have been made to suggest a Cornish derivation). Very recent attempts by some to render Falmouth in Cornish as "Aberfal" are somewhat absurd as the town never had a Cornish name, and, with one possible exception, *aber*, "river-mouth" does not occur in Cornish place names.

FLUSHING: named after the Dutch port of Vlissingen (Flushing), this was previously known as Nankersey, LC *nans kersack*, "reed-bed valley".

GADLES: OC *cadlis*, "camp".

THE GEDGES: LC *gedgez*, "left", perhaps in the sense of this reef being left dry by the receding tide.

GLASNEY: MC *glasneth*, "green place".

ST GLUVIAS: after the church saint, Gluvias, reputedly a Welsh priest.

GOODAGRANE: MC *godegh garan*, "crane's lair".

GOONHINGEY: LC *goon hengy*, "old house downs".

GOONLAZE: LC *goon laze*, "grey-green downs".

GOONVEAN: LC *goon vean*, "little downs".

GORRANGORRAS: *Gone angoras* C16. LC *goon an goras*, "the weir downs". The "weir" was probably the defensive line of angled stakes set across the Penryn River at this point and shown on Lord Burghley's map of 1580.

GWEALMELLIN: LC *gweal melin*, "mill field".

GYLLYNGDUNE: LC *(an) gilan down*, "the deep inlet".

GYLLYNGVASE: LC *(an) gilan vaze*, "the shallow inlet". Pronounced "gil-ing-VAIZ".

HALVOSSO: *Hayfossou* C14 shows that this name does not contain *hal/hale*. MC *havosow*, "summer pastures".

HANTERTAVIS: this name, which is LC *hanter tavas*, "half-tongue", was originally applied to a natural rock formation.

HERNISS: LC *heer nans*, "long valley".

KERGILLIACK: LC *kea gilliack*, "cockerel's hedge".

KERNICK: LC *kernick*, "little corner".

LAITY: this is not pronounced "LAI-it-ee", but "LAI-tee". MC *leth-ty*, "milk-house, dairy".

MABE: although the church saint is St Laud, a C6 Breton bishop, it was also known as *Lavabe* C16, MC *lan Vabe*, "Mabe's church site".

MAENPORTH: a modern reversal of the correct form, LC *porth mean*, "stone cove". Pronounced "MAIN-porth".

MANKEA: LC *mean kea*, "stone hedge".

MAWNAN: named after the church patron, Maunan. The nearby village of MAWNAN SMITH was named after a C17 smithy.

MEAN TOLL: LC *mean tol*, "holed stone", or LC *mean toll*, "bound-stone".

MENEHAY: MC *meneghy*, "sanctuary" or, possibly, "glebeland".

MONGLEATH: MC *mengleth*, "quarry".

MYLOR: from St Melor and pronounced "MEI-ler", rather than the "MEI-law" which is beginning to creep in.

MYLOR BRIDGE: so named in C18, this was formerly *Ponsnowythe* C16, LC *pons noweth*, "new bridge".

NANCENOY: LC *nans Noy*, "Noah's/Noy family's valley".

PARKENGEW: LC *park an gew*, "field by the paddock".

PELLYN WARTHA: MC *pen lyn wartha*, "higher pool-end".

PENARROW POINT: LC *pen- erow*, "acre headland". Another example where the addition of "Point" to the name is unnecessary.

PENBOTHIDNO: LC *pen- bethidniow*, "meadows' end". Traditionally pronounced "p'n-DID-na".

PENCOOSE: LC *pen- cooz*, "end of a wood".

PENDENNIS: LC *pen- dinas*, "cliff castle headland".

PENJERRICK: *Pennanseyryk* C16. LC *pen- nans*, "valley end/head", and an obscure word, possibly a stream name meaning "little fresh one" (LC *earick*).

PENMENOR: *Penmenemur* C14. LC *pen- mean mere*, "great stone head".

PENRYN: MC *penryn*, "promontory." Spoken with the stress on "-ryn".

PENWARNE: LC *pen- wearn*, "alders' end".

PENWERRIS: MC *pen weras*, "end of a slope".

PERRANARWORTHAL: "peh-run-er-WER-dhel". MC *Peran Arwothal*, "St Perran in the Manor of Arwothal"; the manor name is MC *ar wothal*, "beside a flood-plain".

PERRANWELL: Eng., "St Perran's well".

POLGWIDDEN COVE: LC *por gwidn*, "white cove".

POLKANUGGO: LC *poll kernogow*, "frogs' pool". Pronounced "pol-ka-NUG-oe".

POLWHEVRAL: MC *pol whevrer*, "lively pool". The ending with L did not occur before the C17. The traditional pronunciation of this name is "WER-vel".

PONJEVERAH: possibly LC *pons haverow*, "bridge by summer fallow land".

PONSANOOTH: older forms of this name, such as *Ponsonwoth* C16, show this name to be LC *pons an woth*, "the stream bridge".

PORTHALLACK: LC *porth hallack*, "cove by a marshy place".

PORTH NAVAS: LC *porth an davas*, "the sheep's cove".

PORTH SAXON: the Ordnance Survey spelling for what is locally pronounced "per-SAU-z'n". LC *porth Sausen*, "Saxons'/Englishmen's cove".

PRISK COVE: LC *prisk*, "thicket".

PULLA CROSS: LC *pollow*, "pools"; and abbreviated Eng., "crossroads".

RAME: possibly a family name or OE *ramm*, "ram".

RETALLACK: LC *res tallack*, "roach ford", the fish name recorded in OC as *talhoc*, and meaning "big-browed".

RETANNA: LC *res tanow*, "narrow ford".

ROSEMANOWAS: LC *rose menewez*, "hillspur of awl-shaped rocks".

ROSEMERRYN: LC *rose Merryn*, "Merryn's hillspur".

ROSEMULLION HEAD: LC *rose mellian*, "clover promontory".

ROSKROW: LC *rose crow*, "roughland with a hut". Pronounced "r's-KRAOU".

SEWRAH: This has recently undergone an excruciating spelling change to *Seauwraugh*. LC *res wrah*, "hag's ford".

SPARGO: MC *spern cor*, "thorn hedge".

TREBAH: *Trevraybo* C14. MC *tre Worabo*, "Gorabo's farm".

TREBARVAH: MC *tre berveth*, "inner/middle farm".

TREGENVER: MC *tre Genver*, "Kenver's farm". The personal name is descended from Bryth. *Cuno-moros*, "sea hound/chieftain", the name of a C6 Dumnonian king.

TREGEW: LC *tre- gew*, "farm by a paddock".

TREGONIGGIE: LC *tre- genegi*, "farm by reed-beds". Pronounced "treg-en-IG-ee".

TREMOUGH: MC *tre mogh*, "pigs' farm".

TRENGILLY: LC *tre- an gilly*, "farm by the grove".

TRENGOVE: LC *tre- an gove*, "the smith's farm".

TRENOWETH: LC *tre- noweth*, "new farm".

TREVALES: LC *tre(a)v aulz*, "hillslope farm".

TREVERVA: MC *trev Urvo*, "Urvo's farm".

TREVETHAN: LC *tre- vethan*, "meadow farm".

TREWARDREVA: LC *tre- wodreva*, "farm by a smallholding". Pron. "trooer-DREV-a".

Glasney College and The Miracle Plays

According to the legend recounted in a 15th century document, Walter Bronescombe, Bishop of Exeter, received a vision in which he was instructed by St Thomas the Martyr (Thomas a Becket) to build a collegiate church in the woods of Glasney, by Penryn, in the west of his diocese. There, in the place called Polsethow, he would find a hollow willow tree, the bole of which would house a bees' nest. If the instruction was carried out, it would fulfill the old Cornish prophecy, *In Polsethow ywhylyr anethow*, "In Polsethow shall be seen marvels (or dwellings)".

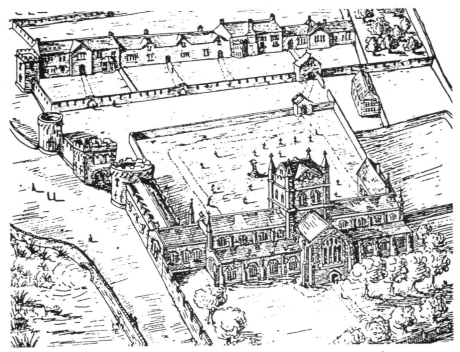

Reconstruction of Glasney College from a 16th-century original

The willow tree was duly found, and its bole was preserved in the church which was built on the site. Penryn's street called Bohill is said to be a contraction of "Bole Hill" in memory of this relic. The church, founded in 1265, was built on low-lying, marshy ground at the head of a tidal creek – a poor choice in view of the number of repairs required through settlement of the foundations – and its plan was based on that of Exeter Cathedral. It was built of granite, embellished with Caen stone.

The Collegiate Church of St Thomas at Glasney (MC _glasneth_, "green place") rapidly grew to include a Bishop's Palace, a half-acre cemetery, refectory, chapter house, dormitories, a school, almonry and detached infirmary. A large area of the adjoining wooded countryside became a Deer Park, enclosed by a pale, and the seaward side of the church complex was defended by a massive wall and three embattled towers.

The College was endowed for thirteen secular canons, one of whom was appointed Provost, or President, and for the same number of vicars. It was entitled to the tithes of no less than fourteen parishes and became a renowned place of learning. However, life at Glasney was not always as pious as it should have been: there are frequent mentions of poaching, theft of timber and other misdemeanours by the Glasney personnel. The last but one Provost, Sir James Gentle (1526-46) was formally accused of letting the College degenerate so that "the service is not ministered as it hath been" and, with his servants, of being, "men of great pleasures, more like temporal men than spiritual, do daily use hawking and hunting and do not only tread and break down hedges, corn and grass of them that be his poor neighbours, and do also kill, drink and joust."

In spite of these lapses, Glasney became renowned as a seat of learning and it was certainly here, and probably during the 14th century, that the great Cornish Miracle Plays were written. These, the sole remnants of written Medieval Cornish, were massive works, taking a whole day to perform. The greatest of all was the cycle of three plays known as the _Ordinalia_. With Latin titles – _Origo Mundi_ (The Beginning of the World); _Passio Christi_ (The Passion of Christ), and _Resurrectio Domini_ (The Resurrection of the Lord), these were works of great sensitivity but also of humour, sometimes a little wicked. For example, the use of English in these plays is given to villainous or ludicrous characters and, indeed, the first character in the _Ordinalia_ to do so is the Devil. Occasionally, a scrap of French is used and there are occasions when a English word is introduced purely in order to fulfil a rhyme. One example of this even mutates the initial letter of the English word in accordance with a grammatical rule of Cornish: _y vody_ is written instead of _y gorf_, "his body", in order to provide an approximate rhyme with _thethy_.

Some of the humour of the _Ordinalia_ gives away the location of the place in which it was composed by introducing well known local place names into its text, most of which occur within a few miles of Glasney itself. Especially worth noting is a piece of irony where, after the building of Solomon's temple, the masons are rewarded with "the parish of Budock and the Careg Royne, with its lands". The Careg Royne is Black Rock, the tip of which protrudes in mid-channel at the mouth of Falmouth harbour.

Pascon Agan Arluth, "Passion of Our Lord" is a further work arranged in eight-line stanzas, with seven syllables per line and of deeper dignity than the *Ordinalia*. It is probable that this was also a produce of Glasney College.

Beunans Meriasek, "Life of St Meriasek" was completed in 1504 by Radulphus Ton, probably a graduate of Glasney and a priest at Camborne, where Meriasek is commemorated. Although still very medieval in form, the language in this play shows traces of change with occasional features being more typical of Late Cornish. In 1611, William Jordan scribed a copy of *Gwreans an Bys*, "Creation of the World", from a lost document tentatively dated at around 1530 and based on *Origo Mundi*.

It can be reasonably argued that Glasney might well have evolved into a Public School, perhaps even a University, if it had not been a victim of the Dissolution of the Monasteries initated by Henry VIII and continued by his successors. Of the great church of Glasney, only an overgrown three-cornered arch remains, neglected and all but forgotten. Carved stones from the church exist in the fabric of later buildings in Penryn itself, and the occasional stretch of boundary wall can be seen.

One of the great medieval seats of learning was wiped off the map. What was its cemetery is a playing field and, in more recent years, the site has been antiquity stripped by unscrupulous officials.

Extracts from The Miracle Plays

From *Origo Mundi*:

Lauar an-nes ov vos vy
A'm bewnans my th'y bysy
A leuerel guyroneth
Thy'so a'n oyl a versy
O dythywys thy'mmo vy
Gans an tas a'y dregereth
Pan vef chacys
Gans an el yn pur thefry
My ha'm gvrek rag gul foly
Helhys warbarth a fuen ny
In mes scon a paradys
Sew olow ov thryys lyskys
Ny dyf guels na flour yn bys
Yn keth forthna may kyrthys
Ha ny ov tos a le-na
My ha'th vam sur kekyfrys
Ty a wylfyth an toknys
Kyn wylly mur volowys
Na thout ny fyth ken ys da.

Say, I being near
To my life's end, I pray him
To say the truth
To thee the oil of mercy
Which was promised to me
By the Father, of His pity
When I was driven
By the angel in very earnest
I and my wife for doing folly
Driven together we were
Quickly out of Paradise
Follow the prints of my feet burnt
No grass nor flower in the world grows
In that same road where I went
And we coming from that place
I and thy mother surely also
Thou wilt see the tokens
Though thou see much light
Fear not, it will not be other than good.

From: *Passio Christi*

Ellas, ellas ogh tru tru	Alas, alas, O sad, sad
Yn ov colon asyw bern	What concern in my heart
Pan welaf ov map ihesu	When I see my Son Jesus
A dro th'y pen curyn spern	With a crown of thorns around his head
Hag ef map dev a vertu	And he the Son of God of power
Ha gans henna guyr myghtern	And withal a true king
Treys ha dyvlef a pup tu	Feet and hands on each side
Fast tackyes gans kentrow hern	Nailed fast with iron nails
Ellas, es byth deyth brues mur a anfues	Alas, thou shalt have on Judgement day
Y kyk ha'y kues	Much misfortune, who sold him
Nep a'n guerthas	Flesh and Fell!
Ogh gouy rak ow map ker	O woe's me for my dear Son
The weles yn keth vaner	To see Him in such a way
May whelaf lemmyn dyghtys.	As I now see treated.

From: *Resurrectio Domini*

Myghtern of guyron ha cref	I am a King true and powerful
Kyns pegh map den a'm sorras	First the sin of mankind provoked me
Er ow fyn travyth ny sef	Against me nothing stands
Porth yfarn me a torras	The gate of Hell I have broken
Hag a thros lyes enef	And I have brought many souls
A ver drok tervyns ha cas	From great evil, tempest and torment
The ioy y tethons gynef	To joy they are come with me
Kemmys a wruk both ow thas	As many as have done the will of my Father
Ow stons a fue crous a pren	My standing was a cross of wood
Kyns en myghtern den ha dev	Before I was a king, man and God
Yn le basnet war ow fen	Instead of a helmet on my head
Curyn aspern lym ha glev	A crown of thorns sharp and stiff
Ol ov ysyly yn ten	All my limbs dragged
Hag a wel the lyes plu	And a sight to many a parish
Yn golon dre'n tenewen	In heart, through the side
The restye syngys ow gu	I felt the spear thrust
Dre ow thrys y tuth vn smat	Through my feet a fellow came
Gans kentrow d'aga gorre	With nails to put them
Y fue ow manegow plat	And my smooth gloves were
Spygys bras dre ow dywle	Great spikes through my hand
Ytha ov fous ha'm brust plat	My robe and my breastplate were
Purpur garow thu'm strothe	Hard purple to wring me
Dre an gos a rak pilat	Through the blood before Pilate
Worto an kyc a glene	The flesh stuck to it
Pan fue an purpur war skwych	When the purple was of a sudden
Kychys the ves gans dyw thorn	Snatched away with both hands
Worto y glynes hardlych	To it stuck closely
Ran a'n kyc bys yn ascorn	A piece of flesh even to the bone

Woge ow da oberow
Dywes a yrhys dethe
Thy'm rosons bystyl wherow
Byth ny fynnys y eve
Gans yu guenys ha marow
Dre an golon me a fue
An tryge deth sur hep gow
Y wruk dasserghy arte.

After my good works
Drink if I required of them
They gave me bitter gall
I would never drink it
With a spear pierced and killed
Through the heart I was
On the third day, surely, without a lie
I did rise again.

From: *Pascon Agan Arluth*

Yn pub gwythres ycoth thys
Gorzye ze zu hay hanow
Ke ze ves omscumvynys
Ze zyvetyth veth yn tewolgow
The vestry a vyth lezys
Neffre war en enevow.

In every act it behoves you
To worship your God and His Name
Go away, accursed
To desert, ever, into darkness
Your mastery shall be lessened
Ever over the souls.

$$* \quad * \quad *$$

Parts of The Body: *Radnow an corff*

ARM: *breh*, dual pl. *deffreh*, f. (brai'h; DEF-rai'h)

BACK: *kein*, pl. *-ow*, m. (kein; KEIN-au)

BODY: *corff*, pl. *-ow*, m. (corf; COR-fau)

BREAST: *brodn*, dual pl. *deffron*, f. (brud'n; DEF-ren)

BUTTOCKS: *patshan*, m.pl. (PAT-shen)

CHEEK: *boh*, pl. *-ow*, f. (bau'h; BAU-hau)

CHIN: *gene* pl. *genow*, m. (gain; GEN-au)

EAR: *scovarn*, dual pl. *dewscovarn*, m. (SKUV-ern; D'YOO-skuv-ern)

ELBOW: *gelen*, dual pl. *dowelen*, m. (GEL-en; DAOU-el-en)

EYE: *lagas*, dual pl. *dewlagas*, pl. *lagadgow* (LAG-az; D'YOO-lag-az; la-GAD-jau)

FACE: *bedgeth*, pl. *-ow*, m. (BED-jeth; b'-JETH-au)

FINGER: *bez*, pl. *-ias*, m. (bez; BEZ-yaz)

FOOT: *trooz*, pl. *treiz*, m. (trûz; treiz)

FOREHEAD: *talle*, pl. *-iow*, m. (tal; TAL-yau)

HAIR: *bleawan*, collective pl. *bleaw*, f. (BLEU-an; bleu)

HAND: *dorn*, dual pl. *doola*, m. (dorn; DÛ-la)

HEAD: *pedn*, pl. *-ow*, m. (ped'n; PED-nau)

KNEE: *pednglin*, dual pl. *pedndowlin*, m. (ped'n-GLIN; ped'n-DAOU-lin)

LEG: *gar*, dual pl. *dewar*, pl. *garow*, f. (gar; D'YOO-ar; GAR-au)

MOUTH: *ganow*, pl. *-ow*, m. (GAN-au; GAN-au-a)

NECK: *codna*, pl. *-how*, m. (COD-na; COD-na-hau)

NOSE: *fregow*, m.pl. (FREG-au) – literally "nostrils".

SHIN: *elesker*, pl. *eleskrow*, f. (el-ES-ker; el-ES-krau)

SHOULDER: *scooth*, dual pl. *dewscooth* (scûth; D'YOO-scûth)

SKIN: *crohan*, f. (KRAU-hen)

THIGH: *morras*, dual pl. *dewvorras*, f. (MOR-az; D'YOO-vor-az)

THROAT: *brandga*, pl. *brandgiow*, f. (BRAN-ja; BRAN-j'yau)

TOE: *bez trooz*, pl. *bezias treiz*, m. (bez TRÛZ; BEZ-yaz TREIZ)

TOOTH: *danz*, pl. *denz*, f. (danz; denz)

5

Place Names around Truro

RIVER ALLEN: a common Celtic river name, but its meaning is unknown.

ST ALLEN: named after the church saint, possibly the Breton St Alan. The churchtown was *Eglosellen* C19, LC *eglos Allen*, "St Allen's church".

ALLET: probably a Celtic river name, meaning "nourisher".

ARRALLAS: LC *arrans les*, "silver court".

BALDHU: a poor respelling of *Baldue* C18, LC *bal due*, "black mine".

BESORE: MC *bos whoer*, "sister's dwelling".

BISSOE: MC *besow*, "birch trees".

BOSKENWYN: MC *bos Kenwyn*, "Kenwyn's dwelling" (but see KEN-WYN).

CALENICK: LC *kelynack*, "holly grove".

CANDOR: LC *cam- dowr*, "crooked river".

CARLAND: LC *corlan*, "sheepfold".

CARLYON: MC *car leghen*, "slab fort".

CARNON DOWNS: LC *carnen*, "little tor", and Eng. "downs". In the C18, this was *Goon Carnon*, LC *goon Carnen*, "downs of Carnen".

CARRINE: MC *car yeyn*, "cold fort".

CARVEDRAS: MC *car Vodras*, "Modret's fort".

CARVOSSA: *Carawoda* C14. Possibly MC *car an vosow*, "fort of the banks", retaining an archaic hard ending to MC *fos*, "wall, bank, dyke".

CHACEWATER: Eng. *chase water*, "stream on hunting land".

CHYBUCCA: LC *chy bucka*, "ghost's/goblin's house".

CHYCOOSE: LC *chy cooz*, "house by a wood".

CHYCOWLING: possibly LC *chy corlan*, "house by a sheepfold".

CHYVELAH: "chei-VEE-la". LC *chy euhelha*, "highest house".

ST CLEMENT: after St Clemens, a C1 Roman Pope.

COMPRIGNEY: LC *clohprednier*, "gallows" – literally "bell-beams"

COOSEBEAN: LC *cooz bean*, "little wood".

COWLANDS: LC *cownans*, "steep-sided valley".

CUSGARNE: LC *cooz garn*, "tor wood".

DEVORAN: LC *devran*, "waters". Pronounced "DEV'ran".

ENYS: MC *enys*, "isolated place".

ST ERME: after St Hermes. The churchtown was known as *Egloserm* C14, MC *eglos Erm*, "St Erme's church".

FEOCK: from St Feoc/Feoca (there is confusion over the saint's gender). The churchtown name was *Lanfioc* C12, "St Feoc's church-site", and this survives as La Feock, pronounced "la-VAIG".

GLOWETH: possibly LC *glow woth*, "coal stream". Pronounced "GLAOU-eth".

GOON GUMPUS: LC *goon gumpas*, "level downs".

GOONVEAN: LC *goon vean*, "little downs".

GREENSPLAT: Eng. "green"; LC *splat*, "plot of land".

GWARNICK: LC *gwernack*, "alder grove".

HALBULLOCK: MC *hal bulyk*, "marsh of earthworms".

HUGUS: "H'YOO-gus". LC *euh gooz*, "above a wood".

IDLESS: *Edelet* C11. An obscure name, unless it is a variant form of ALLET.

KEA: "kee". From St Kei. The original church site at Old Kea (where the ruinous church tower remains) was *Landegei* C12, MC *lan to- Gei*, "church-site of St Kei", with honorific prefix *to-*, "thy" (see TOWEDNACK and LANDEWEDNACK). The parish itself was formerly named after two Celtic saints; *Kycladoca* C14 means "Kei and Ladoca".

KENWYN: although a St Kenwyn is now celebrated here, and with Kenwyn becoming a popular forename, it is probable that no such person actually existed at all. The C13 form, *Keynwen*, strongly suggests MC *keyn wyn*, "white/fair ridge", and it has also been argued that this name descends from that of the *Cenion* river recorded by Ptolemy in C1 AD in the region of the Fal estuary.

KENWYN RIVER: a modern name. Formerly this was *Dower Ithy*, LC *dowr ithiow*, "ivy river".

KERLEY: LC *kear leh*, "slab fort".

KILLIGANOON: LC *killy gnowan*, "nut-tree grove".

KILLIGREW: LC *killy gnow*, "nut grove".

KILLIOW: LC *killiow*, "groves".

LADOCK: from St Ladoca (see KEA). The hard D remains in spite of a softening to *Egloslagek* C14, MC *eglos Lasec,* "St Ladoca's church", and *Lazacke* C16.

LAMBESSOW: MC *lan besow*, "church site by birch trees".

LAMOUTH CREEK: MC *nans mogh*, "pig's valley".

LANGARTH: MC *nans yarth*, "ridge vale".

MALPAS: F. *mal pas*, "bad step". Pronounced "MOE-pus".

MITCHELL: C13/14 forms of this name, *Meideshol/Medeshole*, show that this is Eng., from OE *maegd hol*, "maid's hollow".

NANCASSICK: LC *nans casack*, "mare's valley".

NANKERVIS: LC *nans kervez*, "stags' valley".

NANSALSA: MC *nans alsyow*, "valley of slopes".

NANSAVALLEN: "nans-av-AL-en". LC *nans avallan*, "apple-tree valley".

NANSOUGH: MC *nans hogh*, "pig valley". Pronounced "nan-SOO".

NEW MILLS: Eng. name superceding earlier Cornish one; *Melynewyth* C14, *Melenowith* C16, LC *melin noweth*, "new mill".

PARKENGEAR: LC *park an gear*, "the fort field".

PENAIR: LC *penare*, "promontory/prominent hillspur".

PENCALENICK: LC *pen- kelynack*, "end of a holly grove". Pronounced "pen-k'l-EN-ik".

PENCOOSE: LC *pen- cooz*, "end of a wood".

PENELEWEY: LC *pen- elaw-i*, "end of a place of elms". pron. "pen-a-LOO-ee".

PENPOL: LC *pen- poll*, "end of a pool/creek".

PENSCAWN: LC *pen- scawan*, "elder-tree end".

PILL: Eng. *pill*, "creek".

PLAYING PLACE: Eng. "arena", after a medieval *plain-an-gwary* ("playing place") which formerly existed here. Traces of the amphitheatre were visible earlier this century.

POLSTAIN: LC *poll stean*, "tin pit".

POLSUE: LC *poll jue*, "black pool".

POLWHELE: MC *pol whyl*, "pool of beetles".

PORTH KEA: LC *porth Kea*, "entrance to Kea" (see KEA).

PROBUS: after St Probus. The churchtown was known as *Lanbrebois* C11 and *Lamprobus* C18, MC *lan Probus*, "St Probus's church-site".

REDANNICK: LC *redanack*, "fern-brake".

RESPARVA: MC *res perveth*, "inner/middle ford".

RESTRONGUET: "r'STRON-get". MC *ros troen goys*, "hillspur with a promontory wood". The name curiously retains the hard ending of OC *cuit*, "wood".

RESURRANCE: LC *res arrans*, "silver ford".

SAVEOCK: LC *seviack*, "place of strawberries".

SHORTLANESEND: Eng., "Short's lane end" after local family name. In C16/17 the Cornish *Penfounder/Penvounder* applied here, LC *pen- vounder*, "lane end".

SPARNICK: LC *spernack*, "thorny place".

STITHIANS: from St Stediana, softened to St Stethiana.

THREEMILESTONE: Eng. A C19 settlement which sprang up by the third milestone on the road westward from Truro.

TREFRONICK: MC *tre- vronek*, "farm in a hilly place".

TREGEAGLE: LC *tre- gaggel*, "farm of dung". Properly pronounced "tr'GAA-g'l".

TREGOLLS: *Tragol* C11. LC *tre- goll*, "hazel farm".

TREGAVETHAN: LC *tre- govaithian*, "rich people's farm".

TREGYE: "tr'GEI". LC *tre- gye*, "dog's farm".

TREHANE: *Treyaghen/Trehanna* C14. MC *tre Uanno*, "Uanno's farm".

TREHEVERAS: LC *tre- thevrez*, "well-watered farm".

TRELISKE: *Trelosk* C14. MC *tre losk*, "burnt farm".

TRELISSICK: *Trelesyk* C13. MC *tre Wlesyk*, "Gwledic's farm".

TRELOWTHAS: *Treloudat* C13. MC *tre Loudas*, "Loudat's farm".

TRENITHAN: LC *tre- an eithin*, "farm by the furze".

TRESEMPLE: LC *tre- Sempel*, "farm of the Sempel family".

TRESILLIAN: "tr'ZIL-yan". MC *tre Sulyan*, "Sulyan's farm". The personal name is ancient, from Brythonic *sulo-genos*, "sun-born".

TRESTRAYLE: MC *tre strayl*, "straw-mat farm". Presumably, straw mats were once made here.

TREVASKIS: MC *tre Valscos*, "Maelscoet's farm".

TREVIGLAS: LC *tre(a)v eglos*, "church farm/churchtown".

TREWIRGIE: *Trewithgy* C14. MC *tre Withgi*, "Gwithgi's farm".

TREWITHAN: LC *tre- wethan*, "tree farm".

TRISPEN: contraction of C14 *Trethespan*; perhaps MC *tre Thespan*, "Despan's farm".

TRURO: Cornwall's cathedral city has an intriguingly obscure name, contracted from *Triueru* C12, *Triwereu/Trufru* C13. It is generally agreed that the first element is MC *try*, "three", rather than MC *tre*, "farm, settlement". The second word could be MC *berow*, "turbulence, boiling", and a meaning "three turbulences/torrents" would well describe the three fast-flowing rivers which flow into the tidal creek here. Pronounced "TRAU-ra".

TWELVEHEADS: Modern Eng.name from the 12-headed tin-stamping mill which operated here in the C18/19.

VENTONBERRAN: LC *venton Berran*, "St Perran's well".

VENTONGLIDDER: LC *venton Gleder*, "St Clether's well".

WHEAL BADDON: LC *wheal avadn*, "higher mine".

WHEAL JANE: LC *wheal yein*, "cold mine", or the personal name Jane.

*   *   *

How Cornwall saved the English Language

The Norman Conquest saw the status of the English and their language relegated to the role of the subjugated. The new rulers, themselves descendants of Vikings who had settled in northern France (hence their name, "Nor[se]men]"), spoke a language termed Norman-French and, under their overlordship, this became the official language of the country. English was banned from official use and became regarded as peasant speech. No longer finding a place in the written word, English not only began to die, but was on the verge of extinction.

Shortly after 1300, a campaign to restore English to official status had arisen but authority resisted to the extent that an Act of Parliament in 1332 required French to be taught in all schools. Eight years earlier, Oxford officials had ruled that all conversation in the city must be in either French or Latin. The revival movement seemed doomed.

The tide began to turn at the instigation of two Cornish speaking Cornishmen. John Trevisa of St Mellion (c.1342-1402), a Cornish cleric wrote that John Cornwall, a master of grammar, changed the law in grammar schools with the replacement of French with English, and that Cornwall had taught a fellow Cornishman Richard Pencrych the English language. Pencrych, in turn, instructed others and the knowledge of the English language rapidly grew from there, all at the time when priests at Glasney were composing the *Ordinalia*.

Trevisa himself aided the cause of English in a massive way, translating Ranulf Hidgen's Latin *Polychronicon*, thus providing the English with the largest history and encyclopaedia of the time in their own tongue, this being printed by William Caxton.

Basil Cottle, in *The Triumph of English 1340-1400*, wrote that ". . . we are asked to believe by a Cornishman with a Cornish name that two others from his Duchy were largely responsible for the the redemption of what wasn't even their native tongue, since all three must have been originally Celtic speaking."

The effect of their efforts was remarkable. Support escalated to such an extent that by 1349 the teaching of English in schools was permitted. In 1362 pleas to the Courts of Law, previously only allowed in Latin or French, became acceptable in English and, finally, in 1413, English replaced French as the official language of the Royal court and the ruling classes.

John Cornwall, Richard Pencrych and John Trevisa can rightly be regarded as the saviours of the English language but, at the same time and unwittingly, they had dealt a deadly blow to their own native tongue.

Rebellions

The Reformation initiated by King Henry VIII proved to be a further nail in the coffin of the Cornish language. English had already made a significant inroad into Cornwall and, during Henry VIII's reign, Andrew Borde wrote that: "In Cornwall are two speeches, one is naughty (i.e. corrupted) English, and the other is Cornish speech. And there are many men and women who cannot speak one word of English, but all Cornish".

However, there was no Prayer Book or Bible in Cornish. At this time, Cornwall was staunchly Catholic (a very different picture to the situation only a few centuries earlier) and all services were held in Latin – which most Cornish people did not understand, any more than they could understand English. Henry VIII's hatred of Catholicism, resulting in the Reformation which began in 1533, and the Dissolution of the monasteries, was continued by his successor Edward VI who, in 1547, decreed that *The English Book of Common Prayer* be imposed on Cornwall, and that old customs of the Celtic Chuirch, which had been adopted by the Catholic one, be stamped out. Dr John Moreman, rector of Menheniot, was the first to use the English language in Cornish church services in 1540, instructing his bewildered parishioners in the use of the Lord's Prayer in English.

Opposition to this imposition of an alien language on their culture grew amongst the Cornish people, who found influential leaders in Humphrey Arundell of Helland, and Nicholas Boyer, mayor of Bodmin. A petition was despatched to the King, Article Eight of which strongly stated that: "We, the Cornishmen, whereof certain of us understand no English, utterly refuse this new Service".

The Anglican Church was sympathetic enough to move a resolution to allow Welsh and Cornish children to learn the Premises in the Welsh or Cornish tongues, but this was ignored by the King. In the meantime, the ruthless dismantling of "Popish" symbols and imagery in Cornish churches was under way, overseen by the rather nasty figure of William Body who had leased the archdeaconry of Cornwall from Thomas Winter, an illegitimate son of Cardinal Wolsey. Having stripped a number of churches, Body turned his attention to the church at Helston. Led by Martin Geoffrey, the priest at St Keverne, a thousand people converged on the church. Body escaped to take shelter in a nearby house but the mob dragged him out into the street and with blows delivered by William Kilter and Pascoe Trevian, killed him. These three were later executed.

The uprising which grew from the village of St Keverne revived memories of fifty-two years earlier. Then, King Henry VII had imposed severe taxes in order to finance military action against Scotland. The Cornish were incensed, raised an army of some 15,000 and marched on London. Their leaders were Michael Joseph *"an Gof"* ("the smith"), a St Keverne blacksmith, Thomas Flamank, a lawyer from Bodmin, and Baron Audley. Let down by the men of Kent, who had undertaken to join them, the Cornish rebellion moved on to Blackheath and disaster, for there lay the King's well-disciplined army, 25,000 strong, ready for their march on Scotland. The date was June 16th, 1497.

With 2,000 slain, an Gof gave the order to surrender. He and Flamank were executed at Tyburn, and Baron Audley beheaded at Tower Hill. Nevertheless, just three months later, the Cornish were on the march again, this time in support of the Pretender, Perkin Warbeck. This time, they suffered gallant defeat at Exeter and Taunton.

For the third time in little more than half a century, the Cornish were to march again in the defence of their religion and language, meeting Lord Bedford's army at Exeter, The battle was viciously fought, but the Cornish army was slaughtered. The English army rested for ten days then, under Sir Anthony Kingston, moved into Cornwall. As Peter Beresford Ellis notes in his book *The Celtic Revolution*, a ruthless programme of hangings, confiscations and suppression followed which was "as harsh as anything under Cromwell in Ireland, or Cumberland in Scotland".

With Cornwall reeling from these atrocities, a further blow was dealt to the language when an English playwright produced, in 1550, a play entitled *The Image of Idleness . . . translated out of the Troyance or Cornyshe Tongue by Olyver Old Wanton*. This ridiculed and derided the Celtic tongue of the Cornish and, from that time on, it became seen as the language of the ignorant and the peasant.

When the brief reign of Mary Tudor restored Catholicism as the state religion, Cornish literature enjoyed a brief resurgence when, in 1555, Edmund Bonner, Bishop of London, celebrated the religious change by writing "a profitable and neccesarye doctyne, with certayne homelies adioned thereynto". These twelve homilies were promptly rendered into Cornish by John Tregear, the manuscript of which was discovered in 1949 in Flint, Wales.

This, however, was only a brief spark of hope. The accession of Elizabeth I saw a return to the Protestant faith, and an end to Cornish hopes of a prayer book and bible in their own tongue. John Norden, shortly before 1600, observed that: "Though the husband and wife, parents and children, master and servants, do mutually communicate in their native language, yet there is none of them in manner but is able to converse with a stranger in the English tongue, unless it be some obscure people that seldom confer with the better sort." Already, the bigotry clearly shows through his comments, but he finishes with the sad observation that: ". . . it seemeth, however, that in a few years the Cornish will be, by little and little, abandoned".

* * *

Clothing: *Dilladgow*

BOOT: *bota*, pl. *-s*, f. (BOET-a; BOET-az)

BRA: *jumps*, f.pl. (jumps)

COAT: *cota*, pl. *-s*, m. (COET-a; COET-az)

DRESS: *powz gwreag*, pl. *powziow gwreag*, f. (paouz g'RAI-eg; PAOU-zhiau g'RAI-eg)

HANDKERCHIEF: *nackan*, pl. *-s*, m. (NAK-en; NAK-enz)

HAT: *hat*, pl. *-tez*, m. (hat; HAT-ez)

JACKET: *jacket*, pl. *-s*, m. (JAK-et; JAK-etz)

JUMPER: *frauk*, pl. *-ez*, m. (frahk; FRAH-kez)

MACKINTOSH: *cota stanche*, pl. *cotas stanche*, m. (COET-a STONCH; COET-az STONCH)

SHIRT: *hevez*, pl. *hevedgiow*, m. (HEV-ez; hev-ED-jiau)

SHOE: *esgis*, pl. *skitchow*, f. (EZ-giss; SKITCH-au)

SKIRT: *pillan*, pl. *pillednow*, f. (PIL-HL-an; pil-HLED-nau)

SOCK: *pawgen*, pl. *pawgednow*, f. (PAU-gen; pau-GED-nau)

STOCKINGS: *loder*, pl. *lodrow*, m. (LOD-er; LOD-rau)

SUIT: *dillas*, pl. *dilladgow*, m. (DIL-hlaz; dil-HLAD-jau)

TROUSERS: *lavrack heer*, pl. *lavregow heer*, m. (LAV-rek HEER; lav-REG-au HEER)

UNDERPANTS: *lavrack nessa*, pl. *lavregow nessa*, m. (LAV-rek NEZ-a; lav-REG-au NEZ-a)

VEST: *powz nessa*, pl. *powziow nessa*, f. (paouz NEZ-a; PAOU-zhiau NEZ-a)

Birds: *Ethen*

BIRD: *ethan*, pl. *ethen*, f. (EDH-an; EDH-en)

BLACKBIRD: *mola thue*, pl. *molas due*, f. (MUL-a TH'YOO; MUL-az D'YOO)

BUZZARD: *bargez*, pl. *bargodgas*, m. (BAR-guz; bar-GUD-jaz)

CHOUGH: *chauk*, pl. *-as*, m. (chauk; CHAUK-az)

COCKEREL: *killiack*, pl. *killiogas*, m. (KIL-yak; kil-YUG-az)

CROW: *brane*, pl. *brini*, f. (braan; BRIN-ee)

CUCKOO: *coge*, pl. *cogas*, f. (coeg; COE-gaz)

CURLEW: *gulvinack*, pl. *gulvinogas*, m. (gul-VIN-ek; gul-vin-OG-az)

DUCK: *hoaz*, pl. *heidgi*, m. (hauz; HEI-djee)

GOOSE: *gooth*, pl. *gothow*, f. (gûdh; GODH-au)

GUILLEMOT: *kidda* pl. *-s*, m. (KID-a; KID-az)

GUINEA FOWL: *gleeny*, pl. *gleenez*, m. (GLEEN-ee; GLEEN-ez)

GULL: *goolla*, pl. *-s*, m. (GÛL-hla; GÛL-hlaz)

HEN: *yar* pl. *year*, f. (yar; yair)

KESTREL: *tigry*, pl. *-as*, m. (TIG-ree; TIG-ree-az)

LAPWING: *corniwhillan*, pl. *kerniwhilli*, f. (corn-i-HWIL-an; kern-i-HWIL-ee)

MAGPIE: *pyasan*, pl. *pyas*, f. (pee-AZ-en; PEE-az)

OWL: *ula*, pl. *ulez*, m. (Û-la; Û-lez)

SPARROW: *gulvan*, pl. *-as*, m. (GUL-van; gul-VAN-az)

SWALLOW: *gwennol*, pl. *gwennili*, f. (GWEN-el; gwen-IL-ee)

SWAN: *alarh*, pl. *elerh*, m. (AL-ar'h; EL-er'h)

TERN: *skirret*, pl. *-as*, m. (SKI-ret; ski-RET-az)

THRUSH: *mola looz*, pl. *molas looz*, f. (MUl-a LOOZ; MUL-az LOOZ)

TURKEY: *cock Giny*, pl. *cogas Giny*, m. (cok GIn-ee; COG-az GIN-ee)

WAGTAIL: *stenner*, pl. *stennorian*, m. (STEN-er; sten-ER-yan)

WREN: *gwradnan*, pl. *-as*, f. (g'RAD-nen; g'rad-NAN-az)

6

Place Names of The Roseland

ST ANTHONY IN ROSELAND: from St Antonin.

ANVOASE: LC *an vose*, "the wall/dyke".

ARDEVORA: MC *ar devrow*, "beside waters". Pronounced "ar-DEV-ra"

BLOUTH POINT: MC *blogh*, "bald, bare".

BOHORTHA: MC *buorthow*, "cowsheds".

CAERHAYES: a wealth of early forms, e.g. *Cariheys* C13, *Karieis* C13, *Caeryhaes* C14, draw possible parallels with the Breton CARHAIX. The first element is undoubtedly MC *car*, "fort"; the second is less clear. It may be MC *eys*, "corn".

CAMERANCE: LC *cam- weras*, "curving ground".

CARAGLOOSE POINT: LC *carrack looz*, "grey rock".

CARGURREL: in its present form, this name is LC *kear gurroll*, "fort of a ship", but it replaces the older form, MC *cruk geler*, "coffin barrow/tumulus" by association with the nearby hill fort now called DINGEREIN CASTLE (see below), and the legend that King Gerent's body was rowed from here in a silver ship with golden oars to be buried with the fabulous ship in the great barrow across the bay called Carne Beacon (see CARNE below).

CARNE: LC *carn*, not, in this case, meaning a natural tor, but a massive Bronze Age barrow or "cairn".

CARN PEDNATHAN: LC *carn pedn ethan*, "bird's head outcrop".

CARRICKNATH POINT: LC *carrack nath*, "puffin rock".

CARVINACK: "car-VIN-ek". LC *kear veinack*, "stony fort".

CARWARTHEN: MC *car Warthen*, "Gwarthen's fort".

CASTLEZENS: LC *castell zenz*, "saints' castle".

CORNELLY: named after St Cornelius. Pronounced "corn-EL-ee"

CREGOE: LC *cregow*, "barrows/tumuli".

CRIGMURRIAN: LC *creeg murrian*, "ants' barrow/tumulus".

CRUGSILLICK: MC *cruk Selec*, "Selec's barrow/tumulus".

CUBY: "KYOO-bee". Named after St Kyby, said to have been the son of Selyf (possibly St Selevan), son of King Gerent of Dumnonia, and also commemorated at Caergybi, Wales.

DINGEREIN CASTLE: the current name of this hill fort was coined in the C19 from LC *deen Gerens*, "Gerent's hill fort".

EGLOSMERTHER: LC *eglos merther*, "church on a saint's grave".

ELERKEY: OC *elehrc-i*, "place of swans". This was the former manorial name of Veryan parish, now relegated to a mere place name in Veryan village.

ST EWE: after St Ewa. The churchtown was *Lanewa* C14, MC *lan Ewa*, "St Ewa's church site".

FENTONGOLLAN: MC *fynten Golan*, "St Colan's well", or MC *fynten gollan*, "hazel well".

GERRANS: pronounced with a hard G. Named from St Gerent, believed to have been King Gerent I of Dumnonia (C6), son of Erbin and father of Selyf (St Selevan ?), Yestin (St Just?) and Cado, who succeeded him as king according to the available genealogies.

GREEB POINT: LC *(an) greeb*, "the reef/crest".

GROGOTH: MC *(an) gruk goth*, "the old barrow/tumulus", or "barrow by a stream".

GWENDRA: *Wenetyr* C13. MC *gwyn dyr*, "white/fair land".

JACKA POINT: MC *chogha*, "chough".

ST JUST IN ROSELAND: from St Just, probably the same saint commemorated in Penwith. The former name of the churchtown, *Lansioch* C13, *Lansiok* C17, MC *lan Sioc*, "Sioc's church site", survives as LANZEAGUE (see below).

KIBERICK COVE: LC *keberack*, "place of driftwood".

KILLIGERRAN HEAD: LC *kil Gerens*, "Gerent's ridge"

LAMORRAN: MC *lan Moren*, "Moren's church site".

LANZEAGUE: MC *lan Sioc*, "Sioc's church site" (see ST JUST IN ROSELAND above).

ST MAWES: named from St Maudet. The churchtown was *Lavousa* C15, *Lavowsa* C16, MC *lan Vausa*, "St Mawes's church site".

MELINSEY: LC *melingy*, "millhouse". Pronounced "me-LIN-zee".

MERTHER: MC *merther*, "saint's grave". In C13/14, the churchtown was known as *Eglosmerther*, MC *eglos merther*, "church on a saint's grave".

MESSACK POINT: LC *mesack*, "meadow place".

ST MICHAEL CAERHAYES: "St Michael of Caerhayes" (see CAERHAYES).

J.T. Blight's engraving of St Michael Penkevil

ST MICHAEL PENKEVIL: "St Michael of Penkevil", OC *pen kevil*, "horse's head".

NANCARROW: LC *nans carow*, "stag valley".

NANCEMABYN: LC *nans Mabyn*, "St Mabyn's valley".

NARE HEAD: LC *(an) are*, "the high place".

PEDNVADAN: the late form of earlier *Pentalvan*, MC *pen tal van*, "brow peak headland".

PENCABE: MC *pen capa*, "cape headland".

PENDOWER: MC *pen dowr*, "water's end".

PENHESKEN: LC *penheskan*, "sedge end".

PENNARE: LC *penare*, "prominent headland".

PENVOSE: LC *pen- vose*, "wall's end".

PERBARGUS POINT: LC *por bargez*, "buzzard cove".

PERCUIL: MC *por(th) cul*, "narrow cove". Also spelt PORTHCUEL, both are pronounced "per-KYOOL".

PHILLEIGH: named after St Fili. C14 *St Filius of Eglosros*, including MC *eglos Ros*, "church of Roseland" (see ROSELAND).

PIBYAH ROCK: LC *peeber*, "piper".

PLACE MANOR: LC *plase*, "mansion".

POLGLAZE: LC *poll glaze*, "blue pool".

POLHENDRA: LC *poll hendra*, "old farm pool".

POLMASSICK: *Ponsmadek* C14. MC *pons Madoc*, "Madoc's bridge".

PORTHBEAN: LC *porth bean*, "little cove". Properly, "porth-BEE-an".

PORTHBEOR: perhaps LC *porth mere*, "great cove", but the second element is more likely to be LC *bear*, "short", or *pure*, "clean".

PORTHCUEL: see PERCUIL above.

John Norden's c.1580 map of The Roseland

PORTHLUNEY: MC *porth Luny*, "River Luny cove". The river name appears to be the Cornish equivalent of W. *lyfni*, "smooth river".

PORTHOLLAND: a somewhat obscure place name, and the older forms, *Portalan* C13, *Porthallan* C14, *Porthsalen* C16, do little to help in deciphering it. The most likely explanation is that the word may be LC *hollan*, "salt".

PORTLOE: LC *porth loe*, "inlet cove".

PORTSCATHO: LC *porth scathow*, "cove of boats".

ROSELAND: LC *rose*, in the sense of "promontory", with Eng. "land" added sometime after the C14.

ROSEN CLIFF: LC *rosen*, "little promontory".

ROSEVALLEN: LC *rose avallan*, "apple-tree hillspur".

ROSEVINE: LC *rose vein*, "hillspur of stones".

ROSTEAGUE: "ros-TEEG". LC *rose teag*, "beautiful coastal slope".

RUAN LANIHORNE: MC *Rumon lan Ryhoern*, "St Rumon at Ryhoern's church site". There are still some wholly mistaken lists which give *ruan*, as meaning "river". This is not so, and place names with this word either contain the name of this Breton saint, or LC *royn*, "seal".

SHAG ROCK: Eng., from the seabird.

TOLVERNE: LC *tal- vern*, "hill brow".

TREGASSICK: *Tregossick* C14. MC *tre gorsek*, "farm in a reedy place".

TREGONY: pronounced "TREG-nee", its early spellings *Trefhrigoni* C11, *Trerigani* C11, show that this is MC *tre Rigoni*, "Rigoni's farm".

TREGOTHNAN: MC *tre gothnans*, "farm in a stream valley".

TRELONK: MC *tre lonk*, "ravine farm".

TRENGROUSE: LC *tre- an growz*, "farm by the cross".

TREWARTHENICK: MC *tre Wethenoc*, "Gwethenoc's farm".

TREWITHIAN: MC *tre Wethyan*, "Gwethyan's farm".

TREWORTHAL: MC *tre wothal*, "farm by marshy ground".

TREWORTHEN: MC *tre Worthan*, "Gworthan's farm".

TURNAWARE POINT: possibly LC *torn a vorr*, "junction", from the meeting place of three creeks and the River Fal which, at this point, enters the broad reach of Carrick Roads.

VERYAN: shortened form of St Symphorian, this being mistakenly rewritten as *Seyntveryan* C16 leading to (St) *Verien* C17.

VOSE: LC *(an) vose*, "the wall/dyke".

VOSKELLY: MC *(an) vos kelly*, "the wall by a grove".

ZONE POINT: LC *sawan*, "cliff-chasm", shortened from its C16 name *Savenheer*, LC *sawan heer*, "long/tall cliff-chasm". The "Zoze Point" of late C19 and some C20 maps results from a printing error by the Ordnance Survey.

*   *   *

Some Cornish Proverbs –
Nebas lavarow coth Kernuack

En Have per ko Gwave: In Summer remember Winter.
Debbry morgy en Meez Mea rag tha gweel mawe: Eat a dogfish in May to get a son.
Carenga venga, Covaithias na venga: Love would, Avarice would not.

Morteed a metten traveeth na dale: The morning tide is not worth nothing.

Cabmthavas en metten, glawe boaz etten: A rainbow in the morning, rain is in it.

Cowz nebas ha cowz daa, buz cowz nebas an gwelha: Speak little and speak good, but speak little is the best.

Cowz nebas, cowz daa ha daa veth cowzez arta: Speak little, speak good and good will be spoken again.

Cuzal ha teag, sarra wheag, moaz pell: Soft and fair, sweet sir, goes far.

Ree a edn dra na dale traveeth: Too much of one thing is good for nothing.

An gwreanath ew an gwelha en pub lea trea po pelha: The truth is the best, in every place, at home and further.

Pobell abell a beaw castilli: People afar own castles.

Neb na gare e gwain, coll resteffa: Who loves not gain, let him have loss.

Neb na gare e gye an gwra deveeder: Who loves not his dog will make a sheep-worrier.

Nag eze goon heb lagas na kea heb scovarn: There are no downs without an eye, nor hedge without an ear.

Gwra daa, rag tha honen che an gwra: Do good, for thyself wilt thou do it.

Comero weeth na ra whye gara an vorr goth rag an vorr noweth: Take care you do not leave the old road for the new road.

Bethez gweskez duath ken gweskall eneth: Be struck twice before striking once.

Nag o ve brage na hollan: I am neither malt nor salt.

Thero whye lawhetha an darras po marth ledrez: You are locking the door when a horse is stolen.

Rag pobell thaa nag eze tra e gellas: For good people there is nothing to hide.

Gwary wheag ew gwary teag: Sweet play is handsome play.

Gwave en Have tereba Goluan, ha Have en Gwave tereba Nadelack: Winter in Summer till Midsummer, and Summer in Winter till Christmas.

Ma Whevral lenall an crenniow rag Merh: February fills the reservoirs for March.

Mor menna whye moaz gena ve hannath, me a vedn moaz gena whye avorow: If you go with me tonight, I will go with you tomorrow.

Teag ew hydruk: Beautiful is fragile.

Na vedn nevra doaz vaze a tavas ree heer: No good will ever come of a tongue too long.

Ambossow urt treeher gwreze, anothans nag eze la: Agreements by a conqueror made, from them there is no law.

Dean heb tavas a gollas e deer: A man without a language has lost his land.

Na wrew eva ree, buz eva rag oz zehas, ha hedna mouy po le vedn gweetha corff en ehas: Do not drink too much, but drink for your thirst, and that more or less to keep a healthy body.

Tacklow daa ve gwreze tha voaz gwelhez: Good things were made to be seen.

Flehas heb skeans vedn geel go seeans: Foolish children will do as they wish.

* * *

Cussell Thaa Rag Pewa Benag:

Ma leeas gwreag lacka vel zeag,
Gwell gerez vel comerez:
Ha ma leeaz benen pecarra'n gwenen:
Gye vedn gweras tha go theez dendall
    peath an beaz.

Flehas heb skeans vedn gweel go seans,
Buz mor krown'gye pedery pan dale go gwary,
Ha madra taa pandreeg seera ha daama,

Na rellons moaz than cooz tha cuntell go booz,
Buz gen nebas lavirians
Gye venga dendall go booz ha dillas.

Kasowo tha ve, che dean mar feer,
Tha leb eze mere a peath ha leeas teer:
Ha me reeg clowas an bobell champla
Ha theze tha che ethick gwreag daa;
Hye ore gweel padn daa gen e glawn,
Ha et e olas hye dalvea gawas tane.

Na dale deez perna kinnis war an saw,
Na moaz cuntell an dreiz dro than keow,
Rag hedna vedn boaz cowzez dro than pow.
Gwell hye bea perna nebas glow:
Hedna vedn goz tubma athelhar ha araage,
Ha whye ell eva cor gwelha mars eze dew brage.

Good Advice For Whoever

There are many wives worse than draff,
Better left than taken,
And there are many women like the bees:
They will help their men to earn wealth.

Silly children will follow their fancy,
But if they reflect what their play is worth,
And mark well what their father and mother
                    have done,
They would not go to the wood to get their food,
But with a little effort
They would earn their food and clothing.

Listen to me, thou man so wise,
Who has much wealth and much land:
For I heard people mention
That thou hast an excellent wife;
She can make good cloth with her wool,
And in her hearth she should have fire.

Men should not buy fuel by the load,
Nor go gathering thorns round the hedges,
For that will be gossiped around the country.
It would be better to buy some coal:
That will warm you behind and before,
And you can drink best beer if you have malt.

Na dale dew gweel treven war an treath:
Dreth hedna whye vedn kelly mere a peath. .
Buz mor menno derevall warbidn an pow yein,
Whye dalvea gawas an brossa mein,
Ha rina vedn dirria warbidn moer ha gwenz:
Nag eze droeg veth gwreze lebmen na kenz!

You should not build houses upon the sand:
Through that you will lose much wealth.
But if you wish to build against the cold,
You should fetch the largest stones,
And they will endure against sea and wind:
No harm has been done now or before!

James Jenkins, c.1700

*   *   *

Sea Creatures: *Bestas an moer*

COD: *barvas*, pl. *barvasi*, m. (BAR-vaz; bar-VAZ-ee)

CRAB: *canker*, pl. *cenkras*, m. (KAN-ker; KEN-kraz)

CUTTLEFISH: *padalenkan*, pl. *-s*, f. (pad-el-EN-kan[z])

DOGFISH: *morgy*, pl. *morgean*, m. (MOR-gee; mor-GAA-an)

DOLPHIN: *morah*, pl. *-as*, m. (MOR-a'h; mor-AH-az)

FISH: *pesk*, pl. *puscas*, m. (pesk; PUS-kaz)

JELLYFISH: *mulagowla*, pl. *-s*, m. (mul-a-GAOU-la[z])

LIMPET: *lagas davas*, pl. *lagadgow devas*, m. (LAG-az DAV-az; la-GAD-jau DEV-az)

LOBSTER: *legast*, pl. *legesti*, m. (LEG-est; leg-ES-tee)

MACKEREL: *breal*, pl. *brili*, m. (BRAI-el; BRIL-ee)

OCTOPUS: *guzzalezza*, pl. *gezzalezza*, f. (guz-a-LEZ-a; gez-a-LEZ-a)

PILCHARD: *hernan*, coll.pl. *hearn*, f. (HERN-an; hairn)

SALMON: *sowman*, pl. *-s*, m. (SAU-man[z])

SHRIMP: *beevinbovin*, pl. *-as*, m. (BEE-vin-BOE-vin; BEE-vin-boe-VIN-az))

WHALE: *morvel*, pl. *-as*, m. (MOR-val; mor-VEL-az)

7

Place Names of St Agnes & Perranporth

ST AGNES: after the C4 martyr St Agnes. The alternative name for the churchtown was _Bryanek_ C13, _Bryanick_ C19, possibly MC _bre Ann-yk_, "little Agnes's hill".

BAWDEN ROCKS: in C18, these were _Bawden/Boen Rocks_, possibly LC _bowen_, "cow", although the intrusive D would be curious. An alternative name "Man and his Man" is Eng., whilst a further Eng. name, "Cow and Calf" echoes the possible Cornish one.

BOLINGEY: LC _belingy_, "mill-house".

BOLSTER: a contraction of LC _both lesster_, "hump like a boat". Close to Bolster Farm, an isolated section of the great Romano-British (?) earthwork of the same name closely resembles an upturned boat. The name has also been transferred to the legendary giant who built the earthwork, and who was bested by St Agnes herself. In C17, the earthwork was known as _Gorres_, LC _(an) gorras_, "the weir/dam", from its resemblance to an earthen dam.

CARINES: _Crouwortheynys_ C14, _Crowarthenes_ C15. MC _crow orth enys_, "Crou near an isolated place". This was one part of an estate named _Crou_ C14, MC _crow_, "hut"; the others being Colgrease, MC _crow greys_, "middle Crou", and Carevick, _Crowwarthevyke_ C16, MC _crow orth ewyk_, "Crou near (place of) roe deer".

CARN CLEW: LC _carn cloh_, "bell outcrop", or LC _carrack lew_, "coloured rock".

CARN GOWLA: possibly LC _carn golva_, "lookout outcrop".

CARN HAUT: LC _carn hat_, "hat/hood-shaped outcrop".

CHAPEL PORTH: a modern name with the usual Cornish word order reversed, LC _porth chapall_, "chapel cove", from the former site of St Agnes's chapel on the clifftop.

CHYNHALE: LC _chy an hale_, "house by the marsh".

CHYVERTON: "CHIV-er-tun". MC _chy war ton_, "house on pastureland".

CLIGGA HEAD: LC _cleger_, "cliff/crag".

COOSEWARTHA: LC _cooz warha_, "higher wood".

COSTISLOST: possibly LC _cooz an looz_, "the grey wood", but it is more likely to be Eng., describing land which was a poor investment.

CRANTOCK: from St Carantoc. The churchtown was known as *Langorroc* C11, *Lancorru* C14, MC *lan Gorroc*, "Corroc's church site". The name Corroc may have been a pet form of Carantoc.

CUBERT: from St Cubert. The old name of the churchtown was *Lanowyn* C17, now surviving as Lanlovey. MC *lan Owen*, "Owen's church site".

ELLENGLAZE: LC *elin glaze*, "green corner".

ENGELLEY: MC *an gelly*, "the grove".

GOONBELL: LC *goon bell*, "far downs".

GOONHAVERN: *Goenhavar* C14. LC *goon havar*, "fallowland downs". Pronounced "gûn-HAV-ern".

GOONINIS: LC *goon ennis*, "remote/isolated downs".

GOONLAZE: LC *goon laze*, "grey-green downs".

GOONVREA: LC *goon vrea*, "hill downs".

HOLYWELL BAY: modern Eng. name, from a holy well in a sea cave on the beach. The Cornish name for this bay was *Porraylan* C17, sometimes corrupted to "Porth Island". LC *por hayl-in*, "little estuary cove".

KELSEY HEAD: named from the former manor of Kelsey, perhaps MC *kelghjy*, "circle-house".

LAMBOURNE: *Lanbron* C14, MC *lan bron*, "church-site on a hill".

LANTEAGUE: "lan-TEEG". LC *nans teag*, "beautiful valley".

LIGGER POINT: possibly LC *cleger*, "cliff/crag", or MC *leghow*, "slabs".

MARAZANVOSE: LC *marhas an vose*, "market with a wall". Pronounced "mar-a-zan-VOEZ".

MINGOOSE: LC *mean gooz*, "wood by a stone".

NAMPARA: LC *nans bara*, "valley of bread".

NANCARROW: LC *nans carow*, "stag valley".

PEN-A-GADER: MC *pen an gader*, "headland of the chair".

PENHALE: LC *pen- hale*, "marsh end".

PENHALLOW: LC *pen- hallow*, "marshes' end".

PENWARTHA: MC *pen wartha*, "higher end".

PERRANCOOMBE: modern name reversing the usual Cornish word order, LC *coom Perran*, "St Perran's valley".

PERRANPORTH: a C19 name which again reverses the order from the normal Cornish manner, LC *porth Perran*, "St Perran's cove". In C16, this was *St Perin's creeke*. The name is usually pronounced "peh-ren-PORTH", rather than "PEH-ren-porth".

PERRANZABULOE: "peh-ren-ZAB-yoo-loe". Latin, *Peran in sabulo* C16, "St Perran in the sand", translating the C15 *Pirran in treth*, MC *Peran yn treyth*, "St Perran in the sand". The former church site in the sandhills to the west was *Lanpiran* C11, OC *lan Piran*, "St Perran's church site".

PONSMERE: LC *pons mere*, "great bridge".

PORTH JOKE: LC *porth chauk*, "chough cove". Sometimes spelt POLLY JOKE, LC *poll an chauk*, "the chough's cove".

PORTHTOWAN: "porth-TAOU-an". LC *porth towan*, "sandhill cove".

REEN: LC *reen*, "hillspur".

REJERRAH: "r'JEH-ra". An ancient name, recorded in 960 as *Hryd worwig*, and as *Retworoc* C14. MC *res Worroc*, "Gorroc's ford". The personal name might be the same as *Corroc*, which is linked with Crantock (see CRAN-TOCK).

ROSE: LC *rose*, "roughland".

ROSEMUNDY: LC *rose mungy*, "roughland with an ore-house".

STAMPAS FARM: LC *stampez*, "stamping mill".

TOWANWROATH: LC *tol an wrah*, "the hag's hole" or, perhaps, "the giant's hole" as there are a number of late examples of LC *gwrah*, normally "hag, witch, crone", being applied to a giant. In this case, the giant would be Bolster, who was duped by St Agnes into bleeding himself to death in a clifftop hole which, unknown to him, opened to the sea.

TREAMBLE: MC *taran bol*, "thunder pool".

TRESAWSEN: LC *tre- Sausen*, "Saxons'/Englishmen's farm".

TREVALSA: MC *trev alsyow*, "farm by slopes".

TREVAUNANCE: MC *trev war nans*, "farm on a valley".

TREVELLAS: possibly LC *tre(a)v elez*, "angels' farm".

TYWARNHAYLE: MC *chy war an hayl*, "house on an estuary", but strangely retaining the OC form of *chy*.

VENTONGIMPS: LC *venton gumpas*, "well in a level place".

WHEAL KITTY: LC *wheal Kitty*, "Kitty's mine".

WHEAL VLOW: LC *wheal vlou*, "blue mine".

ZELAH: "ZEE-la". Possibly OE *sele*, "hall", but this is a long way west for such an archaic Eng. word. It is more likely to be MC *seghla*, "waterless place" (i.e. with no water supply of its own).

*　　*　　*

Cornish in the 16th & 17th centuries

By the year 1500, the evolutionary processes of the language was again beginning to show changes. The stressed sounds of *m* and *n* were becoming *bm* and *dn*, for example, MC *cam*, "curved" became LC *cabm*, and MC *pen*, "head", had become LC *pedn*. In fact, place name evidence suggests that this change was taking place at an even earlier date, with names such as Delawhidden, Treliddon and Gradna occurring in places in East Cornwall where the language is supposed to have become moribund well before 1500.

Denied a Prayer Book and Bible, regarded as unrefined by the gentry and ruling classes and faced with the relentless advance of English, it is remarkable that the westward retreat of the Cornish language was not more rapid than it was. Undoubtedly such works as John Tregear's translation into Cornish of Bishop Bonner's Homilies in the late 1550s, and the continuation of Miracle Play performances served to delay the demise of the language. From the late 16th century and into the 17th, the state of Cornish is best described by commentators of the time:

1572:   The Depositions of the Bishop's Consistory Court at Exeter recorded a case of defamation when William Hawysh deposed that on *dew whallon gwa metton in eglos de Lalant*, "All Saints' morning in Lelant church", Agnes Davey was called "whore" and "whore bitch", these being "in English and not in Cornowok".

1595:   In the same records at Exeter, a girl from St Ewe testified that two of the witnesses had been speaking together in both English and Cornish.

1602:   Richard Carew of Antony in *The Survey of Cornwall*: "But the principal love of this (Cornish) language lived in Dr Kenall the civilian (Vicar of Gwennap, died 1592) and with him lieth buried for the English speech doth still encroach upon it and hath driven the same into the uttermost skirts of the shire. Most of the inhabitants can speak no word of Cornish but very few are ignorant of the English . . . and yet some so affect their own to a stranger, they will not speak it for, if meeting them by chance you enquire the way or any such matter, your answer shall be *Meea navidna cowzasawzneck*, "I can speak no Saxonage" (in fact, Carew had this slightly wrong: LC *me na vadna cowz a Sowznack* means "I will not speak the English"). In his *Survey*, Carew also mentions the continuing use of the Plain an Gwary amphitheatres.

1610:   John Norden, *Speculi Britanniae Pars* (compiled c.1584): "The Cornish people, for the most part, are descended from the British stock ... but, until of late years, retained the British speech corrupted (i.e. independently developed) as theirs is of Wales ... But of late, the Cornish men have much conformed themselves to the use of the English tongue and their English is equal to the best, especially in the eastern parts; even from Truro eastwards it is in manner wholly English. In the west part of the Country, as in the Hundreds of Penwith and Kerrier, the Cornish tongue is most in use amongst the inhabitants ..."

1644:   Richard Symonds, *Diary of the Marches of the Royal Army during the Great Civil War*: "This language is spoken altogether at Goonhilly and around Pendennis, and at Land's End they speak no English. All beyond Truro they speak the Cornish language."

c.1645. William Jackman, vicar of Feock and chaplain of Pendennis Castle, customarily used Cornish for the Words of Administration at Holy Communion in his church because the older parishioners could not understand English.

1667:   John Ray's *Itinerary* recorded that the only man who could write Cornish (that he knew of) was Dick Angwin of St Just in Penwith. Few children could speak it, "so that the language is like in a short time to be quite lost".

1680.   William Scawen: "'Tis observed also elsewhere in this county further west, where the Cornish has been most spoken, that the English thereabouts is much better than the same in Devon, or the places bordering them, by being most remote from thence whence the corruption proceeds.
"... For we have some among these few that do speak Cornish who do not understand English ... and those may be many in some of the western parts to whom Mr Francis Robinson, parson of Landewednack, told me he had preached a sermon not long since in the Cornish tongue, only well understood by his auditory."

1695.   William Camden, *Brittania* (original 1586, but as added to by E. Gibson): "Their language, too, is the English and (which is something surprising) observed by travellers to be more pure and refined than that of their neighbours Devonshire and Somersetshire. The most probable reason seems to be this: that English is an introduced, not original, language, and those who brought it in were the Gentry and Merchants who imitated the dialect of the Court, which is the nice and accurate . . . The old Cornish is almost quite driven out of the Country, being spoken only by the vulgar in two or three parishes at the Land's End, and they, too, understand the English. In other parts, the inhabitants know little or nothing of it so that in all likelihood a short time will destroy the small remains that are left of it. Tis a good while since that only two men could write it, and one of them no scholar or grammarian, and then blind with age."

1695.   Cheston Marchant, an old lady of Gwithian, died. A centenarian, she could speak only Cornish and understood not a word of English.

*   *   *

Some conversational phrases: *Nebas lavarow holanack*

Greetings

Hi! Hello there!: *You!* (yoo)

Hello, friend: *Ha, soce!* (ha, soess)

Hello, John: *Ha, Jooan!* (ha, JOO-an)

What cheer?: *Lowena tha whye* (lew-EN-a tha hwei); *Betho whye lowenack* (BETH-o hwei lew-EN-ek)

Good day: *Durdathawhy* (der-DADH-a-HWEI)

Good morning: *Metten daa tha whye* (MET-en DAA tha hwei)

God bless: *Darzona* (dar-ZON-a)

Good evening: *Gothewhar vaze* (guth-YOO-hwer VAAZ)

Invitations

Come in: *Deeo agye* (DEE-o a-JEI)

Won't you sit down?: *Setha vedo whye?* (SEDH-a VED-o hwei)

Will you have a bite to eat?: *Vedo whye cawas tabm?* (VED-o hwei KAOU-az TAB'm)

Will you have a drop?: *Vedo whye cawas badna?* (VED-o hwei KAOU-az BAD-na)

Will you have something to drink?: *Vedo whye eva badna?* (VED-o hwei EV-a BAD-na)

Will you have a cup of tea/coffee?: *Vedo whye cawas bolla a tay/coffy?* (VED-o hwei KAOU-az BÛl-a a TAA/COF-ee)

Will you have a glass of wine/of beer/of cider?: *Vedo whye cawas gwedran a ween/a cor/a cyder?* (VED-o hwei KAOU-az GWED-ren a WEEN/a COR/ a SEI-der)

Could you do with a glass of spirits?: *Vedo whye usia gwedran a spur?* (VED-o hwei YOO-zee-a GWED-ren a SPUR)

Come close to the fire: *Deeo neaz than tane* (DEE-o naiz dhan TAAN)

Call me up sometime: *Gwro creia ve neb preze* (G'roe CREI-a vee neb PRAIZ)

Come and see us/me sometime: *Deeo tha gon/ve gwelhas neb preze* (DEE-o dha gun/vee GWEL-hlaz neb PRAIZ)

Enquiries

How are you?: *Fatlagena whye?* (fat-la-GEN-a hwei)

How are you doing?: *Fatla era whye a keel?* (FAT-la EH-ra hwei a KEEL)

How is/are your wife/husband/children/father/mother?: *Fatla gen oz gwreag/gour/flehas/seera/daama?* (FAT-la gen uz g'RAIG/GOO'r/FLAI-naz/ZEE-ra/DAA-ma)

Where do you live?: *Pelea ero whye treegas?* (p'LAI-a EH-ro hwei TRI-gaz)

Where's that?: *Pelea ew hedna?* (p'LAI-a yoo HED-na)

Are you married?: *Ero whye demithez?* (EH-ro hwei d'MIDH-ez)

Have you any children?: *Eze flehas tha whye?* (aiz FLAI-haz tha hwei)

How many children have you?: *Pes floh eze tha whye?* (pez flo'h aiz tha hwei)

How old are they/is he/is she?: *Pes blouth enz/ewa/ew hye?* (pez blûdh enz/YOO-a/ew hei)

Where do they/does he/does she go to school?: *Pelea iggans/iggeva/igge hye noaz than scoll ?* (p'Lai-a ID-janz/ID-je-va/ID-ja hei mahz than skoel)

What is your address?: *Drew goz trigva?* (droo guz TRIG-va)

Have you a phone?: *Eze telephone tha whye?* (aiz TEL-e-foen tha hwei). Some revivalists have created a word *pellgows*, "far speaking", to represent a telephone. This is somewhat unnecessary for the word "telephone" is a modern word culled from Greek and, with minor variations of spelling, has become international. To do other than adopt the international word would be rather a contrivance].

102

What is your number?: *Drew goz never?* (droo guz NEV-er)

Do you have a sheet of paper?: *Eze vollan paper gena whye?* (aiz VUL-an PAA-per GEN-a hwei)

Do you have a pen?: *Eze quillan gena whye?* (aiz KWIL-an GEN-a hwei)

Are you Cornish?: *Kernuack o whye?* (ker-NOO-ek oe hwei)

Compliments

I'm very glad to see you: *Tho ve per looan tha gwelhas whye.* (tho vee per LOO-an tha GWEL-hlaz hwei)

I'm glad to see you in good health: *Tho ve looan goz gwelhas en ehas daa.* (tho vee LOO-an guz GWEL-hlaz en AI-haz daa)

You speak good Cornish: *Thera whye clappia Kernuack daa* (THEH-ra vee CLAP-ya ker-NOO-ek daa)

Responses

Well enough, thank goodness!: *Daa lowar, merastadew!* (daa LAOU-er, mer-AS-ta-DYOO)

I have my health, thankfully!: *Ma a ehas thebm, merastadew!* (ma a AI-haz THEB'm mer-AS-ta-DYOO)

He/she has his/her health: *Ma e ehas dotha/dothy* (ma ee AI-haz DOE-dha/DOE-dhee)

He/she is not very well: *Nag ewa/ew hye buz gadgack* (nag YOO-a/yoo-HEI buz GAD-jek)

My address is . . .: *Ma trigva thew . . .* (ma TRIG-va th'YOO)

My number is . . .: *Ma never thew . . .* (ma NEV-er th'YOO)

I will, thank you: *Me a ra, gwra 'massi* (mee a rah, g'rah-MASS-ee)

Requests

Please lend me . . .: *Peidgy culla tha ve . . .* (PED-jee KUL-a tha vee)

Hand me that book, please: *Dro thebm an leverna, mor pleag* (droe THEB'n an LEV-er-NA, mor PLAIG)

Please & Thank You

Please . . . (before request): *Peidgy. . .* (PED-jee)

. . . please (after request): . . . *mor pleag* (mor PLAIG)

Thank you: *Durdaladawhy* (der-DAL-a-da-HWEI)

Thanks very much: *Merastawhy* (mer-AS-ta-HWEI)

Farewells

Goodbye: *Benetugana* (ben-e-t'yoo-GAN-a); *Dew boz geno* (d'YOO buz GEN-oe)

Till next time/See you again: *Tereba nessa* (t'REB-a NEZ-a)

Goodnight: *Ternestatha* (ter-nu-STA-dha); *Noze daa tha whye* (nauz DAA tha hwei)

Take care: *Comero weeth* (kum-EH-roe WEETH)

*   *   *

Stearan Lesky

Shooting Star

Me zavas dadn an ebbarn clere an noze,
Settez oll andro gen sterrez gulow,
Anella whath an delkiow
Cregy bith mar guzal en gweeth ethez.

I stood beneath the clear sky of the night,
Set all about with bright stars,
Breathing the breath of the leaves
Hanging ever so still on the scented trees.

Thera edn stearan mesk angye
Passia, ha gonz aise, tectar an rerol,

O gwidn, o glaze, o gwear, oyrack entye,

Meer, ottave!" hevely laull.

There was one star among them
Did surpass, and with ease, the beauty of
      the others,
Which was white, was blue, was green,
      golden for sure,
"Look, here I am!" seeming to say.

Na olgama tha veaz trailia a goolack,
Glenez prest urt hye sevilliack,
Buz wharea me as gwelhas hye
Killynia tua ve pecarra lagas lesky.

I could not turn away my gaze,
Ever clinging to her unmoving,
But presently I saw her
Slanting towards me like a burning eye.

Ha me reeg poonia raage,
A doola stous deraage,
Ha e hatsha nenna,
Ha e sendgy en ma devra,
Buz, ah! hye loskas, hye loskas,
Hye loskas tidn heb truath ry,
Ha lesky meaz an golan ve.

And I ran forward,
My hands outstretched,
And caught her then,
And clasped her to my breast,
But oh! she burnt, she burnt,
She burnt painfully, mercilessly,
And burnt away my heart.

Richard Gendall

8

Place Names around Newquay

BEDRUTHAN STEPS: pronounced "b'DRUH-dhan", and not "bed-ROOTH-an". This coastal feature is named after a nearby farm, recorded in C14 as *Bodruthyn*, OC *bod Ruthin*, "Ruthin's dwelling". The "Steps" are variously claimed to be the precarious steps leading down the cliff to the beach, and the line of great sea-stacks, resembling giant stepping stones.

BENALLACK: LC *banollack*, "broom-brake".

BOGEE: MC *bos ge*, "dwelling by a hedge".

BOSWORGEY: MC *bos Worgi*, "Gorgi's dwelling".

CARGOLL: *Cargaule* C13. MC *car gawl*, "cabbage fort".

CARLOGGAS: MC *car logas*, "fort of mice".

CARNANTON: *Carneton* C14. LC *carn*, "tor/cairn"; Eng. *tun*, "farm".

CARNEWAS: LC *carn hewas*, "summer farm tor/cairn".

CHYTANE: LC *chy tane*, "house of fire".

COLAN: namee after the church saint, Colan.

ST COLUMB MAJOR: from St Columba. The parish was *St Colombe the Over* C16.

ST COLUMB MINOR: from St Columba. *Colombe the Nether*, C16. Both St Columbs are pronounced "KOL'm".

COSWARTH: possibly MC *coys wartha*, "higher wood".

DEGEMBRIS: *Tykambret* C14. OC *ti Kambret*, "kambret's house".

DENZELL: *Dinneshal* C13. MC *dyn ysal*, "low fort".

ENGOLLAN: LC *an gollan*, "the hazel tree".

ST ENODER: from St Enoder. The churchtown was Heglosenuder C11, OC *egglos Enoder*, "St Enoder's church".

ST EVAL: "EV-el". From St Uval.

FISTRAL BAY: a totally baffling name which has defied all attempts to find its meaning. *Fistal Bay* C19.

FRADDON: *Frodan* C14. A fossilised Old Cornish name; OC *frod-an*, "stream place".

GLUVIAN: possibly a personal name.

GOENROUNSAN: MC *goen rounsan*, "ass downs".

GOONHOSKYN: LC *goon hesken*, "sedge downs", or "Hoskyn's downs" (the surname Hoskyn derives from *heskan*). "gûn-HOS-ken".

INDIAN QUEENS: first named c.1800, after its inn. Despite some accounts, there is no known connection with the American Indian princess Pocahontas.

KESTLE MILL: LC *castell*, "castle".

LANHERNE: *Lanhernen* C11. MC *lan Hernan*, "Hernan's church site".

LUSTY GLAZE: possibly LC *lost an glaze*, "the grey-green tail (promontory)".

MAWGAN-IN-PYDAR: from St Maugan, and including the name of the former Hundred in which it was situated (see PYDAR).

MAWGAN PORTH: wrongly reversed from its C18 form LC *Porth Mawgan*, "Maugan's cove". In C14, the name of the cove was *Porthglyvyen*, MC *porth Gluvyan*, "cove of Gluvian".

MELANCOOSE: LC *melin cooz*, "wood mill".

MELLANVRANE: LC *melin vrane*, "crow mill", or "Bran's mill".

RIVER MENALHYL: misspelling of former name, MC *melyn hayl*, "estuary mill".

MOUNTJOY: C13 *Meyndi/Meyndy*. MC *meynjy*, "house of stones".

NEWLYN EAST: named after St Neulina. The churchtown was *Eglosnyulyn* C15, "St Neulina's church site". The "East" was added after 1888 to differentiate the village from the port of Newlyn near Penzance, whose name has a wholly different meaning.

NEWQUAY: Eng., dating from c.1600. Its former name was *Tewynplustri* C14, possibly MC *tewyn por(th) lystry*, "sand-dunes by a cove for ships", though O.J.Padel disputes this on grounds that are perhaps too academically rigid.

PARK HEAD: named after nearby farm from c.1870. It was formerly *Pentir* C14, MC *pentyr*, "headland", and *Pencarne* C17, LC *pen- carn*, "outcrop head".

PENTIRE: MC *pentyr*, "headland". Popularly pronounced "pen-TEIR", even though it should be "pen-TEER".

PORTH: LC *porth*, "cove, landing place".

PYDAR: MC *peder*, "four"; the fourth of the nine (originally six) Cornish Hundreds.

QUINTRELL DOWNS: from family name Quinterell.

RETALLICK: *Res helec* C13. MC *res helyk*, "willows ford".

RIALTON: Eng., "royal farm".

ROSECLISTON: MC *res cellestron*, "ford of pebbles".

ROSEWIN: MC *ros wyn*, "white valleyside".

RUTHVOES: MC *ruth vos*, "red wall".

STEM POINT: MC *stum*, "bend".

SUMMERCOURT: Eng., "summer courtyard".

TALSKIDDY: MC *tal skeudy*, "hillbrow of shadows".

TOWAN: LC *towan*, "sand-dune(s)".

TREAGO: MC *tre Jago*, "Jago's farm". pronounced "TRAI-goe".

TREBUDANNON: "tre-bud-AN-en". MC *tre Pedanan*, "Pedanan's farm".

TREDINNICK: MC *tre redenek*, "fern-brake farm".

TREGAIR: MC *tre gair*, "farm by a fort".

TREGOOSE: LC *tre- gooz*, "wood farm".

TRENANCE: LC *tre- nans*, "valley farm".

TRENCREEK: LC *tre- an creeg*, "farm by the barrow/tumulus".

TRENITHAN: LC *tre- an eithin*, "farm by the furze".

TRENOON: LC *tre- an oon*, "farm by the downs".

TRERICE: MC *tre res*, "farm by a ford".

TRETHERRAS: LC *tre- thew res*, "farm by two fords".

TREVARREN: MC *tre Veran*, "Meran's farm". The personal name might be the same as that of St Merryn.

TREVITHICK: MC *tre Vuthek*, "Budec's farm".

TREVORRICK: *Treworrech* C13; MC *tre Worec*, "Gorec's farm".

TREWINCE: MC *tre uyns*, "farm in wind".

WATERGATE BAY: Eng., "sluice-gate".

WHEAL ROSE: LC *wheal rose*, "hillspur mine", or "Rose's mine".

WINNARD'S PERCH: Eng., from dialect *winnard*, "redwing".

*   *   *

Trees, flowers & plants: *Gweeth, bledgiow ha lozow*

ALDER: *gwernan*, coll.pl. *gwearn*, f. (GWER-nen; gwairn)

ASH: *enwethan*, coll.pl. *enweeth*, f. (en-WEDH-en; en-WEETH)

BEECH: *fawan*, coll. pl. *faw*, f. (FAOU-en; faou)

BLACKTHORN: *drean*, pl. *drein*, m. (DRAI-en; drein)

BRACKEN: *redanan*, coll. pl. *redan*, f. (r'-DAN-en; RED-en)

BRAMBLE: *dreizan*, coll.pl. *dreiz*, f. (DREI-zen; dreiz)

CLOVER: *mullionan*, coll.pl. *mullion*, f. (mul-YON-en; MUL-yen)

DAISY: *cadga*, s. & pl., f. (KAD-ja)

DAISY (OX-EYE): *cadga vroaz*, s. & pl., f. (KAD-ja vrauz)

DANDELION: *danzlew*, pl. *denzlew*, m. (danz-LEU; denz-LEU)

DOCK: *tavolan*, coll.pl. *tavoll*, f. (tav-OL-en; TAV-el)

ELDER: *scawan*, coll.pl. *scaw*, f. (SKAOU-en; skaou)

ELM: *elan*, pl. *elow*, f. (EL-en; EL-au)

FLAG IRIS: *lastran*, coll.pl. *laister*, f. (LAS-tren; LAAS-ter)

FLOWER: *bledgan*, pl. *bledgiow*, m. (BLED-jan; BLED-jau)

GORSE: *eithinan*, coll.pl. *eithin*, f. (ei-THIN-en; EI-then)

HOLLY: *kelynan*, coll.pl. *kelyn*, f. (k'-LIN-en; KEL-en)

NETTLE: *linadgan*, coll.pl. *linas*, f. (lin-AD-jen; LIN-az)

OAK: *derowan*, coll.pl. *derow*, f. (d'-RAU-en; DEH-rau)

PLANT: *lozoan*, coll.pl. *lozow*, f. (l'-ZHOE-en; LOZH-au)

PRIMROSE: *briallan*, coll.pl. *briallow*, f. (bree-AL-en; bree-AL-au)

ROWAN: *kerthan*, coll.pl. *kerth*, f. (KER-then; kerth)

THORN: *spernan*, coll.pl. *spearn*, f. (SPERN-an; spern)

TREE: *gwethan*, coll.pl. *gweeth*, f. (GWEDH-en; gweeth)

VIOLET: *meilhionan*, coll.pl. *meilhion*, f. (meil-he-ON-en; MEIL-hee-en)

WILLOW: *helagan*, coll.pl. *helack*, f. (HEL-a-gen; HEL-ek)

Sky & weather: *Ebbarn hag awall*

CLOUD: *commolan*, pl. *commol*, f. (cum-OL-en; CUM-el)

CLOUDY: *cumolack* (cum-OL-ek)

DARKNESS: *tewldar*, m. (TEUL-der)

DEW: *glooth*, m. (glûth)

FROST: *reaw*, m. (reu)

HAIL: *kezzar*, f. (KEZ-er)

ICE: *clehy*, m. (KLEE-hee)

LIGHT: *gulow*, m. (GÛL-au)

LIGHTNING: *lowas*, m. (LAU-az)

MIST: *newl*, m. (neul)

MISTY: *newlack* (NEU-lek)

MOON: *loer*, f. (LAU-er)

RAIN: *glawe*, m. (glaou)

RAINBOW: *cabmthavas*, m. (cab'm-DHAV-az)

SKY: *ebbarn*, f. (EB-ern)

SNOW: *err*, m. (er)

STAR: *stearan*, pls. *sterrez/sterradnow*, f. (STAIR-en; STEH-rez/steh-RAD-nau)

STORM: *hagarawall*, pl. *-ow*, f. (HAG-er-AOU-el; HAG-er-aou-EL-au)

SUN: *howl*, m. (haoul)

SUNNY: *howlack* (HAOU-lek)

THUNDER: *taran*, f. (TAR-en)

WEATHER: *awall*, f. (AOU-el)

WIND: *gwenz*, m. (gwenz)

WINDY: *gwindgack* (GWIN-jek)

*   *   *

The Late Renaissance

Gwreans an Bys, "Creation of the World" (subtitled "Creacion of the Worlde with Noyes Flude"), transcribed by William Jordan of Helston in 1611 from an older source, was the sole Cornish manuscript written in the first half of the 17th century. Based on the *Origo Mundi*, from the *Ordinalia*, its character is noticeably medieval, although Jordan himself was responsible for introducing hints of the Late Cornish of his time. With the language on the wane, a situation worsened by the Civil War, it seemed that the continuation of Cornish literature was at an end.

It was William Scawen, a vice-warden of the Stannaries, who instigated a resurgence in the writing of Cornish. He not only realised that a vital part of the Cornish heritage was on the brink of death, but listed sixteen reasons for this sorry state of affairs. Among these were: the lack of a definitive Cornish alphabet; the loss of contact between Cornwall and Brittany; the demise of the *Gwaryow Mere* ("Great Plays"), the Miracle Plays whose performances ceased in the 1620s, sixty years before Scawen wrote; the burning or loss of ancient Cornish records in Restormel Castle and other repositories, presumably during the Civil War; the suppression of the remnants of early Celtic church practices from church services (colourfully put as the suppression of Druidic practice by Christianity); apathy among Cornish people resigned to Anglicisation; the influx of strangers to Cornwall; the failure to teach the Lord's Prayer in Cornish; and the lack of surviving literature.

Scawen encouraged his contemporaries to resume writing in Cornish, a call which was taken up by a group of people in the region of Penzance, still a stronghold of spoken Cornish, and, over the next half century, a flood of material, new and old, flowed from the pens of these men. Foremost among them was John Keigwin of Mousehole (1641-c.1710), a master of five languages including his native tongue, and a nephew of Scawen; the Boson family of Newlyn, merchant and landowner Nicholas, his son John (1665-c.1720) and cousin Thomas; William Gwavas of Paul (1676-1741), a barrister; Oliver Pender of Mousehole; James Jenkins of Alverton, Penzance; William Rowe, a Sancreed farmer; the Rev. Henry Usticke of St Just; John Tonkin of St Just; and his namesake Thomas Tonkin of Trevaunance, St Agnes. Of these, Keigwin, Rowe and Jenkins were almost certainly native speakers. Nicholas Boson, who taught John and Thomas, was brought up by a mother who expressly forbade the use of Cornish in the family household, even to instructing the Cornish speaking servants to speak to her son only in English – an

William Gwavas, from a portrait by unknown artist (C. Weatherhill)

indication of the social stigma then being attached to the old language. After a schooling in France, Nicholas returned to learn Cornish from his neighbours.

Unlike the literature of Middle Cornish, which consists purely of religious verse, that of Late Cornish comprised of a rich variety. It was intended to translate the Bible but, although it proved too huge a task, Keigwin and John Boson succeeded in translating Genesis, while Rowe translated a number of chapters from Genesis, and the Gospel of St Matthew. Gwavas, who learned his Cornish from John Boson, produced and collected a mass of items, from personal letters, verses, proverbs and even a complete record of a legal dispute of his against local fishermen and merchants (including Keigwin and Nicholas Boson) over the payment of fishing tithes. A valuable scrap in Gwavas's collection is a letter in Cornish written to him by an unnamed Newlyn man, enclosing a translation of Psalm 100 and stating that ministers still sung that Psalm in Cornish at Paul church, half a century after the use of Cornish in church services had reputedly died out with Mr Robinson's last Cornish sermon at Landewednack in 1678.

Tonkin collected songs and verses in Cornish, whilst Jenkins composed them. Nicholas Boson, however, firstly produced a folk-lore compilation entitled *The Dutchesse of Cornwall's Progresse to see the Land's End and to visit the Mount*, mostly in English, but including snippets of Cornish. His best known work was a complete folk-tale known as *John of Chyanhor*, or *The Three Points of Wisdom*, a story with international equivalents, notably *The*

Servant's Good Counsels. Only verses 1 to 14 survive, these in John Boson's hand, but the whole story was recorded by Edward Lhuyd in his own phonetic spelling system. This same story was retold in the 20th century by Robert Morton Nance who discarded Boson's Cornish for his own Unified spelling and grammar system which was based on medieval Cornish, thereby destroying the original character of the story which is related in Modern (Late) Cornish after the next place name section. A further valuable work of Nicholas Boson is his *Nebbaz Gerriau dro tho Carnoack* ("A Few Words about Cornish").

The variety of Late Cornish literature gave for the first time a clear indication of how vernacular Cornish was spoken. Thanks to the phonetic records of Edward Lhuyd, who consulted with Keigwin, Usticke, Jenkins and Nicholas Boson, the pronunciation of Cornish is known for the first and only time in its long history. Containing half as many words again as the total of Middle Cornish texts, Late Cornish surprisingly included far less in the way of loan words. A recent survey compares the medieval *Beunans Meryasek*, with the Late Cornish works of William Rowe and Nicholas Boson (not including *Jooan Chy a Horr*), and examining those words beginning with A, B, G (very typical of Cornish) and S. No less than 44% of those in the medieval work were English loan words, as opposed to just 12% in the Late works.

In the light of these facts, it beggars belief that, apart from Henry Jenner's intentions, the modern revival movement has virtually ignored Late Cornish, despising it as "too much influenced by English", and "incomplete", and preferring to base a reconstituted language on the medieval texts. It was not until the 1980s that Late Cornish underwent serious, in-depth studies, dispelling the myths and representing it as the full, rich and authentic tongue it is.

9

Place Names of St Austell, Par & Mevagissey

ST AUSTELL: from St Austol. Pronounced "sin-TOS'l".

BARGOES: MC *bar coys*, "wood top".

BISCOVEY: "bis-kuv-AI". *Bosconevey* C13, *Boskennevey* C14. MC *bos Kenevy*, "Kenevy's dwelling".

BLACK HEAD: Eng., "black headland".

ST BLAZEY: from St Blaise. The churchtown was known as *Landrayth* C13, MC *lan dreyth*, "church site on a beach", which it was until the silting-up of the former tidal estuary here. The nearest beach is now a mile away.

BODINNICK: "b'DIN-ik". OC *bod*, "dwelling"; MC *eythynek*, "furzy".

BOJEA: "b'JAI". OC *bod yuv*, "lord's dwelling".

BOSCOPPA: MC *bos Coppa*, "Coppa's dwelling".

BOSWINGER: MC *bos Wengor*, "Gwengor's dwelling".

BRANNEL: The preserved name of a former Domesday manor. MC *bron-el*, "place of hills".

BUGLE: C19 settlement, named in Eng. c.1840 after its inn, whose sign depicted a coaching horn.

BURGOTHA: MC *bar gothow*, "summit of geese".

BURNGULLOW: LC *bern gulow*, "hill of light".

CADYTHEW ROCK: probably MC *carrek thu*, "black rock".

CALLYVARDER ROCK: *Killiwarther* C17. MC *kyl an wartha*, "the higher ridge".

CARBEAN: LC *carn bean*, "little tor". "car-BEE-an".

CARCLAZE: LC *creeg laze*, "grey-green barrow/tumulus".

CARLOGGAS: MC *car logas*, "fort of mice".

CARRICKOWEL POINT: LC *carrack awall*, "weather rock", or LC *carrack euhall*, "high rock".

CARRUGGATT: *Keirhulgat* C13. MC *cair ughel goyt*, "high wood fort".

CARTHEW: MC *car thu*, "black fort". Pronounced "car-THEU".

CASTLE GOTHA: LC *castell gothow*, "castle of geese".

CHARLESTOWN: named after Charles Rashleigh of Menabilly (1747-

1825), this harbour was formerly known as *Polmear* (earlier, *Portmoer* C14), LC *porth mere*, "great cove". Porthpean, LC *porth bean*, "little cove", lies close by to the west.

CHEGWINS: MC *chy an guyns*, "house in wind".

COLDVREATH: LC *killy vrith*, "dappled grove".

CREAK-A-VOZE: LC *creeg a vose*, "barrow/tumulus by the wall".

CREED: after St Crida.

CRINNIS: *Caryhunes* C14, *Caryones* C15. Possibly MC *car an enas*, "the lambs' fort".

ST DENNIS: although the isolated hilltop church is dedicated to St Dionysius, this patronage has been influenced by its siting within an Iron Age hill fort, LC *dinas*.

THE DODMAN: Padel suggests that this imposing headland takes its name from the Dudemann family, one of whom farmed nearby in the C15. Equally possible is a derivation from LC *tubman*, "mound", referring to the great Iron Age cliff castle rampart crossing the headland, whose former name is preserved in that of the nearby farm PENARE (see below).

DOMELLICK: OC *dun Maeloc*, "Maeloc's fort", perhaps referring to the hill fort in which St Dennis church is sited. This Domesday manor is Geoffrey of Monmouth's "Damelioc" in the account of King Arthur's conception at Tintagel.

DRINNICK: LC *dreinack*, "place of thorns".

DUPORTH: modern reversed form of LC *porth due*, "black cove".

ENNISCAVEN: LC *ennis scawan*, "remote place with an elder tree".

FOXHOLE: Eng., "fox's hole", the name of an old tinwork being transferred to the present village.

GALOWRAS: LC *gulow res*, "ford of light".

GARGUS: MC *(an) gar goys*, "the fort in a wood".

GARLENICK: "gar-LEN-ek". MC *(an) gorlanyk*, "the little sheepfold".

GAVERIGAN: MC *gover gwyn*, "white stream".

GOONAMARTH: LC *goon a marth*, "the horse downs".

GORRAN CHURCHTOWN: after St Guron, who moved here from Bodmin. An earlier name was *Langoron* C14, MC *lan Guron*, "St Guron's church site".

GORRAN HAVEN: Eng., "harbour of St Guron", but formerly named after another Celtic saint: *Porthjust* C14, *Porth East* C18, LC *porth East* (pron. "AI-est"), "St Just's cove".

GOSS MOOR: LC *goss*, "sedge", with Eng. "moor" in the older sense of "marsh".

GRAMPOUND: F. *grand pont*, "great bridge", translating the C14 Cornish name *Ponsmur*, MC *pons meyr*, also "great bridge".

GRIGLANDS: LC *griglan*, "heather bush".

GWINEAS/GWINGES: MC *guynsys*, "windswept".

HELIGAN: LC *helagan*, "willow tree".

HENMOOR: *Hyndemore* C13. Eng., from OE *hindes mor*, "hind's moor".

HENSBARROW: *Hyndesbergh* C13. Eng, from OE *hindes beorg*, "hind's barrow/tumulus".

HEWAS WATER: LC *hewas*, "summer farm"; with Eng. "water", here meaning "stream".

HOLMBUSH: Eng., "holly (OE *holegn*) bush".

KARSLAKE: Eng., from OE *caerse laec*, "cress stream".

KILGOGUE: MC *kelly gog*, "cuckoo grove".

KILHALLON: possibly MC *kelly henlan*, "grove by a former church site".

LANHADRON: *Nansladron* C14. MC *nans ladron*, "thieves' valley".

LANJETH: MC *nans yorgh*, "roebuck valley".

LOCKENGATE: Eng., "locking gate", a former turnpike tollgate.

LUXULYAN: pronounced "luk-ZIL-yen". MC *lok Sulyen*, "Sulyan's chapel/cell". The personal name is an ancient one, from Brythonic *sulo-genos*, "sun-born".

MAENEASE POINT: possibly LC *mean esse*, "corn stone". An alternative name for the headland is Pen-a-maen, LC *pen- a mean*, "headland of the stone".

MELEDOR: *Maenleder* C14. MC *men leder*, "stone on a slope".

MENACUDDLE: LC *mena gothall*, "hillside with a thicket".

MENADUE: LC *mena due*, "black hillside".

MENEAR: LC *menheer*, "standing stone".

MENNA: LC *mena*, "hillside".

METHROSE: MC *methros*, "mid-heath".

MEVAGISSEY: "mev-a-GIZ-ee". MC *Meva hag Isy*, "Saints Meva and Isy (earlier, Ida)". The churchtown was named *Lammorek* C13, surviving as Levorrick, MC *lan Morec*, "Morec's church site". The harbour was Porthilly (*Porthiley* C17), LC *porth hily*, "saltwater cove".

ST MEWAN: named after St Mewan, companion of St Austol.

MOLINGEY: LC *melingy*, "millhouse". Pronounced "m'LIN-jee".

MOLINNIS: LC *moel ennis*, "bare isolated place".

NANPEAN: "nan-PEE-an". LC *nans bean*, "little valley".

NANPHYSICK: MC *nans fugyk*, "happy valley".

NANSCAWEN: LC *nans scawan*, "elder tree valley".

NANSLADRON: MC *nans ladron*, "thieves' valley".

PAR: LC *por*, "cove, landing place".

PENARE: LC *penare*, "prominent headland".

PENHAVER POINT: possibly LC *pen- hevva*, "shoaling headland", or LC *pen- havar*, "end of fallowland".

PENHELLICK: LC *pen- helack*, "willows end".

PENPILLICK: LC *pen- pilack*, "heaped end".

PENRICE: MC *pen res*, "end of a ford".

PENSTRAZE: LC *pen- straze*, "end of a flat-bottomed valley".

PENTEVALE: MC *fynten Vale*, "source of the River Fal".

PENTEWAN: MC *pen tewyn*, "end of a sand dune".

PENVENTON: LC *pen- venton*, "well-head".

PENWITHICK: MC *pen uythek*, "end of a wooded place".

POLGOOTH: LC *poll gooth*, "goose pool".

POLMEAR: LC *porth mere*, "great cove".

POLSTREATH: MC *pol streyth*, "stream pool".

PONTS MILL: MC *pons*, "bridge", with Eng., "mill".

PORTMELLON: LC *porth melin*, "mill cove".

PRIDEAUX: F. *pres d'eaux*, "near the waters". Locally pronounced "PRID-iks".

RESCORLA: LC *res corlan*, "ford by a sheepfold".

RESTOWRACK: LC *rose dowrack*, "roughland in a watery place".

RESUGGA: MC *ros ogo*, "hillspur by a cave".

RETALLICK: *Retelek* C13. OC *ret heloc*, "ford with willows".

RETEW: LC *res tew*, "wide ford". Pronounced "r'TEU".

J.T. Blight's 19th century engraving of Roche Rock

ROCHE: F. *roche*, "rock", after the astonishing chapel-crowned pinnacles outside the village.

ROSEMELLYN: LC *res melin*, "mill ford".

STENALEES: LC *stenack laze*, "grey-green tinwork". Usually pron. "sten-a-LEEZ". Contrast with Stenagwyn near St Stephen in Brannel which is MC *stenak gwyn*, "white tinwork".

ST STEPHEN IN BRANNEL: after the church saint, Stephen, with the name of the Domesday manor of Brannel added (see BRANNEL). The churchtown was also known as *Egloshellens* C19, LC *eglos Helens*, "St Helen's church".

STICKER: MC *stekyer*, "tree-stumps".

TOLGARRICK: LC *tal- garrack*, "hillbrow with a rock".

TREBILCOCK: LC *tre- bilgack*, "farm in a place of heaps". Pronounced "tr'BIL-cok" and never "tr'BIL-coe", as some have claimed.

TREGARRICK: LC *tre- garrack*, "rock farm".

TREGIDGEO: LC *tre- gridgow*, "farm in a folded landscape". "tr'GID-joe".

TREGONGEEVES: MC *tre Gentevas*, "Kentevas's farm".

TREGONISSEY: MC *tre goen Isy*, "farm on St Issey's downs".

TREGOSS: LC *tre- goss*, "sedge farm".

TREGREHAN: LC *tre- grehan*, "farm of skins/hides". "tr'GRAI-en".

TRELOWTH: MC *tre Leueth*, "Leueth's farm".

TREMODRETT: OC *treu Modret*, "Modret's farm".

TRENANT: OC *treu nant*, "valley farm".

TRENARREN: *Tyngharan* C14. MC *dyn garan*, "crane's fort", or *dyn Geren*, "Gerent's fort". This might refer to the Iron Age cliff castle on Black Head, half a mile to the south-east.

TRENEAGUE: Treneneyke C14. Possibly MC *tre an ewyk*, "the hind's/doe's farm". pronounced "tr'NEEG".

TRENOWTH: LC *tre noweth*, "new farm".

TRENYTHON: MC *tre an eythen*, "farm by the furze".

TRETHURGY: LC *tre- dowrgy*, "otter farm", but a personal name, *Dourgi*, could be involved.

TREVERBYN: MC *trev Erbyn*, "Erbin's farm".

TREVISCOE: a softened form of *Tref otcere* C11, OC *treu Otcer*, "Otcer's farm".

TREWOON: LC *tre- woon*, "downs farm". Pronounced "TROO-en".

TYWARDREATH: OC *ti*, "house"; MC *war dreyth*, "on the beach". Pronounced "tie-wor-DRETH".

VENTONWYN: MC *(an) vynten wyn*, "the white well".

VICTORIA: C19, named after the inn.

VOUNDER: LC *vounder*, "lane".

*   *   *

Daralla Jooan Chy A Horr:
The Tale of John of Chyanhor

This is the famous folk tale first rendered in Cornish by Nicholas Boson of Newlyn sometime between 1660 and 1700, although according to Edward Lhuyd's own testimony, that it was written about 40 years before his own visit, a date in the 1660s is probably the best guess. Nicholas Boson's original is lost and only verses 1 to 14 survive in the hand of his son John, transcribed soon after 1700. The whole story was recorded by Lhuyd in his own phonetic script, which shows that it was orally related to him. The home of the story's hero, Chyanhor (LC *chy a horr*, "the ram's house") has vanished from the map but is shown on the 1839 Tithe Apportionment above a beautiful valley in the parish of St Levan, only a couple of miles from Land's End. The site is now occupied by a lovely old thatched cottage named Mount Whistle. This story is here retold, with English translation, in authentic Modern Cornish for the first time since 1700:

En termen eze passiez thera treegas en Sent Levan dean ha benen en telhar creiez Chy a Horr.

In times gone by, there lived in St Levan a man and woman in a place called Chyanhor.

Ha an wheal a cothas scant, ha meth an dean tha e wreag, "Me a vedn moaz tha wheelas wheal tha weel, ha whye ell dendall goz Bownas ubma."

And the work fell scarce and the man said to his wife, "I shall go to look for work to do, and you can earn your living here."

Kibmias teag eve a gomeras, ha pell tha east eve a travalias, ha war an duath e reeg doaz tha chy teeack ha reeg wheelas enna wheal Tha weel.

He took fair leave and walked far to the east, and eventually he came to a farmer's house and asked there for work to do.

"Pana wheal 'lesta geel?" meth an teeack. "Pub wheal oll," ameth Jooan. Enna gye vargidnias rag try penz an vlethan gubber.

"What work can you do?" said the farmer. "All kinds of work," said John. Then they agreed on wages of three pounds a year.

Ha pa thera duath an vlethan, e veister a thesquethas dotha an try penz. "Meer, Jooan, meth e veister, "ubma tha gubber, buz mor menta ry e thebm arta, me a theska theez kensa point a skeans."

And when it was the end of the year, his master showed him the three pounds. "Look, John, " said his master, "here are your wages, but if you will give them to me, I will teach you a first point of wisdom."

"Drew hedna?" meth Jooan. "Na," meth e veister, "ro e thebm, ha me a vedn laull theez."

"What is that?" said John. "No," said his master, "give it to me, and I will tell you." "Here you are, ther

"Comero e than," meth Jooan. Nenna meth e veister, "Kebmer weeth na ra whye gara an vorr goth rag an vorr noweth."

Nenna gye a vargidnias rag blethan mouy, rag pecare gubber. Ha pa thera duath an vlethan, e veister e droze an try penz. "Meer, Jooan," meth e veister, "ubma tha gubber, buz mor menta ry e thebm arta, me a theska kene pint a skeans."

"Pandrew hedna?" meth Jooan. "Na," meth e veister, "ro e thebm, ha me vedn laull theez." "Comero e than," meth Jooan. Nenna meth e veister, "Kebmer weeth na ra whye ostia en chy lebma vo dean coth demithez tha benen younk".

Enna gye a vargidnias rag blethan mouy. Ha pa thera duath an vlethan, e veister a throze an try penz. "Meer, Jooan," meth e veister, "Ubma tha gubber, buz mor menta ry e thebm arta, me a theska theez an gwelha point a l skeans oll."

"Pandrew hedna?" meth Jooan. "Na," meth e veister, "ro e thebm, ha me a lavar theez." "Comero e than," meth Jooan. Nenna meth e veister, "Bethez gweskez deweth ken gweskall eneth, rag hedna ew an gwelha point a skeans oll."

Lebmen Jooan, e na venga servia na velha, buz e venga moaz tua tha e wreag. "Na," meth e veister, "gwreew moaz chy, ha ma gwreag ve a pobas metten, ha hye ra geel tezan ragez, tha thoen drea tho tha wreag."

Ha angye a urras an nawe penz en dezan. Ha pe reeg Jooan comeras e kibmias, "Ubma," meth e veister, "ma tezan ragez tha thoen drea tho tha wreag; ha po che ha tha wreag an moyha looan warbarth, nenna gwreew trehy an dezan, ha na henz."

Kibmias teag e comeras, ha tew ha trea e travalias, ha war an duath e reeg doaz tha goon Sen Eler, ha enna eve a vettias gen try vertshant a Tretheen, teez plewe, toaz drea meaz an Feer Careesk.

said John. Then said his master, "Take care not to leave the old road for the new road."

Then they agreed on a further year, for the same wages. And when it was the end of the year, his master gave him the three pounds. "Look, John," said his master, "Here are your wages, but if you will give them back to me, I will teach you another point of wisdom."

"What is that?" said John. "No," said his master, "give it to me, and I will tell you." "Take it, then," said John. Then said his master, "Take care you do not lodge in a house where there may be an old man married to a young woman."

Then they agreed on a further year, and when it was the end of the year, his master gave him the three pounds. "Look, John," said his master. "Here are your wages, but if you will give them back to me, will teach you the best point of wisdom of all."

"What is that?" said John. "No," said his master, "give it to me, and I will tell you." "Take it, then," said John. Then said his master, "Be struck twice before striking once, for that is the best point of wisdom of all."

Now John did not wish to serve any longer, but wanted to go back to his wife. "No," said his master, "go into the house, for my wife is baking this morning, and she will make a cake for you to take home to your wife."

And they put the nine pounds in the cake. And when John took his leave, "Here," said his master, "is a cake for you to take home to your wife; and when you and your wife are at your happiest, then you shall cut the cake and not before."

He took fair leave, and went towards home, and eventually came to St Hilary Downs, and there he met with three merchants of Treen, local men, coming home from Exeter Fair.

"Ha, Jooan!" meth angye. "Deeo gena nye. Looan oan nye tha goz gwelhas whye. Pelea ve che mar bell?"

Ameth Jooan, "Me a ve servia, ha lebmen theram moaz drea tha a wreag." Ha meth angye, "Ewh barra nye, ha welcom che aveth."

Angye a comeras an vorr noweth, ha Jooan a gweethas an vorr goth, ha moaz reb keaw Chyoon.

Ha nag o vertshants gellez pell thurt Jooan buz leddarn a glenas ort angye.

Ha angye a thallathas tha weel crei, ha genz an crei a reeg an vertshants geel, Jooan a greias awethe, "Leddarn! Leddarn!"

Ha genz an crei a reeg Jooan geel, an leddarn a forsakias an vertshants. Ha pe reeg angye doaz tha Varhajeu, enna angye a vettias arta.

Ah, Jooan," ameth angye. "Sendgez oan nye tha whye! Na veea rago whye, nye a veea teez oll diswreze! Deez barra nye ha welcom che a veth."

Ha pe reeg angye doaz than chy lebma guffia angye ostia, ameth Jooan, "Me dale gwelhas an ost an chy."

"An ost an chy?" ameth angye. "Pandra venta geel gen an ost an chy? Ubma ma gon ostez nye, ha younk ew hye. Mor menta gwelhas an ost an chy, ke than gegen, ha enna che en cave."

Ha pe reeg e doaz than gegan, enna e welhas an ost an chy, ha dean coth o e, ha gwadn, a trailia an bere.

"Ah!" ameth Jooan. "Ubma na vadna ve ostia buz en nessa chy." "Na whathe," meth angye, "gwraze cona abarha nye, ha welcom che a veth."

Lebmen, an ostez an chy, hye a cussillias gen nebon vaanah a era en trea, tha destrea an dean coth en gwily en termen an noze, ha ressa angye suppoga ha goera a faut war an vertshants.

"Hallo, John!" they said. "Come with us. We are glad to see you. Where have you been for so long?"

Said John, "I have been in service, and now I am going home to my wife." And they said, "Come along with us, and be welcome."

They took the new road and John kept to the old road, and went by Chyoon hedges.

And the merchants had not gone far from John when robbers fell upon them.

And they began to raise a hue and cry, and with the cry the merchants raised, John cried out also, "Thieves! Thieves!"

And with the cry that John made, the thieves left the merchants. And when they came to Marazion, there they met up again.

"Oh, John," they said. "We are obliged to you! Had it not been for you, we should have been completely ruined men! Come along with us and you will be welcome."

And when they came to the house where they were to ask lodgings, John said, "I must see the landlord."

"The landlord?" they said. "What do you want with the landlord? Here is our landlady, and she is young. If you want to see the landlord, go to the kitchen and you'll find him there."

And when he came to the kitchen, there he saw the landlord, and he was an old man, and weak, turning the spit.

"Oh!" said John. "Here I will not lodge, but in the next house." "No matter," they said, "Have supper with us, and you'll be welcome".

Now, the landlady plotted with a certain monk that was in town, to murder the old man in bed during the night, and they would implicate and place the blame upon the merchants.

Ha po thera Jooan en gwily, thera tol en talle an chy. Ha eve a welhas gulow, ha e savas aman ameaz e wily, ha eve a gazowas, ha e glowas an maanah laull, ha trailiez e gein ghan tol. "Metessen," ameth eve, "ma nebonen en nessa chy a reeg gwelhas gon hagaroberow." Ha genz hedna, an gwadngurty genz e follat a thestreas an dean coth en gwily.

Ha genz hedna, Jooan, genz e golhan, trohas der an tol meaz a kein goon an maanah, pees per rond.

Ha nessa metten, an gwadngurty hye a thallathas tha weel crei ter tho e thermaze hye destreas ha rag na era dean na floh en chy buz an vertshants, angye dale cregy rakta.

Enna angye a ve comeras, ha than clohprednier gye a ve ledias, ha war an duath Jooan a theath war ago fidn.

"Ah, Jooan!" meth angye. "Ma calish luck tha gye. Ma gon ost nye destreas newher, ha nye dale cregy rakta!"

"Whye oll?" Meero whye an justiziow," ameth Jooan. "Gortero, an theez, rag rima na reeg an drogober!"

"Pew a ore," meth angye. "pew a reeg an drogober?" "Pew a reeg an drogober?" meth Jooan, "Menas me a theffa ha prevy pew a reeg an drogober, me a vedn cregy rakta!"

"Lavaro, thanna," meth angye. "Newher," meth Jooan, "po thera ve et a gwily, me a welhas gulow, ha me a savas aman, ha thera tol en talle an chy."

"Ha nebon maanah a trailias e gein warbidn an tol. "Metessen," meth eve, "ma nebonan en nessa chy a ell gwelhas gon hagaroberow." "

"Ha genz hedna, gen a holhan me a trohas " der an tol, meaz a kein goon an maanah, pees per rond. Ha rag geel a gerriowma tha voaz prevez, ubma ma an pees et a fokkat tha voaz gwelhas."

And when John was in bed, there was a hole in the gable of the house. And he saw a light, and got out of bed, and he listened, and he heard the monk talking with his back turned to the wall. "Perhaps," he said, "somebody in the next house might see our evil deeds." And with that, the wicked wife and her fellow murdered the old man in the bed.

And with that, John, with his knife, cut through the hole from the back of the monk's gown, a perfectly round piece.

And next morning, the wicked wife began to raise a hue and cry about her murdered goodman and since there was neither man nor child in the house but the merchants, they must hang for it.

Then they were taken and led to the gallows and eventually John came upon them.

"Oh, John!" they said. "We've had hard luck. Our landlord was murdered last night, and we must hang for it!"

"All of you? See you justices," said John. "Wait, people, for these did not do the evil deed!"

"Who knows," they said. "who did the evil deed?" "Who did the evil deed?" said John. "Unless I stop and prove who did the evil deed, I will hang for it!"

"Speak, then," they said. "Last night," said John, "when I was in bed, I saw a light, and got up, and there was a hole in the gable of the house."

"And a certain monk turned his back to the hole. "Perhaps," he said, "someone in the next house can see our evil deeds." "

And with that, with my knife I cut through the hole, from the back of the monk's gown, a perfectly round piece. And that these words can be proved, here is the piece in my pocket to be seen"

Ha genz hedna, an vertshants a ve freas ha an venen han maanah a ve comerez ha cregez.

Nenna angye a theath warbar meaz tha Varhajeu, ha war an duath gye reeg doaz tha Cooz Kerniwhilli en Borrian.

Nenna thera vorr thiberh, ha an vertshants a venga arta tha Jooan moaz drea barha angye, buz rag an termen e na venga, buz e venga moaz drea tha e wreag.

Ha po tho eve gillez thurt an vertshants, eve a thelledgas an termen, malava preva era e wreag gweetha cumpas et e gever, era po nag era?

Ha pe reeg e doaz than darras, eve a venga clowas dean orrol en gwily. Eve a wasky e thorn war e thagier tha thestrea an theaw, buz e brederas ter gotha thotha boaz avisshez deweth ken gweskall eneth.

Ha eve a theath ameaz arta, ha nenna e gnackiez. "Pewa eze enna, en bar Dew?" ameth hye. "Mars o whye Jooan, deeo agye!" "Doroy an gulow, thanna," meth Jooan. Nenna hye throze an gulow.

Ha pe reeg Jooan doaz chy, meth eve: "Pe riga ve doaz thon darras, me a venga clowas dean orrol en gwily."

"Ah, Jooan," meth hye, "Pe rigo whye moaz kerr, thera ve gellez try meez gen floh, ha lebmen ma tha nye meppig wheag en gwily, tha Thew ro bo gorzehez!"

Meth Jooan, "Me vedn laull theez; a veister ha veistrez roze thebm tezan, ha lavaras thebm pa vo me ham gwreag an moyha looan warbarth tha terry an dezan, ha na henz. Ha lebmen ma caze tha nye rag boaz looan!"

Nenna gye a dorras an dezan, ha thera nawe penz en dezan. Ha an muna angye a gavas, han bara gye a thabbras, ha na ve edn froth na mikan na tra war an norveaz. Ha andelha ma duath ma daralla thothans.

And with that, the merchants were freed and the woman and the monk were taken and hanged.

Then together they left Marazion and at last came to Lapwings' Wood in St Buryan.

There the road divided and the merchants wanted John to go home with them, but for the time being he would not, but would go home to his wife.

And when he had left the merchants, he took his time, so that he might prove that his wife was keeping faith with him, was she or was she not?

And when he came to the door, he thought he could hear another man in the bed. He was clapping his hand to his dagger to kill the pair of them, when he thought how he must be looking twice before striking once.

And he came away again, and then he knocked. "Who is there, in the name of God?" she said. "If you are John, come in!" "Bring the light, then," said John. Then she brought the light.

And when John went indoors, he said: "When I came to the door, I could hear another man in the bed."

"Oh, John," she said. "When you went away, I was three months gone with child, and now we have a sweet little boy in the bed, may God be praised!"

Said John, "I will tell you; my master and mistress gave me a cake, and told me that when my wife and I were at our happiest together to break the cake and not before. And now we have cause to be happy!"

Then they broke the cake, and there were nine pounds in the cake. And they took the money, and they ate the bread, and there was not one bit of strife, nor spite nor anything in the world. And that ends my tale about them.

10

Place Names of Lostwithiel & Fowey

BOCADDON: MC *bos Cadwen*, "Cadwen's dwelling".

BOCONNOC: MC *bos Conoc*, "Conoc's dwelling". Pronounced "b'KON-ek".

BODINNICK: "b'DIN-ek". MC *bos dynyk*, "dwelling by a little fort".

BODITHIEL: OC *bod*, "dwelling"; MC *uethyel*, "place of trees". (G)Uethyel may have been an ancient district name, very possibly that of the former Hundred, later divided into East and West *Wivel*shire.

BODWEN: OC *bod uyn*, "white/fair dwelling". Pronounced "b'd-WEN".

BRADDOCK: Eng., from OE *brad ac*, "broad oak".

BRENEY: possibly MC *brenyow*, "hills".

BURY DOWN: Eng., from OE *byrig dun*, "fort downs".

CARHURLES: MC *car Worlas*, "Gorlas's fort".

CARWEN: MC *car uen*, "white fort".

CASTLE DORE: MC *castel dor*, "earth castle".

COLVITHICK: MC *colluethek*, "place of hazel trees".

CORNAKEE: MC *kernyk ke*, "hedge nook". Pron. "korn-a-KEE".

CRIFT: dialect *croft*, "rough grazing". This word was, in the Late period, absorbed into the Cornish language as: *croft*, plural *croftow*.

FOWEY: named after the river (see RIVER FOWEY). The churchtown was *Langorthou* C14, MC *lan Gortho*, "Gortho's church site". Both town and river are pronounced "foi".

RIVER FOWEY: MC *faw-i*, "beech tree river".

GOLANT: OC *gol nant*, "festival valley". Briefly softened to *Golenance* C15, the OC form survives.

GRIBBIN HEAD: named after the Grebin family in C17. It was formerly *Penarth* C14, MC *penarth*, "prominent headland".

HELMAN TOR: named after the Helman family, with OE *torr*, "rock outcrop".

KILMARTH: LC *kil marth*, "horse's back".

LANKELLY: MC *nans kelly*, "grove valley".

LANLIVERY: MC *lan Livri*, "Livri's church site".

LANREATH: "lan-RETH". *Lanredoch* C11, softening to *Lanretha* C16, MC *lan Rethoc*, "Redoc's church site."

LANSALLOS: *Lanselewys* C13, *Lansalwys* C14. MC *lan Selewys*, "Selewys's church site".

LANTEGLOS: *Nanteglos* C14. OC *nant egglos*, "church valley".

LANTIC BAY: MC *Tallantyk*, "little Talland" (see TALLAND in Section 16, Liskeard and Looe).

LANTYAN: OC *nant iein*, "cold valley".

LANWITHAN: *Lankeweithan* C14. MC *lan ke uethen*, "church site by an enclosure with a tree".

LERRYN: *Leryon* C13. Probably a river name, the meaning of which is not known. However, it might be derived from a Cornish equivalent of W. *lyr*, "flood".

LOSTWITHIEL: MC *lost uethyel*, "tail of district called Guethyel" (see BODITHIEL). Pronounced "lost-WIDH-yel". Early forms all contain *lost-*, so that a derivation from *lys/les*, "court, administrative centre," is unlikely, even though the town was the seat of the Duchy Palace.

MENABILLY: apparently MC *men ebilly*, "colts' stone", although an earlier form, *Menabilyou* C14, would suggest MC *meneth bylyow*, "hillside of heaps".

PENADLAKE: MC *banathlek*, "broom-brake".

PENCARROW: MC *pen carow*, "stag's end/top".

PENKESTLE: MC *pen castel*, "castle top".

PENPOLL: "pen-POL". MC *penpol*, "creek's end".

PENQUITE: OC *pen cuit*, "wood end".

PENVENTINUE: MC *penvyntenyow*, "spring-heads".

PLACE MANOR: MC *plas*, "mansion".

POLDEW: MC *pol du*, "black pool". Spoken with the emphasis on the last syllable.

POLGASSICK: MC *pol casak*, "mare's pool".

POLGLAZE: MC *pol glas*, "blue/green pool".

POLKERRIS: possibly MC *pol kerys*, "fortified pool/cove", or MC *pol Cerest*, "Cerest's pool/cove".

POLRIDMOUTH: *Porthredeman* C15. MC *porth res men*, "stone ford cove".

POLRUAN: *Porthruan* C13. Possibly MC *porth Rumon*, "St Rumon's cove", or MC *porth ruen*, "seal cove".

POLSCOE: MC *pol scath*, "boat cove/pool".

POLVENTON: MC *pen vynten*, "well-head".

READYMONEY COVE: compare POLRIDMOUTH above. MC *res menow*, "ford of stones".

REDMOOR: Eng., from OE *read mor*, "red marsh".

RESTORMEL: MC *ros tor mol*, "roughland on a bare rounded hill". Here MC *tor*, "belly" is used to describe a distinctively shaped hill. Early forms show that the name contains *ros*, and not *res*, "ford".

ST SAMPSON: from the parish saint, Sampson of Dol.

SHAG ROCK: Eng., from the seabird.

TAPHOUSE: Eng., "alehouse".

TORFREY: MC *tor vre*, "belly-like hill (rounded hill)", or MC *towargh vre*, "turf hill".

TREGAMINION: MC *tre gemynyon*, "commoners' farm".

TRENEWAN: *Trenewien* C13. MC *tre Newyen*, "Newyen's farm".

TRETHAKE: MC *tre theg*, "beautiful farm".

TRETHEW: MC *tre thu*, "black farm".

TREVELYAN: MC *tre Velyon*, "Melyon's farm".

TREZARE: *Reswor* C14. MC *res wer*, "green ford".

ST VEEP: named after the parish saint, Vepus.

WILLAKE: Eng., from OE *wid laec*, "wide stream".

ST WINNOW: *S. Winnocus* C12. Winnoc is the pet form of the saint's name Winwalo, and occurs in the west of Cornwall at TOWEDNACK and LANDEWEDNACK. The full name survives at GUNWALLOE.

*   *   *

The House: *An chy*

ATTIC: *tallack*, pl. *-ez*, m. (TAL-ek; TAL-ek-ez)

BATH: *gulva*, pl. *-vaow*, m. (GUL-va; GUL-vaou)

BATHROOM: *rowm gulhy*, pl. *rowms gulhy*, m. (roem GUL-hlee; roemz GUl-hlee)

BEAM: *trester*, pl. *-s*, m. (TRES-ter[z])

BED: *gwily* pl. *-ow*, m. (GWIL-ee; GWIL-yau)

BEDROOM: *chomber*, pl. *-s*, m. (CHOM-ber[z])

CHAIR: *cader*, pl. *-iow*, f. (KAD-er; k'DER-yau)

CHIMNEY: *shimbla*, pl. *-blez*, m. (SHIM-bla; SHIM-blez)

DINING ROOM: *stevall*, pl. *-iow*, f. (STEV-el; stev-AL-yau)

DOOR: *darras*, pl. *derrgow*, m. (DAR-ez; DER-jau)

DOOR (front): *darras raage*, m. (DAR-ez RAAG)

DOOR (back): *darras athelhar*, m. (DAR-ez ath-EL'hler)

DOORWAY: *durns*, m. (dernz)

EAVES: *auvez*, m. (AH-vez)

FIREPLACE: *ollas*, pl. *olladgow*, f. (UL-ez; ul-AD-jau)

FLOOR: *lear*, m. (lair)

GABLE: *talle*, pl. *talliow*, m. (tol; TOL-yau)

GARAGE: *cargy*, pl. *-ow*, m. (KAR-jee; KAR-jau)

GARDEN: *looar*, pl, *-thow*, m. (LOO-er; loo-ARTH-au)

GUTTER: *launder*, pl. *-s*, m. (LAUN-der[z])

HALLWAY: *basefry*, pl. -s, m. (BAZ-a-free[z])

HOUSE: *chy*, pl. *treven*, m. (chei; TREV-en)

KITCHEN: *kegen*, pl. *kegednow*, f. (KEG-en; k'GED-nau)

LANDING: *talfat*, pl. *-ez*, m. (TOL-fat; tol-FAT-ez)

LARDER: *spens*, pl. *-ez*, m. (spenss; SPEN-sez)

LOFT: *tallet*, pl. *-ez*, (TOl-et; TOL-et-ez)

PARLOUR: *heel*, pl. *-ow*, m. (heel; HEEL-au)

PORCH: *portal*, pl. *-s*, m. (PORT-el[z])

RAFTER: *riffell*, pl. *-s*, m. (RIF'l[z])

ROOF: *to*, pl. *-how*, m. (TOE; TOE-hau)

ROOF (slate): *hellin*, pl. *-s*, m. (HEL-en[z])

ROOM: *rowm*, pl. *-s*, m. (roem[z])

TABLE: *bord*, pl. *-ez*, m. (bord; BORD-ez)

WALL: *fose/vose*, pl. *fossow/vossow*, m. (voez; VOZ-au)

WC: *petty*, pl. *pettez*, m. (PET-ee; PET-ez)

WINDOW: *beisder*, pl. *beisdri*, f. (BEIZ-der; BEIZ-dree)

Edward Lhuyd: Cornwall's Debt of Honour

It was during the time of the Late Renaissance of the Cornish language that Edward Lhuyd paid his invaluable visit to the Duchy. Born in Shropshire of Welsh parents in 1660, Lhuyd was appointed Under-Keeper of the Ashmolean Museum, Oxford, in 1684, and Keeper of the museum in 1691. From this time onward, his chief studies were in antiquity and philology and, after assisting with the revision of Camden's *Britannica*, set out on his own major work, the *Archaeologia Britannica*, the first volume of which was published in 1709, the year of his untimely death from pleurisy.

From 1697 to 1701, "honest Lhuyd" as he was dubbed, carried out major studies in all the Celtic countries. In the case of Cornwall, he was anxious to know "what remains of the British language, customes and names of places may be found there", and resolved to visit John Keigwin at Mousehole, among others. He laid the ground for his visit by communicating with Thomas Tonkin of St Agnes and eventually arrived in Cornwall in 1700, accompanied by his helpers David Parry, Robert Wynne and William Jones.

Edward Lhuyd (C. Weatherhill)

Lhuyd stayed for four months, studying antiquities and natural phenomena but, above all, seeking knowledge of a language on the brink of extinction. He was instructed in Cornish grammar by the greatest experts of the time: Keigwin, James Jenkins, Nicholas Boson and Henry Usticke in particular. In Lhuyd's own appraisal, John Keigwin was deemed "without any comparison the most skilfull judge of our age in the Cornish language". A further source of material for Lhuyd was a trio of Cornish manuscripts provided by the Bishop of Exeter, Sir Jonathan Trelawny, which had been translated into English at Trelawny's request by Keigwin.

Lhuyd also visited the western parish of St Just, where a good deal of Cornish was still spoken by the local people, and this he found invaluable in the study of the sounds of the language: the only known study of the pronunciation of Cornish whilst it was still a living language.

Lhuyd's new found knowledge of Cornish enabled him to identify a document found in the Cottonian Library, London by Will Jones. Dating from around 1100, it was a vocabulary thought by some to be Old Welsh but it was Lhuyd who correctly identified it as Old Cornish.

The massive results of Edward Lhuyd's studies were printed in the *Glossography*, the first volume of his projected work but, on hearing that others, notably William Hals, were to produce an English-Cornish vocabulary, he omitted this from the book. In fact, Hals's work turned out to be virtually worthless; a "hodge-podge of Hebrew, Greek, Latin and British words confusedly heaped together" according to William Pryce at the end of the 18th century. However, 200 years after Lhuyd's death, his 172 page notebook containing Lhuyd's draft vocabulary was discovered in the National Library of Wales.

Without Edward Lhuyd, our knowledge of Modern Cornish would have been poor indeed. It is particularly strange that so many scholars of the 20th century have dismissed his spelling of Cornish as "curious" and "highly individualistic", thereby missing the point completely. Lhuyd himself clearly stated that his spelling was not to be taken as an example of Cornish orthography, nor as a suggested revision of it, but as a representation of Cornish pronunciation. In other words, Lhuyd used a phonetic code to record the language, a fact only apparently recognised by O.J.Padel in his *The Cornish Writings of the Boson Family*, in which he reproduces Lhuyd's rewriting of the John of Chyanhor story, and by perhaps the greatest Cornish scholar of our day, Richard Gendall.

*   *   *

Coast & sea: *Morrab ha moer*

BEACH: *treath*, pl. *-ow*, m. (traith; TRAI-thau)

BOAT: *scathe*, pl. *scathow*, f. (skaith; SKATH-au)

BUOY: *bye*, pl. *-s*, m. (bei[z])

CLIFF: *aulz*, pl. *aulgiow*, m. (ahlz; AHL-jau)

CLIFF-CHASM: *sawan* pl. *-ow*, f. (ZAOU-en; ZAOU'nau)

COAST: *morrab*, m. (MOR-eb)

COVE: *por(th)*, pl. *porthow*, m. (por/porth; PORTH-au)

ESTUARY: *hayl*, pl. *-iow*, m. (hail; HAIL-yau)

HARBOUR: *hean*, pl. *-ez*, m. (hain; HAIN-ez)

HEADLAND: *penteer*, pl. *pentiriow*, m. (p'n-TEER; p'n-TI-ryau)

INLET: *lo*e, pl. *-ow*, f. (loe; LOE-hau)

ISLAND: *ennis* pl. *ennesow*, f. (EN-ez; en-EZ-au)

LIGHTHOUSE: *gulowva*, pl. *-ow*, f. (GUL-a-va; GUL-a-vau)

OCEAN: *moer broaz*, m. (mau-er BRAUZ)

PONTOON: *cay neidga*, pl. *cayez neidga*, m. (kai NEI-ja; KAI-ez NEI-ja)

QUAY: *cay* pl. *-ez*, m. (kai; KAI-ez)

REEF: *creeb*, pl. *-ow*, f. (kreeb; KREEB-au)

SAILBOAT: *cowk*, pl. *cucow*, m. (koek; KÛK-au)

SEA: *moer*, pl. *-ow*, m. (mau-er; MAU-rau)

SHIP: *gurroll*, pl. *-ian*, m. (GUH-rel; guh-ROL-yan); *lesster*, pl. *lisstri*, m. (LESS-ter; LISS-tree)

11

Place Names of Padstow & Wadebridge

RIVER ALLEN: originally, the name of the river now called the CAMEL (see below) but transferred to this river in the C19, replacing its earlier name, the *Layne*. The meaning of both Allen and Layne remains unknown, although Allen is a fairly common Celtic river name. Padel suggests an even earlier name for this river, the *Dewi*, from the occurrence of place names which include that word along its course.

RIVER AMBLE: LC *ambel*, "hillslope". It is unusual, but not unknown, to find a place name in its Late Cornish form to the east of the Camel-Fowey line.

BELOWDA: MC *bos Louda*, "Louda's dwelling". Pronounced "b'LAOU-da".

BLABLE: MC *blyth bol*, "wolf-pit".

BODIEVE: OC *bod yuv*, "lord's dwelling".

BORLASE: MC *bor las*, "green bank".

ST BREOCK: from the early Welsh priest Breoc, who went on from here to Brittany (Saint Brieuc). The churchtown was known as *Lansant* C13, *Nanssent* C14, OC *lan sant*, "saint's church site".

BURLAWNE: *Bodlouen* C13. OC *bod lauen*, "happy dwelling".

BURLORNE: either as BURLAWNE above, or MC *bos elowen*, "dwelling by an elm tree".

RIVER CAMEL: MC *cam-el*, "crooked/curved one". This name was originally applied only to the upper reaches of the river, also called the *Allen* before that name was transferred by mistake to the Layne. The estuary was almost certainly known as *Hayle*, MC *hayl*, "estuary, saltings" (see EGLOSHAYLE below).

CANNALIDGEY: MC *canel Isy*, "St Issey's channel". Note the early change in sound of the S to a soft J, a feature of Late Cornish.

CANT HILL: MC *cant*, "border, boundary".

CARHART: MC *car yarth*, "ridge fort".

CASTLE AN DINAS: English "castle", added to MC *an dynas*, "the hill fort".

CATACLEWS POINT: MC *carrek loys*, "grey rock".

CHAPEL AMBLE: LC *chapall Ambel*, "chapel by the River Amble" (see RIVER AMBLE above).

CONSTANTINE BAY: from St Constantine's chapel close by. This was *Egloscontantyne* C16, LC *eglos Constantine*, "St Constantine's church".

CRUGMEER: MC *cruk meyr*, "great barrow/tumulus". Pronounced "krug-MEER".

DEMELZA: MC *dyn Melsec*, "Maeldoc's fort".

DINAS HEAD: LC *dinas*, "fort".

EGLOSHAYLE: MC *eglos Hayl*, "church by the Hayle". This was almost certainly the older name for the Camel estuary, MC *hayl*, "estuary, saltings".

ST ENDELLION: from the church saint, Endelienta.

ST ENODOC: named after the church saint, Enodoc. Pronounced "EN-a-doc".

ST ERVAN: this name derives from St Hermes.

FENTONLUNA: formerly *Fentonlennow*, MC *fynten lynnow*, "spring by pools".

GULLAND ROCK: suggested as Eng. "gull land" by some, but more likely to be LC *goolan*, "gull".

GUNVENA: LC *goon vena*, "hillside downs".

GWENNYMOOR: Eng., "Gwynnowe's marsh (OE *mor*)", from Gwynnowe family of Withiel, recorded in the C16.

HALWYN: *Helewen* C13. MC *hel wyn*, "white hall".

HARLYN BAY: *Arlin* C13, *Arlyn* C14. MC *ar lyn*, "beside a pool".

HAYLE BAY: MC *hayl*, "estuary, saltings", the probable former name of the Camel estuary.

HUSTYN: Eng., *husting*, "meeting place".

ST ISSEY: named after St Isy. The churchtown was *Egloscruc* C12, MC *eglos cruk*, "church by a barrow/tumulus".

ST JIDGEY: a corrupted form of St Issey.

KELLY: MC *kelly*, "grove".

ST KEW: after St Kewa. This was also known as *Docco* C6, *Lannohoo* C11, *St Doquinus* C15; MC *lan Docco*, "Docco's church site".

LANJEW: MC *lyn thu*, "black pool".

LANSEAGUE: "lan-ZEEG". MC *lan Sioc*, "Sioc's church site".

LELIZZICK: *Lanweledyk* C13, the D later softening to S/Z. MC *lan Wlesek*,

"Gwlesek's church site". The Celtic name Gwledic also means "lord, land-owner".

LITTLE PETHERICK: Eng., "Little St Petroc". The churchtown was formerly *Nansenton*, MC *nans fynten*, "well vale".

ST MABYN: named after St Mabena.

MELLINGEY: MC *melynjy*, "millhouse". Pronounced "m'LIN-jee".

ST MERRYN: from St Marina.

ST MINVER: from St Menfreda.

THE MOULS: MC *mols*, "wether sheep".

PADSTOW: shortened form of OE *Petroces stow*, "St Petroc's holy place". An alternative Eng. name, *Aldestowe*, OE *eald stow*, "old holy place" was recorded in the C13. The churchtown's Cornish name, *Languihenoc* C11, *Lanwethenek* C14, contracted to *Lodenek* C16 and *Laffenake* C17. MC *lan Wethenoc*, "Gwethenoc's church site".

PAWTON: *Polltun* C10. MC *pol*, "pool"; OE *tun*, "farm".

PENDOGGETT: OC *pen dui guit*, "end of two woods".

PENMAYNE: MC *pen men*, "top of the stone".

PENNANT: "p'n-NANT". OC *pen nant*, "valley end".

PENROSE: MC *pen ros*, "end of a hillspur".

PENTIRE: MC *pentyr*, "headland". Pronounced "p'n-TEIR" but correct Cornish ought to make it "p'n-TEER".

PENTIREGLAZE: MC *pentyr glas*, "grey-green headland".

POLZEATH: "pol-ZETH". MC *pol seygh*, "dry pool".

PORTGAVERNE: MC *porth gaveryn*, "cove of a little goat (possibly a stream name)". Pronounced "port GAI-vern".

PORTHCOTHAN: MC *porth cuthen*, "cove by a submerged reef".

PORTHILLY: MC *porth hyly*, "saltwater cove".

PORT ISAAC: MC *porth ysek*, "corn cove". Pronounced "port EI-zek" but ought to be "port IZ-ek".

PORTQUIN: MC *porth gwyn*, "white cove".

PRIDEAUX: named after the Prideaux family. Formerly *Gwarthandrea*, MC *gwartha an dre*, "top of the farm".

THE QUIES: MC *gwys*, "sow".

QUOIT: Eng. dialect word for a Neolithic dolmen, one of which (The Devil's Coit) formerly stood here. The word was adopted into Late Cornish as a feminine noun, *coyt*, as in a field name at Lanyon near Penzance, *Goon an Goyte*, "the dolmen downs".

RETIRE: OC *ret hir*, "long ford".

ROCK: Eng. "rock". *Blaketore* C14, "black tor", became *Black Rock* C18 and, finally, Rock.

ROSCARROCK: MC *ros carrek*, "roughland with a rock".

ROSENANNON: MC *ros an onnen*, "valleyside with an ash tree".

RUMFORD: Eng., from OE *rum ford*, "wide ford".

THE RUMPS: Eng., from twin-humped shape of headland.

SKEWES: MC *skeus*, "shade".

TREBETHERICK: MC *tre Bedroc*, "St Petroc's farm". Pronounced "tr'BEDH'rik".

TREDINNICK: *Treredenek* C14. MC *tre redenek*, "fern-brake farm".

TREDRIZZICK: *Tredreyseg* C13. MC *tre dreysek*, "brambly farm".

TREDRUSTON: MC *tre Drustan*, "Drustan's farm". This Celtic personal name, from which Tristan is derived, is found on a C6 inscribed stone at Fowey as *Drustanus*.

TREFREOCK: MC *tre Vreoc*, "St Breoc's farm".

TREGAVERNE: *Tregaveren* C13. MC *tre gaveryn*, "little goat's farm". The second element might be a stream name (see PORTGAVERNE above).

TREGELLES: MC *tre Gelest*, "Celest's farm".

TREGLENNICK: *Tregelennek* C14. MC *tre gelynek*, "holly-grove farm".

TREGOLDS: *Tregatlos* C13. MC *tre Gatlos*, "Catlos's farm".

TREGONETHA: "treg-an-EDH-a". *Tregenhetha* C14. MC *tre Genhetha*, "Kenhetha's farm".

TREGUNNA: MC *tre Gonna*, "Conna's farm".

TRELIGHTS: *Trefflectos* C14, *Treleghtres* C15. MC *tre legh tros*, "slab-foot farm".

TRENTINNEY: MC *tre vyntenyow*, "wells farm".

TREQUITE: OC *treu guit*, "wood farm".

TREVANCE: formerly *Trevantros*, OC *treu vant ros*, "hillspur height farm".

TREVANION: MC *trev Anyon*, "Anion's farm".

TREVANSON: MC *trev Anson*, "Anton's farm".

TREVEGLOS: MC *trev eglos*, "church farm/churchtown".

TREVONE: *Treavon* C14. MC *tre avon*, "river farm".

TREVORRICK: *Treworrech* C13. MC *tre Worec*, "Gorec's farm".

TREVOSE: *Trenfos* C14. MC *tre an vos*, "farm by the wall/dyke".

TREWINCE: MC *tre uyns*, "farm in wind".

TREYARNON: MC *tre Yernan*, "Iernan's farm".

WADEBRIDGE: *Wade* in C14/15; OE *waed*, "ford". Eng. "bridge" added to the name in C15, when the bridge was built.

WEENS: MC *(an) uyns*, "the wind".

ST WENN: named after St Wenna. The churchtown name was *Lantuel* C13, possibly MC *nans tewl*, "dark valley"".

WITHIEL: MC *(an) uethyel*, "the place of trees". This may be connected with the possible district name *Guethyel* (see BODITHIEL and LOSTWITHIEL in Section 10).

WITHIELGOOSE: MC *(an) uethyel goys*, "the wood of Guethyel".

✳   ✳   ✳

Adjectives

ALL: *oll* (ol)	FEW: *nebas* (NEB-ez)	MOIST: *gleab* (glaib)
ANCIENT: *hean* (hain)	FINAL: *dewetha* (dyoo-WEDH-a)	NARROW: *idn* (ID'n)
ANGRY: *serrez* (SEH-rez)	FINE: *braa* (braa)	NEAR: *ogas* (OG-as)
ANOTHER: *orrol* (O-rel)	FLAT: *cumpas* (KUM-pez)	NEW: *noweth* (NAOU-eth)
ATTRACTIVE: *fettow* (FET-au)	FORTIFIED: *kerrez* (KEH-rez)	OLD: *coth* (kauth)
AWFUL: *ethick* (EDH-ek)	FREE: *frank* (frank)	ONLY: *ednack* (ED-nek)
BAD: *droeg* (droeg)	FRESH: *ere* (air)	OPEN: *gerrez* (GEH-rez)
BALD: *moel* (moel)	FULL: *lean* (lain)	PLEASANT: *wheag* (hwaig)
BARREN: *threas* (thrai-ez)	GLAD: *looan* (LOO-en)	POOR: *bohodgack* (b'HOD-jek)
BEAUTIFUL: *teag* (taig)	GOOD: *daa* (daa)	PRIVATE: *prevath* (PREV-eth)
BEST: *gwelha* (GWEL'hla)	GREAT: *mere* (mair)	PUBLIC: *an pobell* (an POB'l)
BETTER: *gwell* (gwel)	HAPPY: *looan* (LOO-en)	PURE: *pewer* (PYOO-er)
BIG: *broaz* (brauz)	HARD: *calish* (KAL-ish)	QUICK: *iskez* (IS-kez)
BLEAK: *idniall* (ID-nee-aul)	HEAVY: *poez* (poez)	REAL: *gweer* (gweer)
BREAKNECK: *crackia codna*	HIGH: *euhall* (YOO-hel)	RIGHT: *cumpas* (KUM-pez);
(krak-ya COD-na)	HOT: *tubm* (tûb'm)	RIGHT-HAND: *athehow* (a-DHAI-hau)
BROKEN: *terrez* (TEH-rez)	ILL: *clave* (clauv)	RIPE: *arvez* (AR-vez)
BURNT: *leskez* (LES-kez)	JAGGED: *dengack* (DEN-jek)	ROUGH: *garow* (GAH-rau)
CHEAP: *raze* (raaz)	KIND: *kerengack* (k'REN'jek)	SAD: *trawethack* (tr'WEDH-ek)

CLEAN: *glane* (glaan)
CLOSED: *degeas* (d'GAI-ez)
COLD: *yein* (ein)
DANGEROUS: dantell (DAN-tel)
DARK: *tewl* (tyool)
DEAD: *marow* (MAH-rau)
DIRTY: *plous* (plooz)
DRUNK: *methow* (MEDH-au)
DRY: *zeah* (zai'h)
EACH: *keniffer* (KEN-e-ver)
EXPENSIVE: *keef* (keev)
EXTREME: *pelha* (PEL'hla)
FAMOUS: *fauge* (fawzh)
FAR: *pell* (pel)
FAT: *tew* (tyoo)

LARGE: *broaz* (brauz)
LAST: *dewetha* (dyoo-WEDH-a)
LASTING: *dirriez* (DI-ree-ez)
LATE: *holerh* (HOL-er'h)
LEFT-HAND: *agleth* (a'GLAITH)
LIGHT (weight): *scave* (scaav)
LITTLE: *bean* (BEE-an)
LONG: *heer* (heer)
LOST: *kellez* (KEL-ez)
LOVELY: *teag* (taig)
LOW: *esall* (EZ-el)
MANY: *leeas* (LEE-az)
MIDDLE: *creaz* (krai-ez)
MISTY: *newlack* (NYOO-lek)
MIXED: *melliez* (MEL-yez)

SCARCE: *scant* (scant)
SINGLE: *ednack* (ED-nek)
SLOW: *lent* (lent)
SMALL: *bean* (BEE-an)
SMOOTH: *leven* (LEV-en)
SOFT: *medall* (MED-al)
SOME: *nebas* (NEB-az)
STRONG: *creav* (kraiv)
TINY: *miniz* (MIN-iz)
TRUE: *gweer* (gweer)
WARM: *tub'm* (tb'm)
WIDE: *ledan* (LED'n)
WONDERFUL: *barthedgack*
(bar-THED-jek)
YOUNG: *younk* (yûnk)

*   *   *

The Legend of Dolly Pentreath

The doubtful fame of "Old Doll" of Mousehole as the last native speaker of Cornish was unwittingly begun by Admiral Samuel Barrington who, in 1746, sailed to Brittany and afterwards wrote to his brother, historian Daines Barrington, describing how one of his crew, a Cornish speaking sailor from Mount's Bay, had made himself understood by the Bretons.

It took Daines Barrington twenty-two years to follow this up but finally, in 1768, visited West Cornwall to find out if anyone could still speak the old language. He was directed to Mousehole, and to an old fish seller (jowster) called Dolly Pentreath.

"I desired to be introduced as a person who had laid a wager that there was no-one who could converse in Cornish; upon which Dolly Pentreath spoke in an angry tone of voice for two or three minutes, and in a language which sounded very like Welsh. The hut in which she lived was in a narrow lane, opposite to two rather better cottages, at the doors of which two other women stood, who were advanced in years, and who I observed were laughing. Upon this I asked them whether she had not been abusing me, to which they answered: "Very heartily, and because I had supposed she could not speak Cornish." I then said that they must be able to talk the language, to which they answered that could not speak it readily, but they understood it, being only ten or twelve years younger than Dolly Pentreath."

Dolly Pentreath: after 1776 portrait by John Opie (C. Weatherhill)

Barrington gave his address concerning Dolly to the Society of Antiquaries in 1773, adding further information that he had received the previous summer after enquiring as to whether Dolly was still alive. It had come in the form of a letter from a gentleman who lived within three miles of Mousehole:

"Dolly Pentreath is short of stature, and bends very much with old age, being in her eighty-seventh year, so lusty, however, as to walk hither to Castle Horneck, about three miles, in bad weather, in the morning and back again. She is somewhat deaf, but her intellect seemingly not impaired; has a memory so good that she remembers perfectly well that about four or five years ago at Mousehole where she lives she was sent for by a gentleman who, being a stranger, had a curiosity to hear the Cornish language which she was famed for retaining and speaking fluently, and that the innkeeper where the gentleman came from attended him.

"She does indeed talk Cornish as readily as others do English, being bred up from a child to know no other language; nor could she, if we may believe her, talk a word of English before she was past twenty years of age, as her father being a fisherman, she was sent with fish to Penzance at twelve years old and sold them in the Cornish language which the inhabitants in general, even the gentry, did then well understand. She is positive, however, that there is neither in Mousehole nor in any other part of the county, any other person who knows anything of it, or at least can converse in it. She is poor and maintained partly by the parish, and partly by fortune telling and gabbling Cornish."

The letter writer had been Dr Walter Borlase, brother of the famous Cornish antiquary Dr William Borlase who, although Rector of Ludgvan just a few miles away, had heard of no-one who could speak Cornish in his time.

Barrington himself doubted Dolly's claim to be the last remaining Cornish speaker, recalling the two younger women who, at the very least could understand the tongue, but did not follow this up other than to publish a letter written to him in 1776 by a sixty-five year old Mousehole fisherman, William Bodinar. The letter was in Cornish and claimed that four or five old people in the village could still speak the language. However, he had not been brought up to speak Cornish but had learned it as a boy when at sea with older fishermen.

Dolly Pentreath was, without doubt, not the last of the native Cornish speakers. However, she was certainly one of the very last to have been brought up to speak only Cornish. Who she was is something of a mystery; recollections of her life seem to be a mass of contradictions. It would seem that she was the Doaryte Pentreath, daughter of Nicholas, baptised in Paul church in 1692 (in which case she was 80, not 87, when Walter Borlase wrote of her). There is no-one of her name in the Paul burial records but an entry for December 1777, for the burial of Dorothy Jeffery, is followed by a footnote in a different hand: "This is the famous Dolly Pentreath (her maiden name) spoken of by Daines Barrington in the "Archaeologica".

However, there is no record of any marriage of Dolly to a man named Jeffery but she did have an illegitimate son, John, in 1729 (a John Jeffery's burial at Paul is recorded only a year after Dolly's death). Nevertheless, in what was apparently the last year of her life, Dolly received immortality in the form of a portrait painted by John Opie (the original hangs on St Michael's Mount).

Unbelievably, Barrington did not record a single word of Dolly's tirade and the only Cornish words reputed to been uttered by her were written down a century later in William Bottrell's *Traditions and Hearthside Stories of West Cornwall* (1870): the insult *Cronack an hagar due!* (This does not mean "The ugly black toad!" as so many translate it, but "You ugly toad!" Also enjoying renown as a wise-woman, Dolly the Spring as she was reportedly known, would, for reasons both right and wrong, be remembered long after her death.

In 1860, a monument to Dolly was erected in Paul churchyard (for a while on the wrong grave) by philologist Prince Louis Lucien Bonaparte; this includes a verse from Exodus rendered into Cornish. A Truro engineer named Thompson, reputedly fluent in Cornish, had at the time of Dolly's death composed a Cornish epitaph for her. It was never to appear on her grave but became well known for claiming that she had been aged 102 (probably poetic licence in order to achieve a rhyme). The legend of Dolly Pentreath had been born.

*   *   *

Pader An Arleth

Agon Taze nye, eze en Neve,
Benegas bo tha Hanow.
Tha Gwlaskath gwrenz doaz;
Tha Voth bo gwreze,
En Noer pecarra en Neve.
Ro tha nye an journama gon bara pub death,
Ha gave tha nye gon pehasow
Pecarra tel era nye gava angye
Neb eze peha war agon bidn.
Ha na raze gon lewa en antall,
Buz gweeth nye thurt droeg.
Rag an Gwlaskath Che a beaw,
Han Nearth, han Worrians,
Rag nevra venitha.
Andelna ra bo.

The Lord's Prayer

Our Father, which art in Heaven,
Hallowed be thy Name.
Thy Kingdom come;
Thy Will be done,
On Earth as it is in Heaven.
Give us this day our daily bread,
And forgive us our trespasses
As we forgive those
Who trespass against us.
And lead us not into temptation,
But deliver us from evil.
For Thine is the Kingdom,
The Power and the Glory,
For ever and ever.
Amen.

12

Place Names of Bodmin & Bodmin Moor

ADVENT: from St Adwena.

ALTARNUN: "OL-ter-NUN". Eng., "altar of St Nonna".

BARLENDEW: MC *bar lyn thu*, "black pool summit".

BEARAH: Eng., from OE *bearu*, "grove".

RIVER BEDALDUR: *Mindaldur* C13. Possibly MC *methelder*, "gentleness".

BERRIOW BRIDGE: *Berio* C16. A somewhat baffling name. A plural form of MC *bery*, "kite", might be involved.

BERRY: Eng., from OE *byrig*, "fort".

BLISLAND: *Bloiston* C12, *Bleselonde/Bliston* C13. The Domesday entry has it *Glustone*, with G for B (probably a scribal error). Eng., from OE *Bloias tun*, "Bloia's farm".

BODMIN: *Botmenei* C12. OC *bod menechi*, "monastery dwelling".

BODMIN MOOR: so called only since 1813, an Ordnance Survey invention. It was formerly Fowey Moor, *Fawimore* C12, *Foy Moor* C19, Eng., "moor of the River Fowey" in the tradition of naming a moor after the principal river which rises on it (compare Dartmoor, Exmoor). The Cornish name for the moor was *Goen Bren* C12, MC *goen bren*, "hill downs".

BODRIGAN: "b'd-RIG-en". OC *bod Rigan*, "Rigan's dwelling".

BODWEN: OC *bod uyn*, "white/fair dwelling". Pronounced "b'd-WEN".

BOKIDDICK: *Bochedek* C13. MC *bos Cadoc*, "Cadoc's dwelling".

BOLVENTOR: Eng., "bold venture". A C19 name for the formation of a farm on poor land.

BOWDA: Eng., from OE *bow wudu*, "bend of a wood".

BOWITHICK: MC *bos uethek*, "dwelling in a place of trees".

ST BREWARD: from St Branwalader. *St Brewveredus* C12 ws shortened to *St Breward* C14, then merged with the "saint" element to become *Semerwert* C15 and *Symonward* C16.

BROCKABARROW: Eng., from OE *brocc beorg*, "badger's barrow/tumulus".

BROWN GELLY: MC *bron gelly*, "grove hill". It would appear that today's bare landscape once contained some woodland.

J.T. Blight's 19th century engraving of the holy well at St. Breward

BROWN WILLY: *Brunwenely* C13, MC *bron wennyly*, "swallows' hill". The name is definitely not derived from MC *bron ughella*, "highest hill", as some would have it (although such a meaning would have been apt – at 1377 feet [420 metres], Brown Willy is Cornwall's highest point).

CALLYWITH: MC *kelly ueth*, "grove of trees".

CANAGLAZE: MC *carn an glas*, "the grey-green tor". Pronounced "can-a-GLAAZ".

CARBILLY TOR: MC *carn ebilly*, "colt's tor"; with Eng. "tor" added.

CARDINHAM: "car-DIN-am". MC *car dynan*, "earthwork fortress".

CARGELLEY: MC *car gelly*, "grove fort".

CARNEGLOS TOR: MC *carn eglos*, "church tor", with Eng. "tor" unnecessarily added.

CARWEN: MC *car uen*, "white fort".

CASTILLY: MC *castilly*, "castles".

CASTLE CANYKE: "kas'l KAN-ik". MC *castel keynyk*, "castle on a little ridge".

CHEESEWRING: Eng., "cider-press". The "cheese" is the compressed apple-mulch.

ST CLETHER: from St Cleder.

CODDA TOR: a hill name including OE *torr*, "rock outcrop", but named after Codda farm which was *Stymkodda* C14. Hybrid; MC *stum*, "bend", plus an OE river name of unknown meaning.

COLDQUITE: OC *kil cuit*, "wood ridge".

COLVANNICK TOR: MC *gelvynak*, "curlew"; Eng. *torr*, "rock outcrop".

COSTISLOST: probably Eng., for a farm which proved to be a poor investment.

CROWDY: OC *crouti*, "hovel".

CUTMADOC: OC *cuit Madoc*, "Madoc's wood".

DAVIDSTOW: *Dewstow* C13. OC *Dewi*, "David"; OE *stow*, "holy place". Still locally known as Dewstow.

DE LANK RIVER: *Dymlonke* C17. Possibly MC *dyn lonk*, "ravine fort".

DOZMARY POOL: *Thosmery* C13, *Dosmerypole* C13. A baffling name in which Eng. *mere*, "pool", does not seem to be involved. A possibility is MC *tos mery*, "pleasant drinking bowl".

DUNMERE: OC *dun maur*, "great fort".

EMBLANCE DOWNS: MC *emlow enys*, "isolated slopes".

FENTONADLE: *Fentonadwen* C13. MC *fynten Adwen*, "St Adwena's well".

GARROW TOR: *Garross Moors* C17; *Garrah* C18. MC *garow ros*, "rough hillspur", contracted to Garrow, with Eng. *torr*, "rock outcrop", added in C19.

GLYNN: MC *glyn*, "deep valley".

GONAMENA: MC *goen an meneth*, "the hillside downs". This name shows an earlier than expected dropping of the final TH, normally a feature of Late Cornish.

GOONZION: MC *goen seghen*, "dry-place downs".

HALGAVER MOOR: MC *hal gavar*, "goat's marsh", with unnecessary addition of Eng. "moor" (OE *mor*, "marsh").

HALVANA: MC *hyr veneth*, "long hillside". Another early example of the final TH being dropped.

HANTERGANTICK: MC *hendre gantek*, "old farm near a boundary".

HAWK'S TOR: Eng., "hawk's tor".

HELLAND: MC *henlan*, "former church site".

HENWOOD: Eng., from OE *henn wudu*, "hen's wood".

THE HURLERS: Eng., dating from at least C17. Three stone circles likened to players of the Cornish sport of hurling.

ST INGUNGER: *Stymgongar* C13. MC *stym Gongar*, "St Congar's bend".

INNIS: MC *enys*, "isolated place".

KELLY GREEN: *Keligren* C13. MC *kelly gren*, "aspen grove".

KILMAR TOR: MC *kyl margh*, "horse's back"; Eng. *torr*, "rock outcrop" added in C17.

LAMORICK: MC *lan Morec*, "Morec's church site".

LANEAST: MC *lan Uste*, "St Just's church site". This dedication, to a saint more associated with West Cornwall, is long forgotten. The church is dedicated to Sts. Gulval and Sativola, both of whom are also better known in the Land's End area (Gulval being a current parish; Sativola was the sister of St Paul Aurelian, commemorated at Paul).

LANHYDROCK: MC *lan Hydroc*, "Hydroc's church site".

LANIVET: OC *lan neved*, "church site on a pagan sacred site".

LANLAVERY ROCK: MC *lam*, "leap"; the second element is obscure. It might be MC *lavyrrys*, "troublesome, difficult".

LANTEWEY: MC *nans Dewi*, "valley of River Dewi".

LAVETHAN: formerly *Lanedowan*. OC *nant bedouan*, "birch-tree valley".

LEAZE: *Layes* C17. Eng., from OE *leahs*, "clearings, pastures".

Kilmar Tor

LESKERNICK: MC *lys carnyk*, "ruined fort by a little tor".

LESQUITE: *Lostcoys* C14. MC *lost coys*, "tail of a wood". The second element, *coys*, has reverted to its OC form, *cuit*.

LEWARNE: MC *lan gwern*, "church-site/enclosure with alder trees".

LEY: Eng., from OE *leah*, "clearing, pasture".

MICHAELSTOW: Eng., "St Michael's holy place".

MINIONS: C19 village named after a Bronze Age barrow, *Minnions burroughe* C17 (now "Minions Mound"). The meaning of Minions is unknown, but the village was so named in 1897, replacing its slightly earlier name of "Cheesewring Railway."

NANSTALLON: *Lantalan* C13. MC *lan Talan*, "Talan's church site".

ST NEOT: *Neotestou* C11. OE *Neots stow*, "St Neot's holy place".

NORTH HILL: *Henle* C13, possibly OE *hind leah*, "hind's clearing"; with Eng. "North" added in C13 to contrast with South Hill.

PANTERSBRIDGE: OC *pont Iesu*, "Jesus's bridge", with Eng. "bridge" added later.

John Norden's c.1580 map depicting Bodmin Moor

PENCARROW: MC *pen carow*, "stag end".

PENDAVY: MC *pen Dewi*, "head of River Dewi" – perhaps an early name for the present River Allen.

PENDEWEY: MC *pen Dewi*, "head of the River Dewi".

PENHARGARD: MC *pen hyr yarth*, "end of a long ridge".

PENKESTLE: MC *pen castel*, "castle top".

PENVOSE: MC *pen fos*, "end of a wall/dyke".

POLBROCK: MC *pol brogh*, "badger's pool".

POLGLAZE: MC *pol glas*, "blue pool".

POLVENTON: MC *pol vynten*, "pool by a spring".

REPERRY CROSS: *Redperi* C12. Possibly OC *rit beri*, "kite's ford".

RESPRYN: perhaps MC *res pren*, "timber ford".

ROUGH TOR: *Roghetorr/Rowetorr* C13. Eng., from OE *ruh torr*, "rough outcrop". Pronounced "RAOU-ter".

ROW: C19 name. Eng. "row" (of cottages).

RUSHYFORD GATE: Eng., "gate to a rushy ford".

SHARP TOR: Eng., "sharp outcrop".

SHOWERY TOR: Eng., "showery outcrop".

SIBLYBACK: Eng. from OE *Sibli baec*, "Sibli's ridge".

SLADES: Eng., from OE *slaed*, "shallow valley".

STANNON: *Standon* C15. Eng., from OE *stan dun*, "stone hill".

TAMSQUITE: OC *stum cuit*, "wood bend".

TEMPLE: named after the Kinights Templar, who owned an estate here and founded the church in the C13.

TRAGO: MC *tre Iago*, "Jago's farm".

TREBARTHA: *Triberthan* C11. MC *tre berthen*, "farm in a bushy place".

TREBYAN: MC *tre byan*, "little farm".

TREDARRUP: "tr'DAR-up". MC *tre gortharap*, "very pleasant farm".

TREDENHAM: *Tredynan* C14. MC *tre dynan*, "farm by a fort". Pronounced "tr'DEN-am"

TREDINNICK: MC *tre dynek*, "fortified farm".

TREFFRY: "tr'FREI". MC *tre Fry*, "Fry's farm".

TREGADDICK: MC *tre Gadoc*, "Cadoc's farm".

TREGARRICK TOR: hill named after nearby farm, MC *tre garrek*, "farm by a rock"; plus Eng. *torr*, "rock outcrop".

TREGEAR: MC *tre gair*, "farm by a fort".

TREGEARE: MC *tre gair*, "farm by a fort".

TREGONGER: MC *tre Gongar*, "Congar's farm".

TREGULLAND: MC *tre gollen*, "hazel-tree farm".

TRELAWNY: MC *tre launow*, "farm by clearings".

TRELILL: *Trelulla* C13. MC *tre Lulla*, "Lulla's farm".

TREMABYN: MC *tre Mabyn*, "Mabyn's farm".

TREMAIL: MC *tre Mael*, "Mael's farm".

TREMEER: MC *tre meyr*, "great farm".

TREMORE: *Tremhor* C11. MC *tre an horth*, "the ram's farm". The C11 is extremely early for the last TH to be dropped.

TRENEWTH: OC *treu newyth*, "new farm".

TRESMEER: *Treguasmer* C11. MC *tre Gwasmer*, "Gwasmer's farm".

TREVERBYN: MC *trev Erbyn*, "Erbin's farm".

TREVISQUITE: OC *treu is cuit*, "farm below a wood".

TREVIVIAN: OC *treu hiuin*, "yew farm".

TREWARTHA: MC *tre wartha*, "higher farm".

TREWINT: OC *treu uint*, "farm in wind".

ST TUDY: from the church saint, St Tudi. The churchtown was *Hecglostudic* C11, OC *egglos Tudi*, "St Tudi's church".

TWELVE MEN'S MOOR: owned by the medieval Prior and Canons of Launceston, this area of moorland had 12 tenants, named in 1284 as: Thomas and David of Kelnystok; William Foth; Robert Faber; Jordan and Nicholas Cada; Robert Broda; Walter of La Lak; Robert le Legha; Roger Boglawoda; John Can and William of Trewortha.

UPTON: Eng., from OE *upp tun*, "higher farm".

VENTONHORNE: MC *(an) vynten horn*, "the iron well".

WARLEGGAN: "wor-LEG-an". Possibly MC *war leghan*, "on a stone slab".

WASHAWAY: Eng. term meaning "hollow way".

WELLTOWN: Eng. from OE *wiella tun*, "well farm".

WITHEYBROOK: Eng., from OE *withig broc*, "willow brook".

* * *

Cornish after Dolly Pentreath

Dolly Pentreath died in 1777 but was almost certainly outlived by the two women mentioned by Daines Barrington and who had been ten or twelve years younger than Dolly. Stating that they could understand the language but not easily converse in it, they bear the hallmarks of people who had learned it from their parents but, as it had become so rarely spoken, had become somewhat rusty in its use.

A Mousehole fisherman, William Bodinar, also outlived Dolly by a dozen years and his 1776 letter to Barrington exhibits Cornish of surprisingly good quality and is the last known example of native Cornish prose. It is reproduced below in Bodinar's original spelling:

Bluth vee try egance a pemp. Theara vee dean bodjack an puscas. Me rig deskey Cornoack termen me vee mawe. Me vee de more gen seara vee a pemp dean moy en cock. Me rig scantlower clowes eden ger Sowsnack cowes en cock rag sythen warebar. Na riga vee biscath gwellas lever Cornoack. Me deskey Cornoack moas da more gen tees coath. Nag es moye vel pager po pemp en dreav nye ell clapia Cornoack leben, poble coath pager egance blouth. Cornoack ewe oll neceaves gen poble younk.

My age is sixty-five. I am a poor fisherman. I learned Cornish when I was a boy. I went to sea with my father and five other men in the boat. I hardly heard a single word of English spoken in the boat for as much as a week. I never saw a Cornish book. I learned Cornish going to sea with old men. There are no more than four or five in the village who can speak Cornish now, old people eighty years of age. Cornish is all forgotten by young folk.

Among other Cornish speakers still alive at the time of Bodinar's death in 1789 were a Truro mining engineer named Thompson (who had penned the fanciful Cornish epitaph for Dolly Pentreath), and another engineer, John Nancarrow of Marazion.

Born into a Quaker family at St Agnes in 1734, Nancarrow's childhood was spent in West Cornwall where he learned his Cornish from native speakers. Daines Barrington learned of his fluency in 1777, three years after Nancarrow had left Marazion for America. Two years later, the vicar of Ruan Lanihorne, on the banks of the Fal, was introduced to two Cornish speaking parishioners who told him of a third.

John Nancarrow was last heard of in Philadelphia in 1804, the same year in which it became plain that native speakers of Cornish still survived – with Newlyn fishermen making themselves understood by their Breton cousins by speaking Cornish. Others retained fragments, such as Mrs W.J.Rawlings of Hayle who had learned the Lord's Prayer and the Apostles' Creed in Cornish from her father at some time around 1830. Mrs Rawlings was also mother-in-law to Henry Jenner, the father of the language's revival.

John Davey the elder (1744-1819), of Zennor and St Just, certainly possessed a considerable knowledge of Cornish. It is not known whether this remarkable schoolmaster, mathematician and poet was brought up to be bilingual, which is more than possible, or if he learned his Cornish from others as Bodinar and Nancarrow had done but, as will be seen, he most certainly passed his knowledge on to his son.

A scattering of reports can be found of other 19th century folk with abilities in Cornish: Jane Barnicoat who died in 1837; Ann Wallis (1754-1844); John Tremethack (1765-1852) who taught his granddaughter, a Mrs Kelynack who was still alive in 1875; and Betsy Matthews who died in 1887.

One remarkable account was given to J. Arthur Rablen in 1936 by a retired St Ives policeman named Botheras. He told how, when a youth in Newlyn at some time around 1875, he often went to sea with local fishermen who were accustomed to talking among themselves in Cornish for up to ten minutes at a time. Botheras was well acquainted with local dialect and would clearly have known the difference, therefore this report must be considered reliable.

John Davey the younger (1812-91), of Boswednack near Zennor, learned a good deal of the language from his father and thus might merit the claim of "the last native speaker of Cornish", a distinction which is much argued about. Davey himself claimed to have enough fluency to enable him to converse on simple topics, though who he would have conversed with isn't clear. J. Hobson Matthews, author of *The History of St Ives* (1892), jotted down a rhyme recited by Davey who had learned it from his father. Matthews's transcription was far from perfect, having little or no knowledge of the language, and writing down what he heard. He himself believed it to be a nonsense rhyme, a mere jumble of place names but, in fact, the verse is a satire likening the quality of farmland at Crankan near Newmill, only a mile or two from Zennor, to the surface of the road from Penzance to Marazion:

The Crankan Rhyme

(Matthews)	(Modern Cornish)	(English)
A grankan, a grankan	A Grankan, A Grankan	O Crankan, O Crankan
A mean o gowaz o vean	Warn mean a gawas saw vean	On stone one finds but little
Ondez parc an venton	Hunt drez Park an Venton	Beyond the Well Field
Dub trelowza vean	Neb try lowz a vean	That bears 3 shoots per stone
Far Penzans a Maragow	Vorr Penzans tha Marhajeu	The Penzance to Marazion road
Githack mackwee	Hag ethick mouy gwear	Both greatly more green
A githack macrow	Hag ethick mouy cro	And greatly more fresh
A mac trelowza varrack	A mag try lowz a varrack	Grows 3 shoots per horseman

However imperfect, the Crankan Rhyme can rightly claim to be the last recorded example of traditional Cornish verse but, even as Matthews printed it, the revival of Cornish was well under way. The man most responsible for this was Henry Jenner, born at St Columb near Newquay in 1848 and the son-in-law of Mrs Rawlings of Hayle who had learned fragments of Cornish from her father.

*   *   *

Useful Verbs

Cornish verbs are generally quite simple and much grammar is made up of the use of the various tenses of five irregular auxiliary verbs (*boaz*, "to be"; *gallus*, "to be able"; *geel/gweel*, "to do"; *gothvas*, "to know, understand"; *mennas*, "to want, intend") with the present participle of the primary verb. Generally, the present participle ("crying") of Cornish verbs is the same as the Infinitive ("to cry"). In other words, *creia* can mean both "to cry" and "crying". On occasions, the past participle "cried" is used, generally formed by adding *-ez* to the root of the verb (*creiez*), and the preterite, which states what happened at a particular moment in the past and normally has an *-as* ending. However, and as this book is an introduction to the language, it is far too early to start examining those. The list below gives 130 verb infinitives:

ABLE, TO BE: *gallus* (GAL-uz)
AGREE: *benidnia* (b'NID-nee-a)
ASK: *goofen* (GÛF-en)
BARK: *harha* (HAR-ha)
BE: *boaz* (bauz)
BEAT: *crunckia* (KRUNK-ee-a)
BEGIN: *dallath* (DAL-adh)
BLOW: *whetha* (HWEDH-a)
BOIL: *bridgan* (BRIDG-en)
BREAK: *terry* (TEH-ree)
BUILD: *derevall* (d'REV-ol)
BURN: *lesky* (LES-kee)
BUY: *perna* (PER-na)
CALL: *creia* (CREI-a)
CHOKE: *taga* (TA-ga)

LOOK: *meeras* (MEER-az)
LOSE: *kelly* (KEL-ee)
LOVE: *cara* (KA-ra)
MAKE: *geel/gweel* (geel/gweel)
MELT: *tetha* (TEH-dha)
MIX: *mellia* (MEL-ya)
OPEN: *agery* (a-GEH-ree)
ORGANISE: *compoza* (k'm-POE-zha)
PAINT: *lewia* (I'YOO-ya)
PLAY: *gwary* (GWAW-ree)
POUR: *scullia* (SKUL-ya)
PRAY: *peidgy* (PIDG-ee)
PREPARE: *parra* (PA-ra)
PROTECT: *gweetha* (GWEE-tha)
PROVIDE: *provia* (PROV-ya)

CHOOSE: *dewez* (d'YOO-ez)
CLEAN: *glanhe* (GLAN-hee)
CLOSE: *degeas* (de-GAI-az)
COME: *doaz* (dauz)
CONTINUE: *pedgia* (PEDG-ya)
COPY: *dasscreffa* (da-SKREF-a)
CROSS: *tremena* (tr'MEN-a)
CUT: *trehy* (TREH-hee)
DANCE: *daunsia* (DAUNSS-ya)
DESCEND: *skidnia* (SKID-n'ya)
DIE: *merwall* (MER-wol)
DIG: *pallas* (PAL-az)
DO: *geel/gweel* (geel/gweel)
DRINK: *eva* (EV-a)
DRY: *zeaha* (ZAA-ha)
DWELL: *treegas* (TREE-gaz)
EAT: *debbry* (DEB-ree)
EXPECT: *gwaitia* (GWAIT-ya)
FALL: *cotha* (KUTH-a)
FEEL (health): *omglowas* (um-GLAOU-az)
FEEL (sense): *clowas* (KLAOU-az)
FILL: *lenall* (LEN-ol)
FIND: *cawas* (KAOU-az)
FINISH: *dowethy* (dow-EDH-ee)
FLY: *neidga* (NEI-dja)
FORGET: *nakevy* (n'KEV-ee)
GET: *cawas* (KAOU-az)
GIVE: *ry* (rei)
GO: *moaz* (mauz)
GUARD: *gweetha* (GWEE-tha)
GUESS: *dismiggia* (dis-MIDJ-ya)
HAPPEN: *chaunsia* (CHAUNS-ya)
HAVE: *cawas* (KAOU-az)
HEAR: *clowas* (KLAOU-az)
HIDE: *kitha* (KITH-a)
HIT: *squatchia* (SKWOT-cha)
HOLD: *sendgy* (SEND-jee)
HURT: *browy* (BRAOU-ee)
JUMP: *lebmall* (LEB-mol)
KEEP: *gweetha* (GWEE-tha)

PUSH: *pokkia* (POK-ya)
PUT: *gurra* (GÛ-ra)
REACH: *hetha* (HEDH-a)
READ: *redia* (RED-ya)
RECEIVE: *fanga* (FAN-ja)
REFER TO: *compla* (KOM-pla)
RESEARCH: *sarchia* (SARCH-ya)
RETURN: *dewhelas* (d'yoo-HWEL-az)
RUN: *poonia* (PÛN-ya)
SAY: *laull/lavarall* (lahl/l'VAR-ol)
SEARCH: *wheelas* (HWEE-laz)
SEE: *gwelhas* (GWEL-hlaz)
SELL: *gwerha* (GWER-ha)
SEND: *danen* (DAN-en)
SHOW: *disquethas* (dis-KWEDH-az)
SING: *cana* (CAN-a)
SIT: *setha* (SEDH-a)
SLIDE: *slinkia* (SLINK-ya)
SOAK: *dowrhe* (DAOUR-hee)
SPEAK: *cowz/clappia* (kaouz/KLAP-ya)
STAY: *treegas* (TREE-gaz)
STUDY: *madra* (MAD-ra)
SWALLOW: *clunka* (KLUN-ka)
SWIM: *neidga en dowr* (NEI-dja en DAOUR)
TAKE: *comeras* (kum-EH-raz)
TALK: *clappia* (KLAP-ya)
TEAR: *squardia* (SKWORD-ya)
THANK: *grassa* (GRAS-a)
THINK: *pedery* (p'DEH-ree)
THROW: *towla* (TAOU-la)
TIRE: *skeetha* (SKEE-tha)
TOUCH: *tava* (TAV-a)
TRAVEL: *laviria* (la-VIHR-ya)
TRY: *saya* (SAI-a)
TURN: *trailia* (TRAIL-ya)
UNDERSTAND: *convethas* (kun-VEDH-az)
USE: *usia* (YOOZ-ya)
WAIT: *gurtas* (GUR-taz)
WAKE: *deffeny* (def-EN-ee)
WALK: *kerras* (KEH-raz)

KILL: *latha* (LADH-a)
KISS: *abma* (AB-ma)
KNOW (understand): *gothvas* (GUDH-vaz)
KNOW (recognise): *adgan* (AD-jan)
LAUGH: *wherthin* (HWER-dhin)
LEARN: *desky* (DES-kee)
LEAVE: *gara* (GA-ra)
LIE DOWN: *gorwetha* (gor-WEDH-a)
LIKE: *cara* (KA-ra)
LISTEN: *gasowas* (g'ZAOU-az)

WANT: *menna* (MEN-a)
WASH: *golhy* (GUL-hee)
WASTE: *gwastia* (GWOST-ya)
WELCOME: *welcumba* (wel-KÛM-ba)
WET: *glebia* (GLEB-ya)
WORK: *gonez* (GUN-ez)
WRITE: *screffa* (SKREF-a)

*   *   *

Ula An Cooz

Ha me a moaz en kerras
Tua an drea,
Edn metten have arvis,
Tha dowla lether mouy en poss,
Abew an kea,
Enna drez am scooth, me glowas
Hubbadullia mesk an ethen . . .
Mola looz ha due, ha gwradnan,
Ruddock, tink, pednpaly, gulvan . . .
Pandra whear? ter me an breze.
Eze neb edn pye, po brane, po cathe,
Gwiwer, po nepeth orrol,
Ladra oyow meaz an neith?

Thosympyas me an gwelhas,
En bar zeah clugia . . . Ula!
Cuzal, tewl, misticall.
You! metha ve, scantlowar metha
Tha anella,
Ass o che teag!
Ha trailia an dro e bedn,
Ha merkia ve
Dreath an drokow e lagadgow,
Carra wherthin, ameth e:
"Peea che behatna, boya,
Tho che an kednow ve an journama!"

The Wood Owl

As I was walking
Towards the village,
One morning early in summer,
To put another letter in the post,
Above the hedge,
There over my shoulder, I heard
An uproar among the birds . . .
Thrush and blackbird, and wren,
Robin, finch, titmouse, sparrow . . .
What's up? I think to myself.
Is there some magpie, or crow, or cat,
Squirrel, or something else,
Stealing eggs from a nest?

Suddenly I saw him,
On a dry branch perching . . . An owl!
Still, inscrutable, mysterious.
Hi there! says I, hardly daring
To breathe,
Aren't you beautiful!
And turning his head around,
And marking me
Through the slits of his eyes,
As if laughing, he says:
"If you had been smaller, my lad,
You'd have been my dinner this day!"

Richard Gendall

13

Place Names of Tintagel & Camelford

BARRAS NOSE: MC *bar ros*, "high promontory"; Eng. "nose", for a protruding headland.

BOSCASTLE: Contracted from *Boterelescastel* C14; Eng., "Boterel's castle", from the Boterel/ Bottreaux family.

BOSSINEY: *Boscinii* C14. MC *bos Cyni*, "Cyni's dwelling". Pronounced "b'SIN-ee".

CAIRO: MC *kerrow*, "forts", or MC *carow*, "stag".

CAMBEAK: Eng., "comb beak" or, possibly, MC *cam byk*, "crooked beak".

CAMELFORD: Eng., "ford on the River Camel".

CANWORTHY: *Carnworthy* C14. A hybrid name: MC *carn*, "tor"; OE *worthig*, "farm". Traditionally pronounced "KEN-er-ee".

CARDEW: The stress is put on the second syllable; "car-DEU". MC *car du*, "black fort".

CARWITHAN: MC *car uethen*, "fort by a tree". "car-WIDH-an".

CASTLE GOFF: MC *castel gof*, "smith's castle".

CONDOLDEN: *Goedolghan* C14, *Godelghon* C17. MC *godolghyn*, "hillock". Padel doubts the existence of such a word, but it would seem to be fairly well attested. In this case, the "hillock" would be the large Bronze Age barrow on the summit of the hill. (Compare GODOLPHIN in Section 1).

CRACKINGTON HAVEN: A hybrid name which was *Crakemude/Crackimtona* C12. MC *crak*, "sandstone"; OE *mutha tun*, "river mouth farm". Traditionally pronounced "krak-en-AWN".

DELABOLE: "del-a-BOEL". *Delyou Bol* C13. MC *Delyow bol*, "pool/pit at a place called Delyow (place of leaves)".

DELINUTH: MC *Delyow nowyth*, "new Delyow" (see DELABOLE above).

FORRABURY: *Forbyry* C14. OE *forbyrig*, "outworks, hornworks".

ST GENNYS: named after St Genesius. Pronounced with a hard G.

HALGABRON: MC *hal Gabran*, "Gabran's marsh".

HALLWORTHY: *Halworgy* C15. MC *hal Worgi*, "Gorgi's marsh". This place was also known as *Halldrunkard* C18, *Haldronket* C15; MC *hal dron coys*, "marsh by a hillspur wood". Interestingly, *coys* retains the hard ending of its OC form *cuit*.

HELSBURY CASTLE: a hybrid name. MC *henlys*, "old ruined fort"; OE *byrig*, "fort", with Eng. "castle" being added at a later date.

HELSTONE: MC *henlys*, "old administrative centre"; OE *tun*, "farm".

HENDRABURNICK: this is remarkably far east for a place name to appear in a Late Cornish form; LC *hendra bernack*, "old farm in a place of hills". LC *bern*, "hill" reversed the order of its central letters from MC *bron*.

LESNEWTH: OC *lis newyth*, "new court/administrative centre".

MINSTER: *Tallcarn/Minster* C13. MC *tal carn*, "brow tor", a name now disused; and MC *mynster*, "endowed church".

OTTERHAM: OE *oter hamm*, "meadow on the River Ottery" (OE *oter ea*, "otter water").

PENALLY POINT: possibly MC *pen hallow*, "end of marshes".

PENCARROW: MC *pen carow*, "stag end" or "stag's head".

PENGELLY: MC *pen gelly*, "grove end".

PENTARGON: an obscure name which might derive from MC *pen dowrguen*, "otters' end/head".

REDEVALLAN: OC *ret auallen*, "ford by an apple tree".

SPLATT: MC *splat*, "plot of land".

START POINT: OE *steort*, "tail".

ST TEATH: from St Tetha. Also *Egglostetha* C12, OC *egglos Tetha*, "St Tetha's church". Pronounced "teth".

TINTAGEL: OC *dun tagell*, "fort of a throat" has been suggested, the "throat" describing the narrow neck of the headland, but the G should be hard. However, the name did not appear prior to C12, as *Tintagol*, and a Norman-French origin should be considered, such as that given to a similar site in the Channel Isles, *tente d'agel*, "the devil's stronghold". Professor Charles Thomas considers this remarkable archaeological site to have been the *Duro-cornovium*, "fortress of the Cornovii" of Roman times.

TREBARWITH: MC *tre berveth*, "inner/middle farm".

TRECARNE: MC *tre carn*, "farm by a tor".

TREGARDOCK: *Tragaraduc* C11. MC *tre Garadoc*, "Caradoc's farm".

TREKNOW: OC *treu tnou*, "valley farm".

TREMAINE: MC *tre men*, "farm by a stone".

TRENEGLOS: MC *tre an eglos*, "farm by a church/churchtown".

TRENGUNE: MC *tre an guen*, "farm on the downs".

TRESLAY: MC *res legh*, "slab ford".

TRESPARRETT: MC *ros perveth*, "middle hillspur".

TREVALGA: prior to the C13, the name of this place was *Menalidan*, MC *meneth ledan*, "broad hillside", before it changed to MC *tre Valga*, "Malga's farm".

TREVEIGHAN: MC *tre vyhan*, "little farm".

TREVENA: *Trewarvena* C13. MC *tre war veneth*, "farm on a hillside".

TREVIAN: MC *tre vyan*, "little farm".

TREWARMETT: *Trewerman* C14. MC *tre Worman*, "Gorman's farm".

TREWASSA: MC *tre Wassa*, "Gwassa's farm".

RIVER VALENCY: MC *(an) velynjy*, "the millhouse".

VALLEY TRUCKLE: MC *(an) velyn droghya*, "the tucking mill".

WAINHOUSE CORNER: *Wynehouse* C15. Eng., from OE *winhus*, "winehouse, tavern".

WARBSTOW: *Warberstowe* C14. OE, *Werbergas stow*, "St Werberga's holy place".

WILLAPARK: *Trevilla Park* C19. MC *tre Wille*, "farm of the Wille family" (John Wille recorded here in C14). Eng. "park" lately added.

WORTHYVALE: MC *guartha avallen*, "higher apple tree".

*   *   *

Trelawny

Properly entitled *The Song of the Western Men*, this protest song has become the Cornish National Anthem and is sung from tap-room to Twickenham rugby finals. The English lyrics were penned by the poetic Reverend Robert Stephen Hawker of Morwenstow (1803-75), who expanded on the traditional refrain: "And shall Trelawny die? There's twenty thousand Cornishmen shall know the reason why!"

The Trelawny of the song was Sir Jonathan Trelawny of Trelawne, Pelynt (1650-1721), baronet and Bishop of Bristol at the time that King James II issued his Declaration of Indulgence restoring rights to Catholics. Trelawny was one of seven bishops who protested and, in the words of the King: "My Lord of Bristol was the most saucy of the seven". He was imprisoned in the

Tower of London, an act which enraged the Cornish people, stirring their rebellious blood. Perhaps remembering the three times in 50 years that makeshift Cornish armies had marched in anger across the Tamar in the 15th and 16th centuries, the Court quickly brought Trelawny to trial where he was acquitted.

The song is reproduced here in the Cornish of Sir Jonathan Trelawny's period, alongside Hawker's lyrics. It is not an exact translation for poetic reasons:

The Reverend Robert Stephen Hawker (from a 19th century engraving)

Gen cletha daa en doola leall,
Gweer looan an colan;
Teez Matearn Jamez seer a weall
Pandr'ra Kernowian!
Ew settez telhar ha termen,
Trelawny tha verwall?
Than, igans meel a Kernowian
Vedn guthvas seer an droll!

Trelawny, ea, mor bew,
Trelawny mor marow,
Ma igans meel a Kernowian
Vedn guthvas seer an droll!

Ameth an capten stowt ha creve,
Gwase looan o entye!
"Tour Loundres pea an Garrack Looz,
Trelawny nye a free!
Tremena Tamer nye a ra,
Nagew an Havren stoy,
Onen hag Oll, cowetha daa,
Pew ra gon naha nye?

Tha vose Loundres pera nye doaz,
Dar, tecka weall deffry!
Deeo raage, deeo raage, ownegian faulz,
Ma ubma gwell vel whye!
Trelawny gweethez ew an Tour,
Trelawny ell merwall;
Buz igans meel Kernowian weer
Vedn guthvas seer an droll!"

A good sword and a trusty hand,
A merry heart and true;
King James's men shall understand
What Cornish lads can do!
And have they fixed the where and when,
And shall Trelawny die?
Here's twenty thousand Cornishmen
Shall know the reason why!

And shall Trelawny live?
And shall Trelawny die?
Here's twenty thousand Cornishmen
Shall know the reason why!

Up spake the captain brave and bold,
A merry wight was he!
"If London Tower was Michael's hold,
We'll set Trelawny free!
We'll cross the Tamar land to land,
The Severn is no stay,
With One and All and hand in hand,
And who shall bid us nay?

And when we come to London Wall,
A pleasant sight to view!
Come forth, come forth, ye cowards all,
Here's men as good as you!
Trelawny, he's in keep and hold,
Trelawny, he may die;
But twenty thousand Cornish bold
Will know the reason why!"

*   *   *

The Great Revivalists: Henry Jenner (1848-1934)

Following the revelations of Daines Barrington towards the end of the 18th century, antiquarian interest began to focus once more upon Cornish. In 1790, Dr William Pryce published the *Archaeologica Cornu-Britannia*, which contained Lhuyd's Grammar (under Pryce's own name) and much of the collections of Gwavas and Tonkin. Guilty indeed of having "unscrupulously plagiarised" it, Pryce nevertheless provided a valuable collection of knowledge which enabled Dr Edwin Norris to translate the medieval Cornish miracle plays in the 19th century. Robert Williams produced his *Lexicon Cornu-Bri-tannicum*, while the exotically named Prince Louis Lucien Bonaparte, the Worcester-born nephew of Napoleon increased his own keen interest in the language.

Henry Jenner (C. Weatherhill)

Another 19th century scholar, Whitley Stokes, translated the *Pascon agan Arluth*, while Frederick W. P. Jago published *The Ancient Language and Dialect of Cornwall* and, in 1887, an *English-Cornish Dictionary*. In 1890, the Reverend W. S. Lach-Szyrma's work *The Last Lost Language of Europe* even contained some elementary Cornish lessons. These enthusiastic works, still valuable in their own way, were nevertheless lacking in knowledge and somewhat unreliable but the man who could rightly be called the Father of Cornish Revival, Henry Jenner, was already at work.

Born at St Columb Major, Jenner was a brilliant scholar with a deep interest in the Cornish language, and brought it to national academic attention in 1873 when he read a paper on the subject to the Philological Society. He was then a young assistant keeper of manuscripts at the British Museum where, on the back of an old 1340 charter, he discovered 41 lines of a medieval Cornish play.

Jenner undertook researches throughout Cornwall, interviewing folk who still recalled the language. He also became fluent in Breton and was admitted to the Breton Gorsedd as a Bard in 1901, the year he also brought about the creation of the first Celtic Cornish Society. Two years later, delivering a speech in Cornish before a Breton audience, he was astonished to find that much of what he said had been understood. This encouraged him further. In the following year, Jenner submitted Cornwall's application for membership of the Celtic Congress, a difficult task as many claimed that Cornwall was no longer Celtic. His case, though, was powerful and the Congress voted to accept the application. Cornwall had regained her identity.

So much interest in the language was now apparent that Jenner was persuaded to produce an introductory text-book of the language and, in 1904, his *Handbook of the Cornish Language* became available.

"Why should Cornishmen learn Cornish?" said Jenner. "There is no money in it, it serves no practical purpose, and the literature is scanty and of no great originality or value. The question is a fair one, the answer is simple. Because they are Cornish."

In the production of his handbook, Jenner chose to take up the language where it had left off and based his work on Late, or Modern, Cornish. In fact, he did not keep it entirely within that period and the book did not really contain enough to any student to progress very far. But it was a start, and a vital one.

In 1920, Jenner and Robert Morton Nance initiated the Federation of Old Cornwall Societies which, three-quarters of a century on, flourishes with 44 branches throughout the Duchy, each collecting and collating aspects of local history and culture in accordance with their motto: "Gather ye the fragments that are left that nothing be lost".

An imposing figure, extremely tall and, in his later years, resplendent with flowing white beard and an expression of deep concentration and wisdom, he might have sprung from the age of the druids. In bardic robes, he seemed to be just that as Cornish people saw when Jenner fulfilled a dream and inaugurated the first Cornish Gorsedd, affiliated to both Welsh and Breton Gorsedds, at the stone circle of Boscawen-un, near Land's End in 1928. Jenner himself was Cornwall's first Grand Bard and his choice of this atmospheric site for the first Gorsedd was inspired by the old Welsh Triad that gave "Beisgawen in Dumnonia" as one of the Three Principal Gorsedds (meeting place of bards) of the Island of Britain.

Jenner, who in his lifetime had achieved more for Cornwall than most would have achieved in three, died in 1934, aged 86.

*   *   *

More useful phrases: *Mouy lavarow vaze*

Happy birthday: *Pedn bluth looan tha whye.* (PED'n blûth LOO-an dha hwei)

Happy Christmas: *Nadelack looan tha whye.* (n'DEL-ek LOO-an tha hwei)

Congratulations!: *Comenetha!* (kum-en-EDH-a)

Forgive me/Excuse me: *Peidgy gaffans.* (PED-jee GAF-anz)

Get better soon: *Gwra mendia wharea.* (g'RA MEND-ya HWA-rai)

I'm glad: *Tho ve looan* (thoe VEE LOO-an)

I'm angry: *Engrez o ve* (EN-grez oe vee)

I'm sorry: *Edrack* (ED-rek)

That's kind of you: *Wheag o whye* (HWAIG oe hwei)

I love Cornwall: *Theram cara Kernow.* (THEH-ram KA-ra KER-nau)

Sure enough: *Seer lowar.* (seer LAOU-er)

Can you speak Cornish?: *Ello whye clappia Kernuack?* (EL-oe hwei KLAP-ya ker-NOO-ek)

I can speak Cornish: *Me ore clappia Kernuack.* (mee OR KLAP-ya ker-NOO-ek)

I will not speak English!: *Me na vadna cowz a Sowznack!* (mee NA VAD-na CAOUZ a SAOUZ-nek)

What is the Cornish for . . ?: *Pandrew an Kernuack rag . . ?* (pan-DROO an ker-NOO-ek rag . . ?)

Please speak more slowly: *Peidgy clappia mouy cuzal.* (PED-jee KLAP-ya MOO-ee KUZ'l)

I can't understand: *Na ellam convethas.* (na EL-am kun-VEDH-az)

I know that very well!: *Me ore hedna per thaa!* (mee OR HED-na per DHAA)

Have you eaten yet?: *Eze debbrez thewh whathe?* (aiz DEB-rez th'yoo'h hwaith)

Are you hungry?: *Gwage o whye?* (GWAAJ oe hwei)

Are you thirsty?: *Zehez o whye?* (ZE-hez oe hwei)

Here you are/Take this: *Comero e thewh.* (kum-EH-ro ee th'yoo'h)

Where are you going?: *Pelea era whye moaz?* (p'LAI-a EH-ra hwei MAHZ)

I have a cold: *Ma annez genam.* (ma AN-ez GEN-am)

I have a headache: *Ma droeg pedn genam.* (ma droeg PED'n GEN-am)

That's a pack of lies!: *Hedna ew scavall an gow!* (HED-na yoo SKA-vol an GAOU)

That's worthless: *Podar ew hedna.* (POD-er yoo HED-na)

This thing was made in Hong Kong: *An dra ma ve gwreze en Hong Kong.* (an DRA-ma vee g'RAIZ en Hong Kong)

Who's that?: *Pew ew hedna?* (p'yoo yoo HED-na)

Shut up!: *Tye wharea!* (tei HWA-rai)

Wait a minute: *Gortero edn spyse* (gor-TEH-ro ed'n SPEIZ)

Are you ready yet?: *O whye parrez whathe?* (OE hwei PA-rez hwaith)

Go away!: *Voyd alebma!* (VOID al-EB-ma)

Shove off!: *Ke tha kerras!* (KEE dha KEH-raz)

Don't forget: *Na rewh nakevy.* (na reu'h na-KEV-ee)

14

Place Names around Bude

BUDE: *Bude* C15, *Beede's Haven* C17. The town is probably named after the stream, which was *Bedewater* C16. The meaning is uncertain but may be an equivalent of W. *budr*, "dirty" (compare with the neighbouring RIVER NEET).

J.T. Blight's 19th century engraving of the Chapel Rock, Bude

CLEAVE: Eng., "cliff".

COOMBE: MC *cum*, "small valley", a Celtic word which became part of SW English speech.

COPPATHORNE: Eng., "copped (pollarded) thorn".

DIZZARD POINT: MC *diserth*, "bluff" (literally, "very steep").

EASTCOTT: OE *east cot*, "east cottage".

FLEXBURY: OE *fleax beorg*, "flax hill".

FORDA: *Forde* C14. Eng. "ford".

GOOSEHAM: OE *gos hamm*, "goose meadow".

GRIMSCOTT: OE *Grims cot*, "Grim's cottage".

HELE: Eng., "nook, angle", or perhaps MC *hayl*, "estuary, saltings".

JACOBSTOW: Eng., from OE *Jacobs stow*, "St James's holy place".

KILKHAMPTON: *Chilchetone/Kilcheton* C11. Possibly MC *kylgh*, "circle"; OE *hamm tun*, "meadow farm".

LAUNCELLS: *Lanceles* C13. MC *lan Seles*, "Seles's church site". Pronounced "LAN-selz".

MARHAMCHURCH: *Marwenacherche* C13. Eng., "St Morwenna's church".

MARSLAND MOUTH: OE *mersc land*, "marshland". "Mouth" probably refers to the mouth of the valley.

MILLOOK: possibly MC *melek*, "place of honey".

MORWENSTOW: OE *Morwennas stow*, "St Morwenna's holy place". The pronunciation "MOR-wen-stow" is often heard now instead of the traditional "mor-WEN-stow".

J.T. Blight's 19th century engraving of the holy well at Morwentow

RIVER NEET: an Old Cornish name, perhaps equivalent to the Irish *necht*, "clean". Compare with the adjacent river BUDE, whose name might mean "dirty".

NORTH TAMERTON: Eng. *north Tamer tun*, "northern Tamar Farm".

PENFOUND: OC *pen fau*, "beech end".

PENSTOWE: MC *pen*, "end"; and STOWE (see below), "end of the Stowe estate".

POUGHILL: *Pochahille* C11. OE *Pohas wiella*, "Poha's well". Pronounced "PUF-il".

POUNDSTOCK: OE *pund stoc*, "cattle pound settlement".

SHARPNOSE POINT: Eng., "sharp nose".

STIBB: OE *stybb*, "tree stump".

STOWE: OE *stow*, "holy place".

STRATTON: *Straetneat* C9. OC *strat Neat*, "valley bottom of the River Neet", with addition of OE *tun*, "farm".

TREGOLE: MC *tre goll*, "hazel farm".

TRESKINNICK: MC *ros kenak*, "roughland by a reed-bed".

TREWINT: OC *treu uint*, "wind farm".

WEEK ST MARY: OE *wic*, "village", of St Mary.

WESTCOTT: OE *west cott*, "western cottage".

WHITSTONE: OE *hwit stan*, "white stone".

WIDEMOUTH BAY: Eng. *wid mutha*, "wide mouth".

WOOLLEY: OE *wulf leah*, "wolf's clearing".

YOULSTONE: OE *eald stan*, "old stone".

*   *   *

The Great Revivalists:
Robert Morton Nance (1873-1959)

Born in Cardiff of Cornish parents, Robert Morton Nance was introduced to the Cornish language through Henry Jenner's *Handbook* and the two began to correspond in Cornish in 1909. They became firm friends and attracted other enthusiasts, Richard Hall, W.D.Watson and R, St.V. Allin-Collins among them. It was Allin-Collins who suggested to Morton Nance that the spelling of revived Cornish needed to be standardised, and he set to work.

Strangely, Nance went further. Declining to base his reconstructed language on Late Cornish, as Jenner had recommended, he went back to the Cornish of

Robert Morton Nance (C. Weatherhill)

Cornish of the medieval Miracle plays, borrowing from Old and Late periods, and even Welsh and Breton, as he went. It seems a curious choice to reconstruct a conversational language from the scanned and rhymed texts of religious poetic drama, but he presevered, taking years of intensive work and study before finally producing his new-look, Unified Cornish in 1929 in the publication *Cornish for All*.

Nance was an indefatigable worker and researcher, collecting folk lore, dialect and scraps of the language. One of his most valuable works was the *Glossary of Cornish Sea Words* published posthumously in 1963 by the Federation of Old Cornwall Societies he and Jenner had co-founded in 1920.

Morton Nance's enthusiasm set fire to the revivalist movement which grew at an astonishing rate. Suddenly, and against all the odds, a Cornwall which had all but forgotten its Celtic heritage was proudly Celtic once more.

In 1934, following the death of Henry Jenner, Robert Morton Nance became Cornwall's second Grand Bard of the Gorsedd, a position from which he could further the cause of revived Cornish. As the years went by, a number of noted scholars emerged to stand beside him: A.S.D.Smith, E.G.Retallack Hooper, Edwin Chirgwin, and P.A.S.Pool among them. Nance himself pointed out that: "One generation has set Cornish on its feet. It is now for another to make it walk."

Robert Morton Nance died in 1959, aged 86, and was buried in the churchyard at Zennor where, on his grave, is the inscription: *Oberow y vewnans yu y wyr govath*, "His life's works are his true memorial". This could not have been more appropriate. During his lifetime, and largely because of his own dynamism, Morton Nance saw the moribund Celtic spirit of Cornwall again become vibrant; he saw his Unified Cornish taught in classes from one end of the Duchy to the other; the proud flying of St Piran's flag, the white cross on black background; the rise of political movements whose aim was the defence of the Cornish people's right to be Cornish.

As Berresford Ellis wrote: "Cornwall was the first of the modern Celtic nations to lose its language. Today, there are many lessons which the other Celtic nations can learn from the truly astonishing rebirth of this nation. Just as Cornish was disappearing into the English ethos, a few dedicated men and women snatched at the embers, blew on them and fanned them into a flame that grows stronger with each passing year." Among those few dedicated people, the figure of Robert Morton Nance stood head and shoulders above the rest.

The Landscape: *An Gweall.*

BARN: *skeber*, pl. *skeburiow*, f. (SKEB-er; skeb-ER-yau)

BARROW: *creeg*, pl. *cregow*, m. (kreeg; KRAI-gau)

BRIDGE: *pons*, pl, *ponjow*, m. (ponz; PON-zhau)

CASTLE: *castell*, pl. *castilli*, m. (KAS-tel; kas-TIL-ee)

COPSE: *killy*, pl. *-ow*, f. (KIL-ee; KIL-yau)

DOLMEN: *crumbla*, pl. *crumlehow*, f. (KRUM-bla; krum-LAI-hau)

DOWNS: *goon*, pl. *gunniow*, f. (gûn; GÛN-yau)

FARM: *bargenteer*, pl. *bargednez teer*, m. (bar-gen-TEER; bar-GED-nez teer)

FIELD: *park*, pl. *-ow*, m. (park; PARK-au)

FIELD (open): *gweal*, pl. *gweliow*, m. (gwail; GWEL-yau)

GATE: *yeat*, pl. *yettez*, m. (zhai-et; ZHET-ez)

HARVEST: *trevas*, pl. *trevadgow*, f. (TREV-az; trev-AD-jau)

HEDGE: *kea*, pl. *keow*, m. (kaa; KAA-au)

HILL: *brea*, pl *breow*, f. (braa; BRAA-au); *bern*, pl. *-ow*, m. (bern; BERN-au)

HILL FORT: *dinas*, pl. *dinadgow*, m. (DIN-az; din-AD-jau)

HUT: *crow*, pl, *-iow*, m. (kraou; KRAOU-yau)

LAKE: *loe*, pl. *lohow*, f. (loe; LOE-hau)

LANE: *bounder*, pl. *-iow*, f. (BAOUN-der; baoun-DEH-r'yau)

MARSH/MOOR: *hale*, pl. *hallow*, f. (haal; HAL-au)

MEADOW: *praze*, pl. *prassow*, m. (praaz; PRASS-au)

MILL: *melin*, pl. *melidniow*, f. (MEL-in; mel-ID-n'yau)

MINE: *wheal*, pl. *wheliow*, m. (hwail; HWEL-yau)

POND: *lidn*, pl. *-ow*, f. (lid'n; LID-nau); *pludn*, pl. *-ow*, m. (plûd'n; PLÛD-nau)

RIDGE: *kein*, pl. *-ow*, m. (kein; KEI-nau)

RIVER: *awan*, pl. *awenow*, m. (AOU-an; aou-EN-au)

RIVERBANK: *gladn*, pl. *-ow*, f. (glad'n; GLAD-nau)

ROAD: *vorr*, pl. *vorrow*, f. (vorr; VUH-rau)

ROCK: *carrack*, pl. *carrigi*, f. (KA-rek; ka-RIG-ee)

SCREE: *radgell*, pl. *-ow*, m. (RAD-jel; rad-JEL-au)

SHAFT: *shafta*, pl. *shaftez*, m. (SHAF-ta; SHAF-tez)

SPRING: *venton*, pl. *ventidniow*, f. (VEN-ten; ven-TID-n'yau)

STANDING STONE: *menheer*, pl. *menhirian*, m. (men-HEER; men-HIr'yan)

STONE: *mean*, pl. *mein*, m. (MAI-en; mein)

STONE CIRCLE: *dauns mein*, pl. *daunsiow mein*, m. (daunz MEIN; DAUN-z'yau mein)

STREAM: *gover*, pl. *-ow*, m. (GOV-er; g'VEH-rau)

TOR: *carn*, pl. *-ow*, m. (karn; KAR-nau)

VALLEY: *nans*, pl. *nanssow*, m. (nanss; NAN-sau)

VILLAGE: *trea(v)*, pl. *trevow*, f. (trai(v); TREV-au)

WELL: *peeth*, pl. *-ow*, m. (peeth; PEETH-au)

WOOD: *cooz*, pl. *codgow*, m. (kûz; KOD-jau)

*   *   *

To Neighbour Nicholas Pentreath

The following rhyme was penned by William Gwavas c.1728, at a time when he was waging successful law suits in respect of fishing tithes. A fascinating thought is that the Nicholas Pentreath it addressed might well have been the father of the famous Dolly Pentreath of Mousehole.

Contrevack Nicholas Pentreath,   Neighbour Nicholas Pentreath,
Pa reffo whye doaz war an dreath   When you come upon the beach
Gen puscas, comero whye weeth   With fish, take care
Tha geel cumpas, hedna ew feer;   To do right, that is wise;
Ha cowz meaz, Dega, Dega,   And speak aloud, Tithe, Tithe,
Enna ew oll goz dega gweer.   There is all your true tithe.

15

Place Names around Launceston

BENNACOTT: OE *Binnas cot*, "Binna's cottage".

BOTATHEN: possibly OC *bod eythin*, "dwelling by furze".

BOYTON: OE *Boyas tun*, "Boya's farm".

CARGENTLE: *Karkentel* C13. Possibly MC *car guntell*, "fort of assembling".

CLUBWORTHY: *Clobiri* C14. OE *clob beorg*, "muddy hill". Pronounced "KLUB-er-ee".

COADS GREEN: Eng., "Code's grassy plot", from the Code family recorded in the vicinity in the C17/18.

CURRY: possibly an Eng. stream name, Cory, meaning unknown.

DRINNICK: OC *dreinic*, "thorny place".

DUNHEVED: possibly OC *dun havod*, "fort by a summer farm", but more likely to be OE *dun heafod*, "hill end". Pronounced "dun-HEV-ed".

EGLOSKERRY: "eg-lez-KEH-ree". OC *egglos Keri*, "St Keri's church".

RIVER INNY: OC *en-i*, "ash-tree river".

KENNACOTT: OE *Kennas cot*, "Kenna's cottage".

RIVER KENSEY: possibly OE *Kennas ea*, "Kenna's water".

LANDUE: OC *nant duw*, "black/dark valley". Stress is put on the last syllable.

LANGORE: *Langover* C15. OC *nant guuer*, "stream valley". "lan-GOR".

LARRICK: OC *lanerch*, "clearing".

LAUNCESTON: pronounced "LAN-son", not, as so often heard on the media, "LAWN-ston". MC *lan Stefan*, "St Stephen's church site"; and OE *tun*, "farm". The C14 form *Lanceton*, and the C15 *Lanson*, show how early the present pronunciation was in place.

LAWHITTON: *Landuuithan* C10. OC *nant uiden*, "tree valley".

LEWANNICK: *Lanwenuc* C12. MC *lan Wenoc*, "Gwenoc's church site," named after a Breton saint, although the present dedication is to St Martin.

LEZANT: OC *lan sant*, "holy church site".

RIVER OTTERY: OE *oter ea*, "otter water".

PETHERWIN: OC *Petroc uyn*, "white (i.e. holy) St Petroc".

POLYPHANT: OC *pol lefant*, "toad pool". *Lefant*, which became *lefans* in Medieval Cornish, was obsolete by c.1500, and was replaced by LC *cronack due*, "toad" (as opposed to *cronack melyn*, "frog"). The prsent pronunciation, "POL-i-fant" ought to be "pol-IF-ent".

REZERE: MC *res cair*, "ford by a fort".

TREBEATH: MC *tre beth*, "farm by a grave".

TREBULLETT: possibly MC *tre bulgh*, "gap farm".

TREBURLEY: MC *tre Borlay*, "farm of the Borlay family". The family were recorded in the parish (Lezant) in the C14.

TRECARREL: *Trecarl* C12, *Trekaryl* C13. MC *tre*, "farm", followed by an unknown second element, although OC *karol*, "choir" might suit.

TREGADILLETT: "treg-a-DIL-et". OC *treu Cadwoled*, "Cadwolet's farm".

TREKELLAND: OC *treu keunant*, "ravine farm".

TREKENNER: OC *treu Kenvor*, "Kenvor's farm".

TREWARLETT: MC *tre war legh*, "farm on a stone slab".

TREWIN: OC *treu uyn*, "white/fair farm".

WERRINGTON: OE *Wulfraeds tun*, "Wulfraed's farm"

YEOLMBRIDGE: possibly OE *ea hamm brycg*, "bridge by a river meadow".

*   *   *

The Great Revivalists: Richard Gendall

A member of an old Cornish family, Richard Gendall was born in 1924, the son of the Vicar of St Winnow, and began to learn Cornish at the age of four. This was not Morton Nance's Unified version of the language, which was yet to become available,but Late (Modern) Cornish. However, when the Unified revolution began, Gendall was drawn into it and became proficient at a very early age.

He came to the fore in the language movement in 1952, when he launched an all-Cornish monthly magazine called *An Lef* (The Voice) and, in 1956, a second magazine, *Hedhyu* (Today) which ran until 1961. A third journal, mainly in English, was entitled *New Cornwall*.

A teacher of languages at a number of schools in Cornwall, England, New Zealand and the West Indies (finishing a long career at Helston Grammar – later Comprehensive – School), Gendall was also an accomplished poet, musician and songwriter. Many of the late Brenda Wootton's recorded songs were written by Richard Gendall, who even accompanied her on the LP *Crowdy Crawn.*

It was at Gendall's instigation that the Cornish Language Board was formed in 1967. The Board produced a number of publications such as P.A.S.Pool's *Cornish for Beginners* but its piece de resistance was Gendall's *Kernewek Bew* (Living Cornish), which was accompanied by records and tapes. This book showed that he had not forgotten his roots, with features of Modern Cornish introduced into the Unified.

Then came the turning point of the revival. It was evident that Morton Nance's Unified Cornish was, in essence, an arbitrary reconstruction and aspects of its spelling (in which Nance had decided to replace all letters I and Z with Y and S), its grammar and even its vocabulary consisted of borrowings and inventions. The academic world was sharply critical, most especially Professor Glanville Price in his work *The Languages of Britain*, with the result that the Cornish Language Board found itself at a crossroads. There were now three schools of thought: to continue with Unified Cornish; to rehash it in accordance with Dr Ken George's computer-aided thesis into the likely pronunciation of the medieval tongue, and its startling spelling system; or to pick up Cornish from its last naturally evolved historic form – Modern Cornish. Gendall spoke firmly for the latter case. Inexplicably, the Board ignored him and chose to adopt George's system which, although based on scholarly work was clearly a greater contrivance than Unified Cornish had been. Richard Gendall appeared to fade away and be lost to the language revival.

This was far from being the case. The problem with Modern Cornish, the language as it had been from the 16th century onward, was that no-one had seriously studied it in depth. Even Jenner had only scratched its surface. This was the work that Gendall set himself, supported by a loyal and dedicated team which included his wife, Jan Gendall. Between them, they transformed their originally ruinous medieval home near Menheniot into a cultural research centre. A quiet, studious yet humorous man who shuns the limelight, Gendall set to analysing the mountain of texts which survived from the language's Late period in 1982. He found a vibrant language with a far greater vocabulary than the medieval texts on which Unified and George's Phonemic (now called Common) Cornish were based, and yet containing only a fraction of the loan words from English that featured in the medieval texts. The spelling, too, was rather different from the early periods with some combinations of letters which, at first glance, looked rather influenced by English, but which were, in fact, used to portray very different sounds from their English counterparts. Gendall was also the first to realise the huge amount of aid in grammar and pronunciation provided by Edward Lhuyd who had studied native speakers while the language was still a living vernacular.

A Student's Dictionary of Modern Cornish, produced by Gendall in 1990, was the first to put together the various textual spellings of each word (there was no dictionary of Cornish during the life of the language) and, the following year, *A Student's Grammar of Modern Cornish* detailed the dynamic yet streamlined grammar of the Late period. This was followed by a number of course books. Richard Gendall and his team then set to deciding on a standardised spelling system, a mammoth task in achieving a level of consistency by only using historic precedent and thereby avoiding the pitfalls of invention. It took five years, and the results, instantly recognisable as Modern Cornish, can be seen in the word-lists, phrases, poems and proverbs in this book. Modern Cornish has gained academic and linguistic acclaim and is available to everyone for the first time since the language's decline.

Without doubt, and after more than sixty-five years experience, Richard Gendall is the most fluent speaker of Cornish for more than two hundred years. Others of his team, some much younger such as Neil Kennedy, are also wonderfully fluent in this Celtic tongue and, in 1986, formed the Cornish Language Council, a sister to *Teere ha Tavaz* (Land and Language) which exists to research and promote all authentic facets of Cornwall's culture. The Council produces a quarterly magazine called *An Garrack* (The Rock).

Despite suffering a heart attack, Richard Gendall continues to work and produce and a definitive dictionary of Modern Cornish will soon (1995) be available.

*   *   *

Cornish Pronouns & Prepositions

I: *me/ve* (mee/vee)

YOU (THOU): *che* (chee)

HE/IT: *e/eve* (ai/aiv)

SHE: *hye* (hei)

WE/US: *nye* (nei)

YOU: *whye* (hwei)

THEY/THEM: *angye/gye* (an-JEI/jei)

MY: *a/ma* (a/ma)

YOUR(S)/THINE: *tha/theth* (dha/dheth)

HIS/ITS: *e* (ai)

HER(S): *e* (ai)

OUR(S): *agon/gon* (AG-un/gun)

YOUR(S): *agoz/goz* (AG-uz/guz)

THEIR(S): *ago/go* (AG-oe/goe)

FOR: *Rag*
FOR ME: *ragam/raga ve*
FOR YOU: *ragas/ragas che*
FOR HIM: *ragtha/rag eve*
FOR HER: *ragthy/rag hye*
FOR US: *ragan/rag nye*
FOR YOU: *rago/rag whye*
FOR THEM: *ractans/ractan 'gye*

IN: *En*
IN ME: *ettam*
IN YOU: *ettas*
IN HIM: *etta/etten*
IN HER: *etty*
IN US: *ettan*
IN YOU: *etto*
IN THEM: *ettans*

ON: *War*
ON ME: *warnam/wara ve*
ON YOU: *warnas/warnas che*
ON HIM: *warnotha/war eve*
ON HER: *warnothy/war hye*
ON US: *warnan/wara nye*
ON YOU: *warno/wara whye*
ON THEM: *warnans/war angye*

WITH: *Gen*
WITH ME: *genam/gena ve*
WITH YOU: *genez/gena che*
WITH HIM: *gonga/gonz eve*
WITH HER: *goshy/gonz hye*
WITH US: *genen/gena nye*
WITH YOU: *geno/gena whye*
WITH THEM: *gongans/gonz angye*

FROM: *Thurt*
FROM ME: *thurtam/thurt ve*
FROM YOU: *thurtas/thurt che*
FROM HIM: *thurto/thurt eve*
FROM HER: *thurty/thurt hye*
FROM US: *thurtan/thurt nye*
FROM YOU: *thurto/thurt whye*
FROM THEM: *thurtans/thurt angye*

OF: *A*
OF ME: *ahanam*
OF YOU: *ahanas(ta)*
OF HIM: *(a)notha*
OF HER: *(a)nothy*
OF US: *ahanan*
OF YOU: *ahano*
OF THEM: *(a)nothans/non 'gye*

TO: *Tha*
TO ME: *thebm/tha ve*
TO YOU: *theez/tha che*
TO HIM: *thotha/tha eve*
TO HER: *thothy/tha hye*
TO US: *thene/tha nye*
TO YOU: *thewh/tha whye*
TO THEM: *thothans/tha angye*

* * *

Food & drink: *booz ha dewas*

APPLE: *avall*, pl. *lavallow*, m. (AV-al; la-VAL-au)

BEAN: *favan*, coll.pl. *fave*, f. (FAV-en; faav)

BEER: *cor*, m.(kor)

BREAD: *bara*, m. (BA-ra)

BREAKFAST: *haunsell*, m. (HAUN-sel)

BUTTER: *manin*, m. (MAN-in)

CAKE: *tezan*, pl. *tezadnow*, f. (TEZ-an; te-ZAD-nau)

CARROT: *caretezan*, pl. *caretez*, f. (kar-ET-iz-an; kar-ET-ez)

CEREAL: *esse*, pl, *esow*, m. (ess; EZ-au)

CHEESE: *keaz*, m. (KAA-uz)

CHIPS: *scubmow*, m. (SKUB-mau)

COFFEE: *coffy*, m. (COF-ee)

DINNER: *kednow*, m. (KED-nau)

DRINK: *dewas*, pl. *-ow*, m. (d'YOO-az; d'yoo-WOZ-au)

EGG: *oye*, pl. *oyow*, m. (ei; EI-au)

FISH: *pesk*, pl. *puscas*, m. (pesk; PUS-kaz)

FOOD: *booz*, m. (bûz)

FORK: *forh*, pl. *ferh*, f. (vor'h; ver'h)

FRUIT: *lavallow*, m. (la-VAL-au)

JAM: *kifith*, m. (KIV-ith)

KNIFE: *colhan* pl. *colhednow*, f. (KUL'hlan; kul'hLED-nau)

LOAF: *torth*, pl. *torthow*, f. (tordh; TOR-thau)

LUNCH: *kednow*, m. (KED-nau)

MARGARINE: *gowmanin*, m. (gaou-MAN-in)

MILK: *leath*, m. (laa-uth)

ONION: *onyon*, pl. *-s*, f. (ON-yun[z])

ORANGE: *owravall*, pl. *owrlavallow*, m. (aour-AV-al; aour-la-VAL-au)

PASTY: *hoggan*, pl. *hoggas*, f. (HUG-an; HUG-az)

PEAR: *peran*, coll.pl. *pear*, f. (PAA-ran; paar)

POTATO: *taata*, pl. *tettez*, m. (TAA-ta; TET-ez)

SALT: *hollan*, m. (HUL-an)

SAUSAGE: *goozigan*, pl. *goozigednow*, f. (GÛZH-ig-an; gûzh-i-GED-nau)

SOUP: *isgal*, m. (IZ-gal)

SPOON: *lo*, pl *lew*, f. (loe; lue)

STRAWBERRY: *sevian*, pl. *seavi*, f. (ZEV-yan; ZAA-vee)

SUGAR: *coon*, m. (kûn)

SUPPER: *cone*, m. (koen)

TEA: *tay*, m. (taa)

TOAST: *crazan*, f. (KRAZ-an)

VEGETABLE: *lozoan*, coll.pl. *lozow*, f. (l'ZHOE-en; LOZH-au)

WATER: *dowr*, m. (daour)

WHISKY: *dowrtubm*, m. (daour-TUB'm)

WINE: *gween*, m. (gween)

16

Place Names of Liskeard & Looe

BAKE: OE *baec*, "ridge".

BARBICAN: MC *porth byhan*, "little cove", preserving the old name of West Looe, *Porthbighan* C13; *Portbyhen* C17.

BIN DOWN: *Bundon* C13. OE *Binnas dun*, "Binna's hill".

BLACKATON: *The Blakedowne* C16. OE *blaec dun*, "black hill/down". Locally called *Menadue*, the LC translation of the Eng. name.

BODBRANE: OC *bod Bran*, "Bran's dwelling".

BOKENVER: MC *bos Kenvor*, "Kenvor's dwelling".

BRAY: MC *bre*, "hill".

CANAKEY: MC *carn an ky*, "the dog's tor".

CARADON: *Carnedune* C12. A hybrid name; MC *carn*, "tor"; OE *dun*, "hill". Pronounced "CA-ra-dun".

CARLEON: *Carleghyon* C13. MC *car leghen*, "slab fort".

CARTUTHER: MC *cruk Teudar*, "Teudar's barrow/tumulus".

ST CLEER: named after St Clarus.

CLICKER TOR: MC *clegar*, "crag"; Eng., *torr*, "rock outcrop".

CRUMPLEHORN: nothing to do with nursery rhyme cows, but MC *tre Maelhoern*, "Maelhoern's farm".

CUTPARRETT: *Cut Pervet* C12. OC *cuit pervet*, "middle/inner wood".

DARITE: probably named after the Daryth family, recorded in the vicinity C14-C16.

DOBWALLS: Eng., "Dobb's walls", after a local landowning family C14-C16.

DOUBLEBOIS: F. *double bois*, "two-fold wood". The wood in question is now called Twelvewood; *Twyfeldewood* C14, Eng., "two-fold wood".

DOWNDERRY: first recorded in C17, this is probably an English name, but of obscure meaning.

DRAYNES: MC *dreyn-ys*, "place of thorns". Properly pronounced "DRAI-ness"

DULOE: MC *dew logh*, "two inlets", referring to the branches of the Looe estuary.

FURSNEWTH: possibly MC *fos noweth*, "new wall".

GOLITHA FALLS: obscure; possibly a Cornish equivalent of W. *gorlifo*, "flooding, overflowing".

HALL: Eng., "hall".

HANNAFORE: formerly *Havenfore*. Eng., "haven"; MC *forth*, "road, way".

HENDERSICK: MC *hendre segh*, "old farm without water".

HERODSFOOT: *Heriott foote* C17. A hybrid name, MC *hyryarth*, "long ridge"; Eng., "foot, base".

HESSENFORD: OE *haegtsena ford*, "hags' ford".

KELLOW: MC *kellyow*, "groves".

ST KEYNE: named after the church saint, Keyna.

LAMELLYN: MC *nans melyn*, "mill valley". "la-MEL-in".

LAMMANA: MC *lan menegh*, "monks' church site" (see LOOE ISLAND below).

LISKEARD: "lis-KARD". *Lys Carruyt/Liscarret* C11. The early form suggests OC *lis cervyt*, "stag's court", but the second element could be a personal name, "Cervyt's court".

LOOE: MC *logh*, "inlet". West Looe was *Porth Bighan* C13, *Portbyhen* C17; MC *porth byhan*, "little cove".

LOOE ISLAND: also called St George's Island after 1602, but originally the Island of *St Michael of Lammana* C13, and the *Isle of Lemayne* C16. MC *lan menegh*, "monks' church site", but the name has since been transferred to a mainland location opposite the island.

RIVER LOOE: MC *logh*, "inlet".

LYDCOTT: *Lotcoyt* C14. OC *luit cuit*, "grey wood".

ST MARTIN BY LOOE: *Markstowe* C13. Eng., "St Mark's holy place".

MENHENIOT: *Mahiniet* C13, *Mahynyet* C14. MC *ma Heniot*, "Heniot's place". Pronounced "m'n-HEN-yet".

MERRYMEET: Eng., "happy meeting place".

MILLENDREATH: MC *melyn dreth*, "mill by a beach". Pronounced "mil-en-DRETH".

MORVAL: *Morevall* C13. Eng., *mor*, "marsh"; F. *val*, "valley".

MUCHLARNICK: *Lanher* C11, *Muchele Lanrak* C14. OC *lanerch*, "clearing", with OE *micel*, "great" added in C14.

NEWBRIDGE: so named in C16. Eng., "new bridge".

PELYNT: *Plunent* C11. MC *plu Nent*, "St Nunet's parish". Pronounced "p'LINT".

PENCOOSE: MC *pen coys*, "end of a wood".

PENDRIM: MC *pen drum*, "ridge end".

ST PINNOCK: named after St Pynnoc.

POLMENNA: MC *pen meneth*, "end of a hillside". An early example of final TH being dropped.

POLPERRO: "pol-PEH-ra". *Portpira/Porthpera* C14. MC *porth Pera*, "Pera's cove".

QUETHIOCK: *Quedoc* C13. OC *cuidoc*, "wooded place". Pronounced "GWITH-ik".

REDGATE: Eng., "red gate".

ROSECRADDOCK: *Rescradok* C13. MC *res Caradoc*, "Caradoc's ford".

SANDPLACE: Eng., "sand place"; presumably where sand for the fields was collected by farmers.

SEATON: *Seythen* C17. Named after the RIVER SEATON (see below).

RIVER SEATON: *Seythen* C17. MC *sethen*, "arrow (-like)".

TALLAND: *Portatlant* C11. MC *porth Talant*, "St Talant's cove".

TENCREEK: MC *keyn cruk*, "ridge barrow/tumulus".

TREBROWNBRIDGE: "Bridge of Trebrown". Eng., "bridge" added to farm name, MC *tre bron*, "hill farm".

TREGARLAND: *Crugalain* C12. MC *cruk Alan*, "barrow/tumulus by a stream called the Alan".

TREGRILL: MC *tre Grylle*, "Crylle's farm".

TRELASKE: *Trelosk* C14. MC *tre losk*, "burnt farm".

TRELAWNE: possibly MC *tre laun*, "farm in a clearing".

TRELAY: MC *tre legh*, "slab farm".

TREMAR: MC *tre margh*, "horse farm" or "Mark's farm".

TREMBRAZE: MC *tre an bras*, "the great farm".

TRETHEVY: MC *tre Thewi*, "Dewi's (David's) farm".

TREWIDLAND: *Trewithelan* C13. MC *tre Wethelan*, "Gwethelan's farm".

TREWORGEY: MC *tre Worgi*, "Gorgi's farm".

WIDEGATES: Eng., "wide gates".

WIDLAKE: OE *wid lacu*, "wide stream".

The Sound of Cornish

Much has already been said in this book regarding Edward Lhuyd's study of the pronunciation of living Cornish in 1700. More than a few hints of its delivery can be easily gleaned by listening to two elderly Cornishmen talking together in any West Penwith pub, even though they will be speaking English, but past commentators also made their observations which very much accord with what you would hear in the two old men's conversation:

JOHN NORDEN c.1580: In comparing Cornish to northern and southern Welsh, Norden observed that, "The pronunciation of the tongue differs in all (three) but the Cornish tongue is far the easiest to be pronounced; for they strain not their words so tediously through the throat and so harshly through and from the roof of the mouth; as in pronoucing Rhin they fetch it with Rh (i.e."hr"), and LL with a kind of reflecting of the tongue."

DON ANTONIO ORTES 1600: Many Cornish priests trained in Spain at this time and, on September 7, 1600, one of these, Richard Pentrey, delivered a sermon in Cornish before the Spanish monarchs in Vallodolid. Don Antonio Ortes remarked that the language was "spoken rapidly" which, coming from a Spaniard, must be taken seriously!

RICHARD CAREW 1602: "Cornish is more easy to be pronounced and softer in sound than the Welsh".

WILLIAM SCAWEN c.1680: Cornish ". . . is not to be gutturally pronounced as the Welsh for the most part is, not mutteringly as the Armorick (i.e.Breton), nor whiningly as the Irish . . . but must be lively and manly spoken . . ."

Camborne Hill

One of the most traditional of Cornish songs, this is sung more frequently than Trelawny or any other Cornish song. It originated in honour of Richard Trevithick, to whom the credit for the steam locomotive rightly belongs rather than Stephenson. A trial run of Trevithick's steam engine was held on Camborne Hill, upon which the eyes of his statue forever rest. Those with memories of steam engines at work will understand the meaning of the "white stockings" she (the engine) wore and, of course, her "awld faather, awld man" is Trevithick himself. For poetic reasons, the Cornish translation is not directly that of the English words or, as the Cornish might say: "Tedn zac', but tez near 'nuff".

Moaz aman Brea Cambern, toaz trea,	Going up Camborne Hill, coming down,
Moaz aman Brea Cambern, toaz trea,	Going up Camborne Hill, coming down,
An verth hethas stag,	The horses stood still,
An rosow geath raage,	The wheels went around,
Moaz aman Brea Cambern, toaz trea.	Going up Camborne Hill, coming down.
E lodrow, e lodrow o gwidn,	White stockings, white stockings she wore,
E lodrow, e lodrow o gwidn,	White stockings, white stockings she wore,
E lodrow o gwidn, wos eath thur an jin,	White stockings she wore, the same as before,
Moaz aman Brea Cambern, toaz trea.	Going up Camborne Hill, coming down.
Me oya e seera, taze coth,	I knawed her awld faather, awld man,
Me oya e seera, taze coth,	I knawed her awld faather, awld man,
Me oya e thaze, en band e whethas,	I knawed her awld man, he blawed in the band,
Moaz aman Brea Cambern, toaz trea.	Going up Camborne Hill, coming down.
E voozas an tane gen an glow,	He aived in the coal in the steam,
E voozas an tane gen an glow,	He aived in the coal in the steam,
E voozas gen glow, an jin geath adro,	He aived in the coal, the steam hit the beam,
Moaz aman Brea Cambern, toaz trea.	Going up Camborne Hill, going down.

*   *   *

Present Tense Phrases

How to Say:

What I Am

This tense of the irregular auxiliary verb *boaz*, "to be" is used to describe who or what you are, or what you are like, e.g. I am tall; she is happy; he is old; we are students, etc.

I AM: *tho ve*	I AM NOT: *nag o ve*
YOU ARE: *tho che*	YOU ARE NOT: *nag o che*
HE IS: *thew e*	HE IS NOT: *nag ew e*
SHE IS: *thew hye*	SHE IS NOT: *nag ew hye*
WE ARE: *tho nye*	WE ARE NOT: *nag o nye*
YOU ARE: *tho whye*	YOU ARE NOT: *nag o whye*
THEY ARE: *then 'gye*	THEY ARE NOT: *nag en 'gye*
AM I? *o ve?*	I AM TALL: *Tho ve heer*

ARE YOU? *o che?*   YOU ARE YOUNG: *Tho che younk*

IS HE? *ew e?*   HE IS NOT OLD: *Nag ew e coth*

IS SHE? *ew hye?*   SHE IS NOT A STUDENT: *Nag ew hye deskibel*

ARE WE? *o nye?*   ARE WE OLD? *O nye coth?*

ARE YOU? *o whye?*   ARE YOU READY? *O whye parrez?*

ARE THEY? *en'gye?*   ARE THEY FISHERMEN? *En'gye puscadors?*

Where I am (also what my present position/condition is)

I AM: *thera ve*	I AM NOT: *nag era ve*	AM I? *era ve?*
YOU ARE: *thesta*	YOU ARE NOT: *nag esta*	ARE YOU? *esta?*
HE IS: *ma e*	HE IS NOT: *nag iggeva*	IS HE? *iggeva?*
SHE IS: *ma hye*	SHE IS NOT: *nag igge hye*	IS SHE? *igge hye?*
THERE IS: *ma*	THERE IS NOT: *nag eze*	IS THERE? *eze?*
WE ARE: *thera nye*	WE ARE NOT: *nag era nye*	ARE WE? *era nye?*
YOU ARE: *thero whye*	YOU ARE NOT: *nag ero whye*	ARE YOU? *ero whye?*
THEY ARE: *mown'gye*	THEY ARE NOT: *nag iggan'gye*	ARE THEY? *iggan'gye?*

I AM IN THE GARDEN: *Thera ve en looar*   ARE YOU IN THE HOUSE? *Esta en chy?*

HE IS NOT IN TOWN: *Nag iggeva en drea*   SHE IS LEAVING: *Ma hye gara*

ARE WE GOING TO THE BEACH? *Era nye moaz thon dreath?*

YOU ARE NOT TO RUN IN SCHOOL: *Nag ero whye poonia en scoll*

THEY ARE WALKING BESIDE THE RIVER: *Mown'gye kerras reb an awan*

It's that easy.

17

Place Names of Callington, Saltash & The Rame Peninsula

ALBASTON: OE *Alvas tun*, "Alva's farm".

ANTONY: *Antone* C11. OE *Antas tun*, "Anta's farm".

BATHPOOL: *Bathpole* C15. Eng., "bathing pool".

BONYALVA: MC *banalva*, "place where broom grows".

BOTTERNELL: OC *bod Dornal*, "Dornal's dwelling".

BOTUS FLEMING: "boe-FLEM-en". *Bothflumet* C13. OC *bod Flumiet*, "Flumiet's dwelling".

BRAY SHOP: A C17 place name; Eng., "Bray's workshop".

BURRATON: OE *burh tun*, "farm by a fort".

CADSON BURY: OE *Caddas tun burh*, "fort by Cadda's farm".

CALLINGTON: *Calwetone* C11. OE *calu tun*, "bare hill farm". Early forms of the name provide convincing evidence that Callington can never have been the Kelliwic (Celli Wig) of the Mabinogion, and that the name is not Celtic but English. Pronounced "KAL-ing-tun".

CALSTOCK: *Kalestoc* C11. OE *calu stoc*, "bare hill settlement".

CARGREEN: *Carrecron* C11. OC *carrec ron*, "seal rock".

CARKEEL: possibly MC *car kyl*, "ridge fort".

CARRACAWN: *Caricon* C19. MC *carrek on*, "lamb's rock".

CASTLEWICH: MC *castel wyk*, "castle by a wooded settlement".

CATCHFRENCH: F. *chasse franche*, "unenclosed hunting land".

CAWSAND: *Couyssond* C15. Eng., "cows' sand".

CHILSWORTHY: OE *Ceols worthig*, "Ceol's farm".

CLENNICK: MC *kelynek*, "holly-grove".

COLDRENICK: MC *kyl dreynek*, "thorny ridge".

COLQUITE: OC *kil cuit*, "ridge wood".

COTEHELE: OC *cuit heill*, "estuary wood".

CRAFTHOLE: *Croftilberwe* C14. OE *croft hyll burh*, "croft hill fort".

CUTMERE: OC *cuit maur*, "great wood".

ST DOMINIC: after St Dominica.

DOWNGATE: A C19 Eng., place name, "downs gate".

DUPATH: Eng., "thieves' path".

EDDYSTONE: Eng., "eddy stone".

EDGCUMBE: named after the Edgcumbe family.

EGLAROOZE: MC *eglos ros*, "church on roughland".

ST ERNEY: after St Teyrnon.

FREATHY: named after the Fridia family, recorded in the area in C14 and earlier.

ST GERMANS: from St Germanus of Auxerre. The churchtown was *Lannaled* C10; OC *lan Aled*, "Aled's church site".

John Norden's c. 1580 depiction of the church at St German's

GOLBERDON: OE *Golbers tun*, "Golber's farm".

GUNNISLAKE: OE *Gunnas lacu*, "Gunna's stream".

HARROWBARROW: *Harebeare* C14. Eng., *har bearu*, "grey wood".

HATT: OE *haett*, "hat", from shape of nearby hill.

HAYE: OE *haeg*, "enclosure".

HESKYN: MC *hesken*, "sedge".

HINGSTON DOWN: OE *Hengestes dun*, "Hengest's hill" or "stallion's hill".

INCE CASTLE: MC *enys*, "island, isolated".

ST IVE: "eev". Named after St Ivo.

KELLY BRAY: *Kellibregh* C13. MC *kelly bregh*, "dappled grove".

KILQUITE: OC *cul cuit*, "narrow wood".

KINGSAND: Eng., "King's beach" after the King family, resident nearby in the C16.

KIT HILL: OE *cyta hyll*, "kite's hill".

LANDRAKE: OC *lanherch*, "clearing".

LANDREYNE: OC *nant drein*, "valley of thorns".

LANDULPH: *Landeloch* C11. MC *lan Deloc*, "Deloc's church site".

LANTALLACK: MC *nans Talek*, "Talek's valley".

LATCHLEY: OE *laec leah*, "stream grove".

LINKINHORNE: *Lankinhorn* C12. MC *lan Kenhoern*, "Kenhoern's church site".

LUCKETT: *Lovecot* C16. OE *Leofas cot*, "Leofa's cottage".

RIVER LYNHER: OC *lin-ar*, "lake-like", an apt description of this beautiful winding estuary. The modern pronunciation "LIE-ner" is technically incorrect; it ought to have been "LINN-er".

MAKER: MC *magor*, "ruin".

MARKWELL: *Aelmarches wylle* C11. OE *Aelmarches wyll*, "Aelmarch's well".

ST MELLION: *S. Melanus* C13. St Melan.

MILLBROOK: Eng., from OE *myln broc*, "mill brook".

MOLENICK: OC *melhionic*, "place of clover".

MOUNT EDGCUMBE: named after the Edgcumbe family.

PENLEE POINT: *Penleigh* C14. MC *pen legh*, "slab headland". Another example where "Point" has been unnecessarily added in recent times.

PENSILVA: a C19 place name, MC *pen*, "end, top"; and place name Silva

Downs, the meaning of which is obscure. It could be from Eng. "silver" or from an OE personal name.

PERDREDDA: OC *pedreda*, "four fords".

PILLATON: OE *pil tun*, "farm of posts/stakes".

POLBATHIC: OC *pol bahet*, "boar's pool".

POLDRISSICK: OC *pol dreisic*, "brambly pool".

PORTWRINKLE: *Port Wrickel* C17. "Cove by Trewikkel"; the farm bearing this name was recorded in C12. The meaning is obscure.

RAME: OE *ramm*, "ram".

RAME HEAD: OE *ramms hed*, "ram's head", which also translates its Cornish name *Pendenhar*. This is most unusually in a LC form for a location so far east, *pedn an horr*.

RILLA MILL: *Rillemille* C14. Eng., "mill of Rillaton Manor" (see RILLATON below).

RILLATON: A hybrid name with OE *tun*, "farm", added to MC *res legh*, "slab ford".

SALTASH: *Esse/Aysh/Asshe* C13, *Saltehasche* C14. OE *aesc*, "ash-tree", with Eng. "salt" added in C14, presumably after a local salt works.

SCRAESDON: OE *tun*, "farm", added to MC *crew res*, "weir ford".

SHEVIOCK: MC *sevyek*, "place of strawberries".

SOUTH HILL: Eng, from OE *suth hyll*, "south hill".

ST STEPHENS: named after the parish saint, St Stephen.

STOCKADON: OE *stoc tun*, "farm settlement".

RIVER TAMAR: *Tamaros* C2. A very ancient name, this appeared on Ptolemy's map. The name is of unknown meaning, but it contains the same *tam-* root found in other Celtic river names such as Thames and Tavy. An early Celtic word, *tamo-s*, "supreme" is a possibility. Despite common mispronunciation as "TAIM-ah", it is actually "TAIM-er".

RIVER TIDDY: *Tudi* C11. Another Celtic river name of obscure meaning. The early Celtic word *toto-s*, "people, tribe" is a candidate.

TIDEFORD: Eng., "ford on the River Tiddy". The endless argument over the pronunciation of this name (TIED-ferd v. the correct TIDDY-ferd) is settled by the C14 *Tediford* and C19 *Tidiford*.

TORPOINT: Eng. "point" added to a shortened form of OE *steort*, "tail", a word commonly applied to promontories, e.g. Start Point.

TREGANTLE: *Argantel* C11. OC *argantel*, "silver stream".

TREMATON: *Tref meu tun* C11. Probably OC *treu moch*, "pigs' farm", with addition of OE *tun*, "farm". Unusually pronounced "TREM-a-tun".

TREQUITE: OC *treu cuit*, "wood farm".

WHITSAND BAY: Eng., from OE *hwit sond*, "white sand".

*   *   *

Parra Hearn

Ma canow ve war hearn, gen cowk ha rooz
Comerez en zans* Carrack Looz en Cooz.
Pothew an cucow devethez trea
Durt moer, teez por "Dega, Dega!" creia,
Ha keniffer benen ogas a toaz
Gen kawall ha try canz hearn war e kein
Tha gweel barcadoes en keniffer chy,
Gen ganow leeas, "Hearn! Hearn!- Hollan mouy!"

Pothens sallez daa, edn meez warbar,
Preze ew tha squatchia man, ha tedna kerr.
Oug'hedna, golhy glaneth en dowr sal:
E vedn ry hanow daa tha muzzi oll.
Gurra spladn en balliar, pedn ha teen,
Gubber ha tra vroaz enz rag vertshants feen.

Meero whye rag gwethan, heer tarthack trooz;
Gurra war hedna meanow pemp canz pooz.
Try termen en jeath meero whye dotha.
Rag hanter meez durta saim vedn cotha.
Thew hebma vorr gweer an hearn tha parra;
En marhas, gwelha gye vedn wharra.

Blethan war blethan gwra gurrollian doaz,
Ha gen hearn lean moaz urt Dowr Gwavas.
War duath, gwra gwenz Noor East whetha pell,
Rag an bobell pow tubm debbry oll.
Ma peath hearn pecare oll an beaz
Mouy pobell bohodgack vel pobell broaz.

Pilchard Curing

My verses are of pilchards, with boat and net
Taken in the bay of the Grey Rock in the Wood.
When the boats have come in
From sea, with beach folk, "Tithe, Tithe!" crying,
And every woman coming nigh
With back basket and 300 pilchard on her back
To make up bulks in every building,
With many voices, "Pilchards! Pilchards! More salt!"

When they are well cured, a month altogether,
It is time to break up, and pull away.
After that, wash clean in salt water:
It will give all the maids a good name.
Place gleaming in a barrel, heads out, tails in,
They are income and big business for fine merchant

Look for a pole, thirteen feet long;
Put on this 5 hundredweight of stones.
Three times a day see to them.
For a fortnight oil will fall from them.
That is the proper way to cure the pilchards;
In the market, they will sell better.

Year after year let ships come,
And filled with pilchards go to Gwavas Lake.
Eventually, let a North East wind blow long,
For the people of a warm clime to eat all,
The pilchard business like the whole world is
More to do with the poor than the rich.

John Boson, c.1700

---

*   There is no known copy of this poem in Boson's own hand and a scribe has evidently written *zans*, "holy" in mistake for "bay". Despite this error, John Boson's poem gives such a wonderfully graphic account of work in Cornish fishing harbours 300 yoears ago that you can almost smell the fish!

Talking about the past

How To Say:

What I Was, Have Been (something over and done with)

I WAS: *me ve*	I WASN'T: *na ve ve*	WAS I? *ve ve?*
YOU WERE: *che ve*	YOU WEREN'T: *na ve che*	WERE YOU? *ve che?*
HE WAS: *e ve*	HE WASN'T: *na veva*	WAS HE? *veva?*
SHE WAS: *hye ve*	SHE WASN'T: *na ve hye*	WAS SHE? *ve hye?*
WE WERE: *nye ve*	WE WEREN'T: *na ve nye*	WERE WE? *ve nye?*
YOU WERE: *whye ve*	YOU WEREN'T: *na ve whye*	WERE YOU? *ve whye?*
THEY WERE: *angye ve*	THEY WEREN'T: *na ve angye*	WERE THEY? *ve angye?*

YOU WEREN'T HERE: *Na ve whye ubma.*   THEY WERE WARNED: *Angye ve gwarnez.*
WHERE HAVE YOU BEEN? *Pelea ve whye?* WHEN I WAS A LAD: *Termen me ve mawe.*

What I Did (a useful past tense in Cornish speech where for example, "I ran" is rendered as "I did run". This tense uses the auxiliary verb *gweel/geel*, "to do")

I DID: *me reeg*	I DIDN'T: *na riga ve*	DID I? *riga ve?*
YOU DID: *che reeg*	YOU DIDN'T: *na resta che*	DID YOU? *resta che?*
HE DID: *e reeg*	HE DIDN'T: *na reeg e*	DID HE? *reeg e?*
SHE DID: *hye reeg*	SHE DIDN'T: *na reeg hye*	DID SHE? *reeg hye?*
WE DID: *nye reeg*	WE DIDN'T: *na riga nye*	DID WE? *riga nye?*
YOU DID: *whye reeg*	YOU DIDN'T: *na rigo whye*	DID YOU? *rigo whye?*
THEY DID: *angye reeg*	THEY DIDN'T: *na reeg angye*	DID THEY? *reeg angye?*

I LOST MY WAY: *Me reeg kelly ma vorr* (lit. "I did lose my way")
THE FARMER WAS BUILDING A HEDGE: *An teeack reeg derevall kea.*
DID YOU FIND YOUR DOG? *Rigo whye cawas goz kye?*
WE DIDN'T SEE THE GAME: *Na riga nye gwelhas an gwary.*

SCILLY c.2000 BC

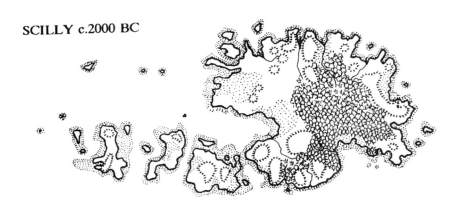

SCILLY c.400 AD

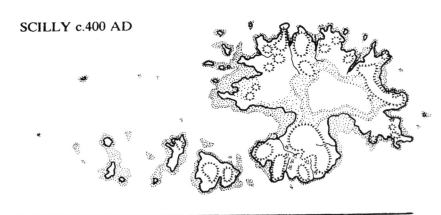

SCILLY TODAY

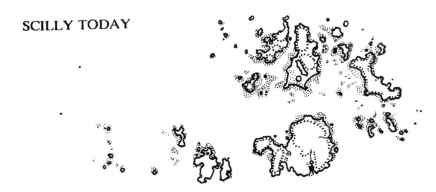

18

Place Names of The Isles of Scilly

Understanding the meaning of a number of place names in the Isles of Scilly (which should never be called "The Scilly Isles") requires a little background knowledge of their history. In brief, these beautiful islands are gradually sinking. At the end of the Neolithic era, 4000 years ago, the main islands of St Mary's, Samson, Bryher, Tresco, St Martin's, the Eastern Isles and the various islets in between formed one single landmass. Gugh and St Agnes formed a peninsula to the main island whilst Annet and the Western Rocks formed smaller islands to the south west. Archaeology suggests that a large part of the main Neolithic island was wooded and supported a herd of red deer.

By the end of the Roman period, c.400 AD, the main island had become a little smaller, with St Agnes and the Gugh being sundered from it to become another island. The low-lying centre of the large island was protected from the sea only by sand dunes, which still exist as submerged sand bars, and, in time, the sea forced its way in. Beneath the shallow central waters lie prehistoric settlements and field boundaries and the submergence of so much of Scilly may explain the origin of the legend of the lost land of Lyonesse.

Place names show that Cornish was extensively spoken in the islands, but its use probably ceased before 1700.

∗   ∗   ∗

ST AGNES: "Saint" was added to the island's name in the C16 to conform to those of other major islands in the group. In the C12, its name was *Aganas/Hagenes/Hagenesse*. A word containing the Scandinavian *nes* is possible, but it is thought that the name is Early Celtic *ek enes*, "off-island". Locally, the island is called "Agnes", without the "Saint".

ANNET: an obscure name; possibly OC *aneth*, "dwelling" although the C14 forms *Anet/Anete* do not show the soft ending which would support this.

BAR POINT: Eng. translation of C17 *Pendrathen*, LC *pen- drethan*, "end of a sand-bar". The notorious sandbank now called the Crow Bar stretches northward from here.

BISHOP ROCK: never "Bishop's Rock", this is a direct Eng. translation of the C14 name *Maenenescop*, MC *men an epscop*, "the bishop's stone".

BOROUGH FARM: Eng. "barrow", translating the C14 name of the holding on this site, *Cheyncruk*, MC *chy an cruk*, "house by the barrow/tumulus".

BROAD SOUND: *Brode Sownde* C16. Eng., "broad sound".

BRYHER: *Braer* C14. OC *breyer*, "place of hills". Pronounced "BREI-yer".

CASTELLA: LC *castilli*, "castles", from shape of rocks.

CRAGYELLIS: *Trigga Hilles* C17. Probably LC *trigva helles*, "old court dwelling place". Submerged prehistoric settlements lie close to this reef.

CREBAWETHAN: LC *creeb a wethan*, "reef with a tree". Presumably these rocks could once support a small tree when a greater area stood above water. "Kreb-a-WEDH-an".

CRIM ROCKS: possibly a contraction of LC *creeban*, "little reef".

CROW SOUND: named after the Crow Rock. This might be Eng., or LC *crow*, "hut", from submerged prehistoric buildings.

EASTERN ISLES: Modern Eng. name for a group of islands which were once low hills in the eastern part of a large island. This area may once have been called *Goonhily* (see GANILLY below).

ENNOR: still surviving as a minor place name on St Mary's, this was most likely the name of the former large main island of which St Mary's was the southernmost part. OC *en noer*, "the land". Compare the name *Mainland* given to the largest of the Orkney and Shetland groups.

GANILLY: MC *guen hily*, "saltwater downs". Pron. "g'NIL-ee".

GANINICK: LC *(an) geninack*, "the place of wild garlic". Pron. "g'NIN-ek".

GARRISON: Eng., from the C16 construction of fortifications.

GIANT'S CASTLE: Eng., "giant's castle". An Iron Age cliff castle, called *Hengastel* in the C14, MC *hen gastel*, "ancient castle".

GREAT ARTHUR: *Arthur/Arthur's Ile* C16. From the personal name Arthur, perhaps the great Romano-Celtic hero himself.

GUGH: LC *keow*, "hedge-banks". Pronounced "g'YOO".

GWEAL: *Gwithiall* C17. LC *gwethiall*, "place of trees".

HANJAGUE: *Ingeak/Hengiack* C17. Possibly LC *(an) wendgack*, "the windy one". Pronounced "han-JIG".

ST HELEN'S: *St Elidius* C12. Named after St Elidius, possibly the Welsh bishop Ilid. An early Christian chapel survives on this island.

HELVEAR: *Hayle Veor* C16. LC *hayl vere*, "great estuary/saltings". A name which harks back to the pre-submergence era of the islands.

HOLY VALE: LC *hale*, "marsh", added to the earlier Norman-French name *La Val*, "at the foot, low-lying".

HUGH TOWN: the principal town of the islands is built on a low-lying sand-spit connecting the main body of St Mary's to a peninsula called The Hugh, OE *hoh*, "heel of land, promontory".

ILLISWILGIG: LC *ennis welgack*, "grassy island".

INNISVOULS: LC *ennis voulz*, "island of wether-sheep".

KITTERN ROCK: OE *cyta aern*, "kite's nest".

LOWER MOOR: A rather characterless Eng. name replacing *Gwernewgavell* C17; LC *gwernow*, "alder-marshes" and LC *gavar hale*, literally "marsh-goat" but meaning "snipe, woodcock".

MAIDEN BOWER: possibly LC *mein mere*, "great stones".

ST MARTIN'S: from the C16, this island has taken its name from the patron of its church, St Martin of Tours. Previously, it was *Brethyoke/Brechiek*, C14, MC *breghyek*, "dappled one".

ST MARY'S: In the C12, the name of the pre-submergence island of ENNOR (see above) was transferred to the largest of its fragments. In the C14, its name changed to that of its church's patron saint.

MEN-A-VAUR: *Menevorth/Menavorth* C17. Probably not LC *mean a vere*, "the great stone", but most likely MC *men ar voth*, "stone facing the hump" – the "hump" being Round Island nearby. The name has no connection with Eng. "man o'war".

MENAWETHAN: LC *mean a wethan*, "the tree stone".

MINALTO: MC *men*, "stone"; and OC *altou*, "cliffs".

MINCARLO: LC *mean carla(th)*, "rayfish stone".

NEW GRIMSBY: *Grymsey* C16. Old Norse *Grimrs ea*, "Grimr's (Odin's) water".

NORNOUR: MC *ar nor*, "facing the land".

NORTHWETHEL: *Arwothell* C16. MC *ar wothel*, "facing watery ground".

OLD TOWN BAY: *Porth Enor* C14. MC *porth Ennor*, "cove/landing place of Ennor".

PARTING CARN: *Perkin Carne* C17. LC *park an carn*, "the tor field".

PELISTRY BAY: LC *por lisstri*, "cove of vessels". The addition of "Bay" is unnecessary.

PENINNIS HEAD: LC *pen- ennis*, "end of the island". Pron. "p'NIN-is".

POPPLESTONE BAY: OE *popelstanas*, "pebbles".

PORTH HELLICK: LC *porth helack*, "cove of willows".

Peninnis Head

PORTH LOO: LC *porth loe*, "inlet cove".

PORTH MELLON: LC *porth melyn*, "yellow cove".

PORTH MINICK: LC *porth meinack*, "stony cove".

ROSEVEAN: LC *rose vean*, "small promontory".

ROSEVEAR: LC *rose vere*, "great promontory".

ROUND ISLAND: *Rownd Ylond* C16. Eng., "round island". Its distinctive shape, and the likely derivation of MEN-A-VAUR (see above) nearby, suggest that its original name might have been MC *both*, "hump".

SCILLY: the name of the archipelago is not easy to unravel and its present form is clearly corrupt. Judging from its ancient forms, *Silimnus* C1, *Sillina* C3, *Sylina* C5, *Sulling* C12 and *Syllingar* C13 (with a Norse plural), it would seem that the C18 LC name *Sillan* is more correct. Perhaps the best explanation of the name has been suggested by Prof. Charles Thomas; that the islands are named after the Romano-Celtic goddess *Sulis* (pronounced "SIL-is"), also commemorated at Roman Bath (Aquae Sulis), and equated by the Romans to Minerva. The Celtic name of the goddess might mean "watcher".

SEVEN STONES: so called on charts since the C16, this dangerous reef between Scilly and Land's End, and the grave of the *Torrey Canyon*, had a Cornish name recorded in the C17 as *Lethas/Lethowsow*, LC *lethedgow*, "milky ones", from the foam which constantly churns about the reef.

SHIPMAN HEAD: the older forms *Shepene/Sheepen* show this to be Eng.. "place of sheep".

SMITH SOUND: Eng., from rocks called *The Smith* and *Great/Little Smith* C16/17. There seeems to be no link with the Lords Proprietor of the islands, the first of which, Augustus Smith, did not take up his post until 1834. The Sound was also *Awana Sound/St Awanaes Sound* C17, from St Awana, now remembered on the adjacent island of St Agnes as St Warna, patroness of shipwrecks.

TEAN: "TEE-an". Named after St Theona, about whom little is known. The ruins of an early Christian chapel remain on the island.

TRENOWETH: LC *tre- noweth*, "new farmstead".

TRESCO: in C12, this was the "Island of St Nicholas", the then Cornish name *Rentemen* (meaning unknown) becoming obsolete. *Trescau*, MC *tre scaw*, "farm by elder trees", appeared as a holding on the island in the C13, the name later becoming that of the island which, briefly in the C16, became *Iniscaw*, LC *ennis scaw*, "island of elder trees".

WHITE ISLAND: *Whites Iland* C17. Eng., "White's island", probably from a personal name.

* * *

A Final Word on Place Names

Deciphering place names, particularly Cornish ones, is not an exact science. So many have changed from their original forms over the centuries that it is often difficult to ascertain what those original forms might have been. Usually this is the fault of scribes, mapmakers and the like, and the trend continues with modern mapmakers changing the spellings of place names on new editions of their maps. Obviously, to find the meaning of a Cornish place name, to merely look up a Cornish-English dictionary is definitely not the road to take.

The derivations in this book are based on the most up-to-date research but that is not to say that opinions will not be revised in the future, as in any study of history and archaeology, for that is precisely what place name research is.

* * *

More Cornish Tenses

How to say:

What I will do

I WILL: *me ra*	I WON'T: *na ra ve*	WILL I? *ra ve?*
YOU WILL: *che ra*	YOU WON'T: *na ra che*	WILL YOU? *ra che?*
HE WILL: *e ra*	HE WON'T: *na ra e*	WILL HE? *ra e?*
SHE WILL: *hye ra*	SHE WON'T: *na ra hye*	WILL SHE? *ra hye?*
WE WILL: *nye ra*	WE WON'T: *na ra nye*	WILL WE? *ra nye?*
YOU WILL: *whye ra*	YOU WON'T: *na ra whye*	WILL YOU? *ra whye?*
THEY WILL: *angye ra*	THEY WON'T: *na rown'gye*	WILL THEY? *rown'gye?*

WILL YOU GO TO TOWN TOMORROW? *Ra whye moaz than dreav avorow?*
YES, I WILL GO TO TOWN TOMORROW: *Ea, me ra·moaz than dreav avorow.*
NO, WE WON'T GO TO TOWN TOMORROW: *Na, na ra nye moaz than dreav avorow.*

What I want to/intend to do

I WANT: *me vedn*	I DON'T WANT: *na vadna ve*
YOU WANT: *che vedn*	YOU DON'T WANT: *na venta*
HE WANTS: *e vedn*	HE DOESN'T WANT: *na vedn e*
SHE WANTS: *hye vedn*	SHE DOESN'T WANT: *na vedn hye*
WE WANT: *nye vedn*	WE DON'T WANT: *na vedon nye*
YOU WANT: *whye vedn*	YOU DON'T WANT: *na vedo whye*
THEY WANT: *angye vedn*	THEY DON'T WANT: *na vedons*

DO I WANT? *vadna ve?*
DO YOU WANT? *venta?*
DOES HE WANT? *vedn e?*
DOES SHE WANT? *vedn hye?*
DO WE WANT? *vedon nye?*
DO YOU WANT? *vedo whye?*
DO THEY WANT? *Vedons?*
I WANT TO SPEAK CORNISH: *Me vedn clappia Kernuack.*
HE DOESN'T WANT TO SPEAK ENGLISH: *Na vedn e clappia Sowznack.*
DO YOU WANT TO SPEAK CORNISH? *Vedo whye clappia Kernuack?*

Select Bibliography

Berresford Ellis, Peter: *The Cornish Language and its Literature*, 1974; *The Story of the Cornish Language* (2nd ed.), 1990

Fudge, Crysten: *The Life of Cornish*, 1982

Gendall, Richard: *A Student's Dictionary of Modern Cornish*, 1990; *A Student's Grammar of Modern Cornish*, 1991; *The Pronunciation of Cornish*, (2nd ed.),1990; *1000 Years of Cornish*, (2nd ed.), 1994

Gover, J.E.B.: *The Place Names of Cornwall*, 1948 (four unpublished vols at Royal Institution of Cornwall, Truro)

Jenner, Henry: *A Handbook of the Cornish Language*, 1904

Lyon, Rod: *Authentic Cornish*, 1989

Morton Nance, Robert: *A New Cornish Dictionary*, 1938, (republished 1990); *A Glossary of Sea Words*, 1963

Padel, O.J.: *Cornish Place Name Elements*, 1985; *A Popular Dictionary of Cornish Place Names*, 1988; *The Cornish Writings of the Boson Family*, 1975

Pool, P.A.S.: *The Place Names of West Penwith*, (2nd ed.), 1985; *The Field Names of West Penwith*, 1990; *The Death of Cornish*, 1975

Thomas, Charles: *Exploration of a Drowned Landscape*, 1985

Weatherhill, Craig: *Belerion: Ancient Sites of Land's End*, 1981; *Cornovia: Ancient Sites of Cornwall & Scilly*, 1985

Whetter, Dr. James: *The History of Glasney College*, 1988

Periodicals

An Garrack: Quarterly magazine of the Cornish Language Council

Journal of The Royal Institution Of Cornwall (yearly)

Old Cornwall: Quarterly journal of the Federation of Old Cornwall Societies

Learning more about Cornish

For further information on the Cornish language and culture: please send an SAE to: Teere ha Tavaz, Tregrill Vean, Menheniot, Liskeard, Cornwall (01579-343366)

For lessons in Cornish, please send an SAE to: The Cornish Language Council, Tregenza Vean, Antron Hill, Mabe, Penryn, Cornwall.

place name note Book

Use these three blank pages to jot down the place names you find on your holiday!

place name note Book

place name note Book

Also of interest:

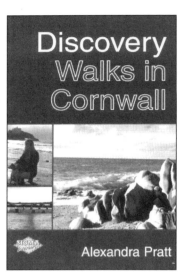

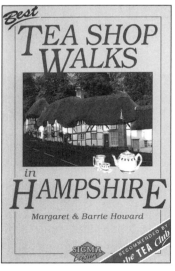

DISCOVERY WALKS IN CORNWALL

Alexandra Pratt

Ever wondered what lies beyond the coastal path? Tired of the usual attractions? This book follows less frequented routes which will take you to Cornwall's secret places. £6.95

THE WATERFALLS OF ENGLAND

Griffith Fellows

If you enjoy country walking, fine scenery and nature and have an interest in geology, natural history or art *The Waterfalls of England* is a must. Ranging from Northumberland in the north to the southern tip of Cornwall, up to 200 easily accessible waterfalls are described and illustrated (many in full colour) for you to enjoy. Clear directions are given to each of the waterfalls and access is graded according to severity. Each waterfall is star rated for attractiveness and appeal. This is a unique illustrated guide which is comprehensively and succinctly compiled to attract the interested reader to the beauty and accessibility of England's waterfalls. £9.95

BEST TEA SHOP WALKS IN HAMPSHIRE

Margaret & Barrie Howard

26 walks, ranging from 4 to 8 miles, form the basis of a thorough exploration of all the county has to offer: landscape, sites of historical interest, and culinary delights. £6.95

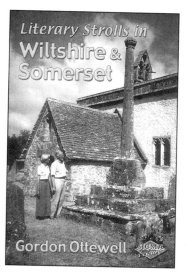

LITERARY STROLLS IN WILTSHIRE & SOMERSET

Gordon Ottewell

This original approach to countryside exploration contains 40 varied and attractive circular strolls, none longer than 4 miles, many with shorter alternatives. In addition to accurate route directions, sketch map and suggestions for parking and refreshments, each stroll description includes a section on a literary connection, together with details of the books or poems referred to. Relevant photographs supplement the text. £8.95

DORSET CHURCH WALKS

Diana Pé

40 superb walks in a varied and beautiful landscape - and all including visits to remarkable churches. Routes range from 2-mile strolls to demanding 13-mile hikes. The special feature of interest on these routes, however, is a visit to a local church. £7.95

COOK WITH CONFIDENCE

Beryl Tate

Beryl Tate is known to millions as 'The Kitchen Doctor' on the BBC's Jimmy Young programme. Beryl reveals how to use professional catering techniques at home, giving the reader greater confidence in tackling what, for many, is a daunting exercise. Beryl broadcasts regularly as BBC Essex radio chef, enjoys giving live cookery talks and demonstrations and has had monthly hour-long sessions on BBC Radio 2's Jimmy Young programme when she has answered listeners' cookery questions. *£7.95*

GAMES TO PLAY WITH YOUR CAT

Paul Berman and Roger Markman
This describes games to give hours of enjoyment for any cat and owner. Most kittens play spontaneously but as a cat grows, these games will give the necessary encouragement to provide hours of extra fun. The games can be played by cat and owner together and some will keep your cat happy for hours while you're out. *£6.95*

WALKS IN MYSTERIOUS HAMPSHIRE

Laurence Main
An original approach to historical walking which intertwines authentic fact with mystical legends - some tragic, some romantic. A superb read for the questing rambler. £6.95

LONESOME RHODES: One Man, Two Wheels & 19,000 Miles

Ashley Rhodes
Picture yourself as the pillion passenger on a bold, brave, daring and defiant journey through the longest continuous landmass in the world ... the Americas. This is the story of Ashley Rhodes and his solo motorcycle odyssey from Tierra del Fuego at the southern tip of South America – a mere stones throw from Antarctica – all the way to Anchorage in the frozen Alaskan north. *£8.95*

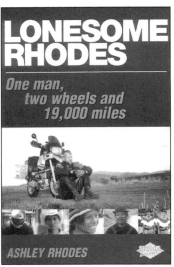

All of our books are available through booksellers. In case of difficulty, or for a free catalogue, please contact:

SIGMA LEISURE, 1 SOUTH OAK LANE, WILMSLOW, CHESHIRE SK9 6AR.
Phone: 01625-531035 Fax: 01625-536800.
E-mail: info@sigmapress.co.uk   Web site: http//www.sigmapress.co.uk
MASTERCARD and VISA orders welcome.